Carolyn Allen

7 8 9 10 11 12 13

THE SOVIET SYSTEM OF GOVERNMENT

THE CHICAGO LIBRARY OF COMPARATIVE POLITICS

ROY C. MACRIDIS, EDITOR

THE SOVIET SYSTEM OF GOVERNMENT

REVISED EDITION

By John N. Hazard

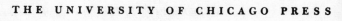

THE UNIVERSITY OF CHICAGO PRESS

Library of Congress Catalog Number: 57-5273

THE UNIVERSITY OF CHICAGO PRESS, CHICAGO 37
Cambridge University Press, London, N.W. 1, England
The University of Toronto Press, Toronto 5, Canada

FOREWORD

The comparative study of political institutions is central to a scientific and systematic approach to politics—to the development of fruitful generalizations and to the careful scrutiny and validation of such generalizations. Comparative study and analysis are perhaps the only valid instruments at the disposal of the student of politics for the careful examination of the policy issues that confront his country. It is, indeed, only through comparison that we can appreciate the multiplicity of the factors that account for a given political phenomenon and accordingly develop a healthy skepticism toward quick and easy "solutions." And comparative study, by giving the student a grasp of foreign political institutions and forms, helps him to re-examine constructively and understand better the political institutions of his own country.

There is today a general consensus among political scientists that in the existing literature in the field of "comparative government" undue emphasis has been placed on the formal and legal institutions of various political systems and that little effort has been made to relate them to what may be called the "contextual" elements of a political system—ideology, social structure, pressure groups, and the like. Those writing in the field have tended to shy away from generalizations and hypotheses and to avoid interpretive studies of the dynamics of a system. The Chicago Library of Comparative Politics, of which Mr. Hazard's book is the first volume in print, is designed to fill this gap in the literature and to provide teachers and students with books that raise questions and call for generalizations.

This series of short studies will include volumes on individual countries and also institutional or functional volumes that cut across country lines and are truly comparative in character. With Mr. Hazard's volume, those in preparation (listed facing the title page of this book) and those still in the planning stage—on the judiciary, on Germany, and on selected non-European countries—the first set of studies will have been realized as a self-sufficient group for purposes of instruction. But each separate volume will also stand independently as a study of its own subject and can be used to supplement the other materials that exist in its field.

It is appropriate that our series should begin with a study of Soviet political institutions, a subject that calls for continuing re-examination and scrutiny. Recent developments in Soviet institutions and policies raise new questions that cannot be answered in terms of the familiar stereotypes. Perhaps the greatest merit of Mr. Hazard's study is that it raises as many questions as it answers and projects both in terms of a bold and imaginative frame. His thesis that the Soviet Union utilizes "democratic forms" operating in a context of what he calls "totalitarian counterweights" and that the interplay between the two constitutes the dynamic of the system is one that may be received with criticism by some of our experts in the field. But none, I hope, will fail to examine carefully the data that Mr. Hazard marshals so carefully, and none can dismiss it without a careful re-examination of his own theoretical assumptions about the nature of the Soviet system.

It is the express purpose of the Chicago Library of Comparative Politics to provide studies that do not duplicate existing texts or monographs; that challenge the reader, the teacher, and the student alike; and that lead to independent and constructive thought. The freshness and, probably, the boldness of Mr. Hazard's study perform this task admirably and bring new insights to the study of the Soviet system that no student can afford to ignore.

ROY C. MACRIDIS

PREFACE

The Soviet system of government provides sharp contrast to the system that has evolved in these United States. For that reason it is an admirable subject for a course in comparative government. Sharp contrasts provoke thought on the structure and functions of political institutions.

Examination of the features of the Soviet state can have a second purpose, also appropriate to a study of comparative government. It can deepen an American's understanding of his own political system. Comparison of American political institutions with those created in the Russian Revolution can be an aid to an understanding of the contrasting elements in our own system that make it the success it is. Study of the Soviet government can be for the able student a means of supplementing his study of the American system of government. The unfamiliar values sustained by Soviet institutions provoke re-emphasis of the values treasured by the Founding Fathers at Philadelphia.

Believing, as the author does, that a text in the field of comparative government should itself be comparative to achieve maximum usefulness, he has pointed out throughout this study the contrasts between Soviet institutions and those of the West. When there are points of similarity in form, these points are also noted, especially when an apparently familiar institution has been reshaped to achieve ends far different from those of a democracy.

The materials chosen for presentation in this study have been selected from the great mass of scholarly works that have appeared since the war. They have been tested against the accounts of former Soviet citizens who have fled to the West. They have been tested also against the author's own knowledge of life in the U.S.S.R., gained as a prewar fellow of the Institute of Current World Affairs of New York. They attempt to portray the Soviet system as it operates and to indicate the pressures that may influence the development of this system in the future.

J. N. H.

PREFACE TO SECOND EDITION

Momentous events have surprised the world since the preparation of the first edition of this book. The year of its publication, 1957, marked the culmination of nearly four years of reconsideration of Stalin's policies and adoption of a new course. Industry was removed from Stalin's system of centralized direction and placed under regional economic councils. Agriculture was reorganized in the next year with equal thoroughness to rid it of control by the machine tractor stations. Violent conflict over issues of economic management and control was revealed in June, 1957, within the Presidium of the Central Committee of the Communist party, ending four years of collective leadership.

The way was opened to further change. Marshal Georgi K. Zhukov was ousted as Minister of Defense in the autumn of 1957, and political education within the Armed Forces was restrengthened. The often arrogant factory manager found himself subjected in late 1957 and 1958 to new controls created by the trade-union shop committees and the Communist party's factory organization in fulfilment of state and party directives. The school system was revolutionized in 1958 to require all but a few students to become familiar with production prior to entering upon intellectual careers.

Law codes were subjected to the revision often promised under Stalin but never achieved. General principles for criminal codes, codes of criminal procedure, and court structure were enacted in 1958 and the law of treason redefined. Other legal principles followed suit. In a much heralded campaign to bring the masses into law enforcement a new form of disciplinary body, the "social assembly," appeared in 1957 and spread to several republics. Vigilantes were organized by the young Communists to patrol public places.

The Communist party was refreshed between its twentieth and twenty-first congresses by the admission of 700,000 bench workmen and dirt farmers to dilute the increasingly intellectual elite group.

While the march of events on the administrative side has been reflected in three annual reprints of the first edition by incorporation of amendments to the U.S.S.R. constitution, the full scope of the changes and their assessment had to await the perspective provided by the passage of time. The revision has been accomplished and is presented herewith to portray Soviet government as it moves into the 1960's.

J. N. H.

TABLE OF CONTENTS

CHAPTER 1

IN THE NAME OF DEMOCRACY

Soviet politicians woo their own people and those of the world beyond Soviet frontiers in the name of democracy. In support of their much-publicized appeal, they point to their espousal of political forms, many of which are familiar to citizens of the ancient democracies of the West and of the emerging republics of southern Asia. They claim to be loyal supporters of some of the fundamental procedures revered by Americans, Englishmen, Frenchmen, Swedes, and Indians. They use much the same vocabulary of politics found in the democracies. Yet, the forms and procedures are manipulated and revised to obtain results very different from those sought outside the Soviet orbit. The Soviet apparatus of government functions to meet the desires of a small group of self-appointed leaders rather than to provide a mechanism through which the general public can select its own leaders and influence the formulation of policy.

Like politicians everywhere, the Soviet leaders are products of historical environment and traditions of political thought. Their environment was the Russian Empire of their childhood, in which most of them lived as the sons and daughters of peasants and working-class families. Their tradition of political thought is that created by Karl Marx. To their historical environment they owe a desire to develop democratic institutions and a lack of personal experience with them. To their historical environment they also owe a craving to improve their economic condition, for their status in the empire was very different from that of the American farmer or workman. To their tradition of political thought they owe a belief that man has at last discovered the rules of social development and can manipulate social forces so as to achieve a goal called "communism."

This tradition of political thought and this heritage of environment have worked together in some instances to establish a fixity of purpose in the minds of Soviet politicians. In other instances, the two currents of influence have created sharp conflicts in attitude, some of which have never been resolved and even today help to explain the contradictions so often noted by foreign observers in Soviet society. A few examples may indicate the points at which the Soviet leadership has fixity of purpose and the points at which there is constant flux.

The Influence of History and Political Theory

Russian history and Marxist political theory have combined to create in Soviet minds a firm resolve to improve economic conditions. History's contribution to this aim was the youthful experience of those who were leaders of the Russian Revolution and also of those who still guide the U.S.S.R.'s destinies. These people were themselves poor during the Imperial period, or, as educated men, they studied the problems of the poor and identified themselves with them. Political theory's contribution was to teach that poverty need not be the lot of man. Marxism held out to its adherents a promise of a society in which every citizen might obtain satisfaction of his needs if capitalism were destroyed and if the working classes were to seize power.

Russian history and Marxist political theory in combination convinced the leaders of the Russian Revolution that capitalism had to be replaced by socialism and that the Imperial state apparatus had to be smashed and replaced by one in which the working classes ruled. A program of action incorporating these elements was expected to improve the economic and political status of both peasants and workmen.

The joint heritage of an Imperial Russia and of Marxist political thought proved not so harmonious when it came time to determine the type of government required in the new Russia. There could be fixity of purpose on an economic program to raise the standard of living, but there was reason for a conflict of views on the manner of putting that program into effect.

The current of Russian history established a strong yearning among the peoples of the empire for democratic institutions. There was ample reason for such aspirations. Up to 1906 there had been no parliament in the Russian Empire. There had been severe limitations upon freedom of speech and of the press, upon freedom of movement, upon the right to form trade unions and co-operative associations, and there had been legal inequality of citizens. Even many of the nobles, who were the privileged class, petitioned the Tsar for reform, but he was reluctant to act. Not until the serious unrest of 1905 did he feel impelled to promise a parliament, and even then he withheld the vote from the entire working class until riots forced him to revise his plan.

The reforms following what has been called the "Revolution of 1905" left much to be desired by those hoping for the development of democratic institutions. The Prime Minister and his cabinet could not be forced to resign by a vote of lack of confidence; the Tsar retained a veto over the acts of his parliament, dissolved it on various occasions when its activity frightened him, and, in the interval between parliaments, governed by decree as he had before 1906. In consequence the Russian Revolution of March, 1917, was fought by forces craving full political democracy. There was a determination on many sides to depart forever from the principle enunciated in Article 4 of the Fundamental Law of the Empire, which read: "To the Emperor of all the Russias belongs the supreme autocratic power. To obey his commands not merely from fear but according to the dictates of one's conscience is ordained by God himself."

The history of the year 1917 only intensified the demand for complete change. While the Provisional Government established at the time of the abdication of the Tsar struggled to make progress with democracy, it was still conducting a very unpopular war, and the country was in economic chaos. Under constant pressure from the center and left, the government tried to introduce reforms, but it was unable to meet the growing hunger for radical change. The masses had tasted blood, and under the leadership of the left they revolted a second time in November, 1917, to establish what they hoped would be a new, democratic type of government that would cope first of all with the pressing economic needs of the times.

Marxist political theory contained much preaching about the desirability of democracy, but it also contained within it the seeds of the negation of democracy. These seeds were to be found in the important role assigned by the theory to "leadership." This factor was taught as essential to the achievement of communism. Marx and his collaborator, Friedrich Engels, had no confidence in the political preparation of the general public for the task of building the kind of society they had planned. Although they wrote for a public in western Europe in which there were already large numbers of sophisticated people, they expected that only a relative few would understand what they were recommending and that still fewer would have the determination and stamina to try to put the Marxist program into effect. The authors of the program expected the great mass of the people to accept passively the inevitable continuance of the capitalist system. They expected that the mass would not rise in revolt against the system unless it were led by the few who were willing and able to take the trouble to understand what had to be done. They called for leadership of the masses toward the goal of communism. They were not content with the mere liberation of the masses from capitalism, to be followed by popular determination of political goals.

Marx's Concept of Democracy

Marx was not preaching democracy in the sense in which it is understood in the countries that have long experienced it, yet he claimed to be a democrat. Such a claim was necessary to win adherents, for democracy was on the lips of all as the aspiration of humanity. Marx held out the goal of economic abundance, which he assumed to be the primary desire of mankind. He seemed honestly to have thought that his analysis of history had discovered the forces that made for social progress, and he counted on the effective manipulation of these forces to achieve economic abundance.

Having assumed that mankind sought abundance and that his analysis of the forces that could provide it was correct, he took a step that has been popular also with other figures in history. He assumed that his system was democratic because it was designed, and in his view it was certain, to achieve maximum benefit for the general public. For him, "democracy" became synonymous with his plan to save the world; it did not mean a mechanism of government to be used by a majority to decide what it wants to do.

Marx was optimistic that if his plan could be introduced and the general public taught to appreciate its virtues, there would come a time when a leadership with the authority required to enforce its decisions would become unnecessary. He did not live to outline his dream of this final period, but his colleague Engels described it as the ultimate "withering away of the state." As Engels conceived of the final stage of government, it was to be a time in which the general public, satiated in its economic needs by the socialistic organization of the economy and trained over the years to understand its duties toward the community, would accept the rules that had been devised to achieve the goal. At that point no police, no courts, no army, no force of any kind would be necessary to restrain dissenters. There would remain only the administrators, and even these might be ordinary citizens taking their turn at the desk. These administrators would channel the flow of goods so as to achieve efficiency of production and distribution and the creation of the cultural media necessary to satisfaction of the mind as well as of the body.

The ultimate goal of a society without institutionalized compulsion looks utopian to students of government in the Western world, and it came during Stalin's declining years to look utopian to Soviet politicians as well. They satisfied their consciences by pushing its achievement so far into the future that it was not an active consideration in their planning. Only since Stalin's death has there been fresh consideration of means through which to reflect the process of withering. But even with the renewed interest in application of theory, this obscure Marxist concept still is of little more than theoretical interest to Soviet authors and approaches rejection in practice. There has been no rejection, however, of the basic theme of "leadership."

For the Russian Marxists the necessity of leadership had even stronger appeal than for those Western workmen who first accepted Marx's plan of action. The Russian Marxists believed that although the masses of Russian peasants and workmen were demanding the right of self-government during the early twentieth century, they were, generally, completely unprepared to govern. In this view, the working masses thought only of what could be gained by self-government: a full stomach, clothes, decent housing, and the essential home conveniences. Few of them were literate, and the Russian Marxists did not expect them to understand how their hopes could be realized.

To Vladimir Lenin, who came forward at the end of the nineteenth century as the most dedicated and vigorous of the Russian school of Marxists, the first task was to spread the new ideas among a limited few whom he planned to organize thereafter into a hard core of dedicated leaders. Lenin had no plan to invite the masses to share in the determination of goals. In his view this was unnecessary, for the goals had been already determined by Marx. Lenin saw his task as the preparation of leaders to execute Marx's plan and not that of preparing thinkers to devise new plans. Lenin called upon the masses to follow those who had mastered Marx and who demonstrated the skill and training necessary to achieve Marx's goals. Lenin was astute enough to know that leaders cannot overthrow governments without masses behind them. Masses were necessary, but their place was to afford weight and not to share in the decision-making process. He and his small body of colleagues were to be the vanguard.

In order to win their confidence in his leadership, Lenin analyzed the mass desires of the Russian people and of the minority peoples who lived on the fringes of the Russian Empire. He knew that the minority peoples wanted to be free of domination by the Great Russians, who had been the core of the Tsarist system of government. He knew that the peasants wanted to be rid of the landlords and to have sole control over the use of the land. He knew that the workmen wanted to be free of the discipline required by factory owners and managers. He knew that by 1917 the soldiers had become tired of war and wanted to go home. It was by playing upon these yearnings that he hoped to win the support of the masses for his plan.

Lenin sought also to win the allegiance, or at least the neutrality, of the educated men, known in the Russian Empire as the "intelligentsia." Many of the educated men had been increasingly active in pressing the Tsar to make concessions leading to a constitutional monarchy. Some were prepared for socialism, but few would have accepted Lenin's concept of government had he disclosed it to them. Most of the educated men sought the democratic determination of goals by democratic procedures. They considered that the means were as important as the ends. They would not accept Lenin's order of emphasis.

Lenin had his fixed ideas of leadership, but he could not swim against the current of history. He had to talk like a democrat in the traditional sense, both before the Russian Revolution and for some months after it, to win the loyalty of the various forces on which he relied for success. Yet he held tenaciously to his belief in a special type of leadership that would not be subject to dismissal by any majority vote of the general public. He enlarged his relatively small group of colleagues, whom he had first helped to organize in 1903, and created an elite to lead. The group came to be known as the "Communist party." He created behind the party a political police, to single out the enemies of his party's program when these enemies became sufficiently threatening. He demonstrated in practice after the Revolution that his view of democracy was quite different from that of many of those from other political groups who had fought with him to overthrow the Tsarist system of government.

The Leadership Circle Is Narrowed

Lenin took the Marxist germinal idea that mankind requires leadership, at least for a time, to guide it toward the goal of communism, and he interpreted it to mean that voices seeking to lead in directions other than his and his party's must be silenced. His development of the Marxist idea of leadership was in the direction of monopoly, restricted to those who had accepted the Marxist goal and who were dedicated to its achievement. Lenin did not go so far as to suggest that he alone had the right to determine policy even for his own party. Although he demanded for himself the loyalty of his colleagues and used political maneuvers to outwit those who opposed his views, he supported the role of the Central Committee of the party as the maker of policy. He may have thought of himself as the first among equals, but he seems not to have desired to assume a role of dictator to all.

Lenin showed his fear of personal dictatorship as the possible outgrowth of what he had done by preparing a political testament on December 25, 1922, only nine days after his second stroke. He called upon his colleagues to avoid a split in the party between Leon Trotsky and Joseph Stalin. He said of Stalin that he had concentrated enormous power in his hands and that it was not certain that he always knew how to use that power with sufficient caution. He said of Trotsky that he had proved in his struggle with the Central Committee that he was distinguished not only by his exceptional abilities but also by his too far-reaching self-confidence and a disposition to be too much attracted by the purely administrative side of affairs.

Lenin had good reason to fear the emergence of a personal dictator, as subsequent events were to show. He had created a mechanism that made personal dictatorship possible, although he had not used it to establish himself. When he died, in January, 1924, there was no device that could be used by the rank and file of the party to hamper the rise of a personal dictator, and there was waiting a man without Lenin's particular willingness to impose self-restraint upon his ambition.

A triumvirate of Lenin's heirs was intrusted by the Communist party with the task of guiding the destinies of the country. Trotsky was omitted from the triumvirate as the result of the maneuvers of those who feared his assumption of power. Gregory Zinoviev, Leo Kamenev, and Stalin became the official leaders, and they described themselves as a "collective leadership." Stalin seems to have accepted the idea of sharing power with two colleagues only because he was not yet strong enough to do otherwise, but he soon exhibited the qualities that Lenin had feared. He began to push his colleagues from the triumvirate. By the beginning of 1926, Stalin and the machine he had created through his position as Secretary-General of the Communist party had established control over the party. Collective leadership was no more, and it was not to be restored until after his death in 1953.

Stalin utilized the opening that Marxist political thought, as developed by Lenin, gave him to justify his personal assumption of power. Yet he had also to consider the stream of Russian history and the desire of the masses for democracy, and he needed also to reduce his enemies abroad and to expand Soviet influence among foreign leftist groups. To win adherents to his system, he had to espouse democratic principles and even to take steps that might be interpreted as leading to the ultimate realization of a government in which the people shared in policy-making and in the choice of leaders.

Stalin seized the propaganda initiative in declaring his regime the most democratic the world had ever seen. He drafted a new constitution in 1936 that opened elections to all and that created a type of parliament more nearly like that known in the West than the one created by the Congress of Soviets at the time of the Revolution. He included within the constitution what he called a "bill of rights," which went considerably beyond the statement of rights adopted soon after the Revolution. He eliminated from the laws the discrimination in securing employment and schooling that had previously operated against those whose background had not been peasant or worker.

At the very moment that professedly "democratic" forms were being developed in an effort to please the masses, there were being established counterweights to prevent any possible use of the forms to influence policy or to select leaders. This was Stalin's way of trying to resolve the conflicts caused by the fusion of democratic yearnings arising from the frustrating Russian historical experience and of his version of the Marxist political concept of leadership. On the one hand, he was trying to satisfy the historic, although inexperienced, craving of the people for democracy, and, on the other hand, he was trying to make certain that no one would challenge his authority to decide what was good for the peoples of the U.S.S.R.

Stalin's Heirs Demand Reform

Stalin's heirs, on his death in March, 1953, seem to have recognized the danger of a successor's assumption of dictatorial power. They soon indicated their appreciation that Stalin had pushed too far the concept of leadership developed by Marx and expanded by Lenin. Lenin had made Marx's idea concrete by establishing a monopoly party, which was to be led, in turn, by a Central Committee. Stalin had created the role of personal dictator over the monopoly party and over its Central Committee.

To meet hostility toward his assumption of dictatorial powers, which is now revealed to have been widespread but unspoken during Stalin's declining years, Stalin's heirs reverted to the expedient adopted in the crisis caused by Lenin's death in 1924. They called for the re-establishment of collective leadership within the Communist party. They indicated their determination to permit no single man to hold all reins of power and to claim all-embracing knowledge. The renunciation of Stalin's type of personal dictatorship received world-wide publicity when the Communist party met in its twentieth congress in February, 1956. Stalin's system was denounced as the "cult of the individual." The official history of the Communist party, in which facts had been distorted to prove Stalin a genius and to villify all those who disagreed with him as enemies of the people, was ordered withdrawn and rewritten. Stalin's heirs said "Never again!"

The collective leadership was short lived. By June, 1957, the members of the collective were intriguing to oust Khrushchev, but he utilized his position as successor to Stalin's power within the Communist party and obtained the support of the army chief to oust his opponents and seize power. He completed the process by dismissing the army chief in November, 1957. He had become supreme, but his power was not as all-embracing as had been Stalin's. The explanation of his remarkable feat lies in the character of the political apparatus he had inherited. The limitation on complete assumption of power is to be found in the changes in the structure of Soviet society and in the temper of the people, who are no longer willing to accept Stalin's type of absolute dictatorship.

Democratic Forms Subject to Counterweights

The Soviet political apparatus can be understood best and criticized most effectively, in my view, if it is described as incorporating democratic forms, counterweighted with totalitarian controls. Such an approach is contrary to the current view of some Western political scientists. They prefer to describe the Soviet system as an autocratic or totalitarian machine masked in democratic phraseology. The reasons for emphasizing democratic forms are several, and they bear stating at the outset.

First, an approach to the Soviet system of government as incorporating democratic forms counterweighted with totalitarian controls facilitates exposure of the Soviet system in terms understandable to every student of democratic systems. If the Soviet system is described as one of institutions of completely unfamiliar form, there is a tendency on the part of beginning students to disbelieve the analysis when subsequent research discloses Soviet references to institutions with familiar names. If the Soviet system provides procedures called "elections" in which all citizens are permitted to vote without restrictions, it seems better to examine these institutions as the forms they are said to be, and then to determine how they are prevented from serving the democratic function of elections, than to deny that there are any elections in the U.S.S.R. If there are parliamentary sittings in which deputies rise to speak and in which legislation is adopted, it seems better to examine this as a democratic form subject to controls nullifying its democratic function than to deny that there is a parliament.

So long as Soviet propaganda appeals to the peoples of the U.S.S.R. and of the world in terms that have established meanings outside the U.S.S.R. and its orbit, the propaganda claims should be met directly with an explanation of how the Soviet institutions with familiar names have been deprived of their familiar functions. The use of entirely different words to emphasize Soviet contrasts may serve a useful purpose in a radio program when there is no time for analysis, but it does not serve the purpose of a textbook.

Second, an approach to the Soviet system as incorporating democratic forms counterweighted with totalitarian controls has been chosen because it permits a student to draw a moral from a study of the Soviet system. The moral is that the existence of a democratic form gives no assurance that it will function automatically in truly democratic fashion. Astute individuals have devised ways of perverting democratic forms so that the mass will remain confident that it is in no danger of losing its voice while it has in fact lost, or is in the process of losing, any real influence on leadership.

A study of the Soviet system suggests the peril-points at which democratic forms can be counterweighted to nullify their function, although the counterweighting may not be noticed at all or may not be appreciated for what it is. Some of the peril-points are indicated in the final chapter in this book. The opportunity of drawing such a moral would be missed if the Soviet system were described as a totalitarian machine masked in democratic phraseology. Such a description can lull the citizen of a true democracy into passivity, on the assumption that his democracy is secure so long as he can still find within it institutions called elections, political parties, parliaments, labor unions, co-operative associations, courts, and codes of law.

Finally, the approach to the Soviet system adopted in this study may facilitate prediction of the future course of events in the U.S.S.R. by providing balanced emphasis upon both means by which the Soviet leaders have ruled. It exposes not only the terror by which the people have been controlled, but it discloses how the Soviet leaders have lessened their task of maintaining order by catering to the democratic aspirations of their people.

Description of the Soviet system as completely lacking in forms which are designed to appeal to the people's desire for democratic participation in government can lead to an underestimation of the importance of measures introduced by the Soviet leaders to avoid pressure for revolution. Proper balancing of the two means by which Soviet leaders have ruled can make it easier to understand why most foreign students of Soviet politics anticipate evolution rather than revolution within the U.S.S.R. during the next twenty years.

The pages which follow will make abundantly clear that the Soviet system of government is not easily characterized. It speaks in the name of democracy, and some democratic forms exist within the system, although presently counterweighted to prevent their democratic functioning. The twentieth Communist party congress suggested that some of the counterweights would be lifted, and there was the beginning of what one Soviet author called a "thaw."

While a thaw has been in process, it is evident that there are some serious obstacles in the way of complete democratic functioning of Soviet institutions. The nature of these obstacles will be made clear in the description of the institutions. Foremost among the obstacles is, however, not an institution but an idea. So long as those who rule the U.S.S.R. have no faith in the capacity of the general public to choose policies wisely, democracy in its true sense can hardly be born. The leadership idea as presently interpreted is the primary barrier to a democratic system. To be a real democrat one must share with Edmund Burke his faith that, although the people may make mistakes, "in all disputes between them and their rulers, the presumption is at least upon a par in favor of the people."

Khrushchev and his colleagues have exhibited no faith in Burke and his willingness to trust the people. It will call for a considerable change in their interpretation of the theory of Marx, as embellished by Lenin and Stalin, before any such faith can be expected to manifest itself. The chapters that follow will indicate such possibilities for change as presently exist. They will also expose the very real limitations upon realization of true democracy, should the new leaders ultimately exhibit a faith in the people or should the educated people become sufficiently persuasive to require the ruling few to let them share in the process of ruling.

CHAPTER 2

THE HARD CORE OF THE SYSTEM

The people cannot be trusted to govern themselves. This is the creed of Khrushchev and of his colleagues, the principle that they have extracted from Marxist political theory as developed by Lenin and Stalin. Leadership is essential, and it must be a special kind of leadership. It must guide the people toward a specific goal, not in response to their present wishes but by molding them so that their wishes coincide with those of the leaders.

A description of the Soviet system of government must begin differently from an account of a democracy. The latter would focus upon the operation of instruments through which the public expresses its will. Western political scientists are now centering their attention upon pressure groups, upon parliaments and their committees, upon law which enables the individual to speak his mind without fear of retaliation. Soviet parliamentary institutions and pressure groups work in reverse, for these serve as focal points from which the influence of leaders is radiated throughout the populace. The key to the functioning of the Soviet system is the leadership group. A study of Soviet political institutions must begin, therefore, with the Communist party.

While the Communist party is called a "political party" in textbooks from the U.S.S.R. and from elsewhere abroad, it is so different from Western political parties that some Westerners have suggested that another term be invented for it. A look at the characteristics of the Communist party as a political organization will both indicate its distinguishing elements and help to suggest the features of Western political parties that are essential to preservation of intraparty democracy and of a political party's function in a democratic system of government.

13

The key terms in any characterization of the Communist party are "centralized structure" and "discipline." Armies too are structured centrally and require discipline of the troops. In considerable degree the Communist party is patterned on an army. It has its officers, from the level of the general staff down to the platoon, and their command is law. Yet the Communist party would not attract members if it were structured completely on army lines. A twentieth-century political party must attract and hold its members on a basis other than that of a military draft or of a system of military discipline and punishment. Ever since the American and French revolutions too many people, even in Russia, have dreamed of democracy and of mass determination of policy to be attracted to a political party without a show of these.

Thus the leaders of the Communist party have been faced with a more difficult task than the organizers of an army. They have found it necessary to provide a mechanism through which the rank-and-file members appear to have the opportunity to choose their own leaders and to influence policy. Having created this mechanism in a form susceptible of democratic use, they have felt it necessary to devise a subtle system of counterweights to prevent an overturn of their leadership and an adoption of policies contrary to their desires. The Communist leaders have devised a name for this system of mass participation subject to counterweight control. They have called it "democratic centralism."

The Formalities of Communist Party Structure

How is the system operated? The democratic feature comprises two elements, the first of which is the choice of officers. Party members at the level that would be called a platoon in an army are given the formal right to elect every year their second lieutenant, who is called, in the Communist party vocabulary, "secretary of the primary party organization." In the large organizations this secretary is aided by an executive bureau, also elected formally each year. The party members in the primary organization, who may be as few as three or as many as one hundred, also are given the formal opportunity to choose a delegate every year to attend a conference of delegates from other primary party organizations within a geographical area corresponding to a city or to a county in a rural area. This conference meets seldom, being required to convene only every year, or every two years in large cities subdivided into boroughs. When the delegates meet they choose from their number a smaller group, called a "district committee," to meet every three months. This committee then chooses its executive bureau, including several secretaries. One of the secretaries is designated "first secretary," and, in practice, it is he who runs the bureau and the affairs of the committee in general.

The large conference of delegates from the various rural and city party organizations within the county also elects a delegate to attend periodically, at intervals of twenty-four months, a superior meeting called a "provincial conference," or, in the small republics not divided into provinces, a "republic congress." In the few cases of very large cities, such as Moscow, the party conference of delegates from below brings together only delegates from the ward party conferences of the city, the wards being in the position of rural counties within the party structure. Such party conferences in the very large cities have the same rights within the party hierarchy as provincial conferences and are represented directly in higher party agencies rather than through the provincial conference of the party organization in the province in which the very large city is located geographically.

When the provincial party conference meets, its delegates take steps similar to those taken in the various county conferences. They choose their own "committee," which, in turn, selects an executive bureau including several secretaries. The provincial committee meets only every four months, but its executive bureau is on call at all times. The provincial party conference in each of the four larger republics also selects a group of delegates to proceed, at four-year intervals, to the capital of the republic within which the province or very large city is situated. Again the same procedure is followed in the choice of an executive body: the republic congress chooses a committee, called in this instance a "central committee," and the central committee then chooses an executive bureau including several secretaries. The delegates to the republic party congress also name a group of delegates to proceed to the quadrennial all-Union congress in Moscow.

To this pattern of ever higher party bodies leading up through the republics to Moscow, an exception is provided by the largest republic, that comprising the Great Russian ethnic element of the population. In this large republic, called the Russian Soviet Federated Socialist Republic, stretching from Leningrad across Siberia to Vladivostok, there is no republic party congress. There is but a co-ordinating committee guiding the provincial conferences. The various provincial party conferences send their delegations directly to the all-Union meeting in Moscow.

The all-Union meeting in Moscow, composed of delegates from republic party congresses and from the various provincial conferences of the Russian Republic, is called "The All-Union Communist Party Congress." It is always of very large size. In 1952 it consisted of 1,192 delegates representing 6,013,259 party members, and 167 delegates representing 868,886 candidate members. In 1956 the congress numbered 1,355 delegates representing 6,795,896 party members, and 81 delegates representing 419,609 candidate members. The extraordinary twenty-first congress in 1959 had 1,269 delegates for 7,622,356 party members and 106 delegates for 616,775 candidate members.

Like the groups at lower levels, The All-Union Communist Party Congress chooses by formal vote its own "committee," which in this case is called the "Central Committee of the Communist Party." As named in 1956, it was composed of 133 members and 122 alternates with the right to attend meetings but not to vote. Vacancies arising in the panel of voting members are filled from the alternate panel. The party congress also names a "central auditing commission," which numbered 63 in 1956. Its task is to check upon the financial affairs of the party.

The Central Committee chooses its steering committee from its own members, and to this group is given the name "Presidium." As named in 1952, the Presidium numbered 25 members and 11 alternates. In 1953 its membership was sharply reduced, as will be elaborated in a discussion of changes made after Stalin's death, but in 1956 the number was again increased.

In addition to the Presidium there is named by the Central Committee a "committee of party control" to police party members against violation of party discipline and to hear appeals against expulsion from the party by lower party organs. This body is permitted to maintain agents at all levels within the party, without formal relationship to the party bosses at those levels.

What has been a considerable staff or "apparatus" serves the Central Committee. Although this staff was to be reduced under resolution of the twentieth party congress, it seems still to be divided into sections, each of which is headed by a member of the Central Committee. The sections have the task of compiling information for the formulation of policy papers. They also see to the execution of party policy decisions by lower party organizations, once they have been adopted. For this purpose they arrange the establishment of analogous sections in republic party committees and even at local party levels. Refugees from the U.S.S.R. have reported that sections have been designated in the recent past for propaganda and agitation, heavy industry, war industry, light industry, finance and trade, transportation and communication, agriculture, science and culture, schools, courts and prosecutors, work among women, military affairs, Komsomol and trade-union relations with the party, personnel, instruction in party organization, and state security. Occasionally evidence of other sections comes to light, as when a Soviet delegation studying housing construction in England in late 1955 included the chief of the housing construction section of the Central Committee of the party as well as the minister of urban and rural construction.

Controls within the Party

The creation of a hierarchy of party agencies is an attempt to meet the desire of the rank and file to share in the selection of its leaders. Share they do, yet there are controls so that this selection cannot result in the overturn of the leaders. It is in the formulation of these controls that Lenin, and subsequently Stalin, showed skill in manipulating democratic forms for their own purposes.

One measure of control is inherent in the nature of this very hierarchy. Because there are no direct elections of top Communist party officials, a wave of mass discontent over party leadership would have to exist for several years and sweep almost the whole country to be reflected in the top echelons. The rank and file can influence only the choice of their committee and of their delegate to the next higher party conference. By their committee they are insulated even from selection of the party secretary, who in practice controls the destiny of a primary party organization. Top party officials are chosen by the small Central Committee of the party, and this in turn can be reconstituted only once in four years by The All-Union Party Congress. Even this opportunity has been withdrawn in the past, because party congresses have been postponed for long periods of time during which the leaders have not had to account even formally to representatives of the rank and file, except at rare intervals.

A second measure of control lies in the nominating and electing procedure within the party. Nominations are prepared by the first secretary at the level of the primary party organization and by the executive bureau at higher levels. These individuals can, and usually do, assure their own election by placing only their own names on the ballot. Until 1939 the rules of the Communist party under which operations within the party were conducted provided that voting upon the nominations should be by a show of hands. Clearly this method of voting, which has been subject to abuse wherever it has been tried, permitted the executive bureau to determine its enemies and subsequently to take measures discriminating against them, if not ousting them from Communist party membership. In 1939 the rules were amended, on the recommendation of Stalin, to introduce secret voting for the executive bureau and for delegates to the higher party conference. It was further required that the vote now be on each name separately rather than on a whole slate. This amendment prevented the secretary from pushing through an unpopular delegate by including his name upon a slate which had to be accepted or rejected as a whole.

The 1939 change in voting procedure seems to have been made as a result of pressure from party members upon Stalin for relaxation of the very strict controls that had tended openly to negate the presence of democracy within the party not only in the eyes of Communist party members within the U.S.S.R. but perhaps even more importantly in the eyes of those who were being wooed by Communist parties in France, Italy, and elsewhere. Stalin conceded the secret ballot probably because of his growing confidence in the effectiveness of his Communist party machine. He had been developing discipline in this machine during the seventeen years of his control over its heart, namely, the general secretariat of the party, and he had completed in 1938 a purge of his most powerful opponents within the party. By 1939 he could afford to appear to be democratic, since he could be sure of the results even when the ballot was secret.

Stalin also may have felt by 1939 that a secret ballot for the various secretaries of the primary party organizations would be a good way to test their political effectiveness. While he could be sure that the rank and file had learned the lesson of the preceding seventeen years, a lesson dramatized by the purge trials of 1936, 1937, and 1938 in which expectable penalties for dissenters on basic issues had been made clear, he could not be sure that his party secretaries at the levels of the primary party organizations and above were not making enemies unnecessarily by being completely arbitrary and unresponsive to demands which should not be ignored. The secret ballot gave Stalin some opportunity to find out from the rank and file itself which party secretaries were so tyrannical that they would be voted against. According to announcements in the Communist party newspapers of the time, there occurred some overturns in the local secretaryships, overturns that the party press hailed for clearing out local party officials who had become drunk with power.

Selection of Party Members

A third measure of control, in addition to the intraparty measures of the multi-stepped system of elections and the self-nominating procedure adopted for these, lies in a careful selection of candidates from among those who express their desire for party membership. Not every applicant is admitted to membership. In 1956 there were only slightly more than seven million members out of a total Soviet population of 120 million over eighteen years of age. This ratio of one to seventeen adults shows quickly the selective nature of Communist party membership.

The small number of members in the Communist party is the result of a selection system devised to eliminate from consideration all but those most devoted to the cause of the party—those who can be expected to be willing and able to accept party discipline. The selection process is placed within the authority of the primary party organizations, which are established at places of employment such as factories, government offices, collective or state farms, divisions of railways, large department stores, universities, and army units. The Communist party leaders have indicated their feeling that those who know a person at work know a great deal about him because the good and the bad in a man or a woman appear more clearly at work than in social activities. Application for membership must be filed, therefore, with the primary party organization at the applicant's place of work, and he is judged by those who in party thinking know him best.

An application must be accompanied by recommendations from three persons who have been members of the Communist party for at least three years. These are not lightly given, because those who recommend and vouch for a candidate are subject to penalties, including loss of their own Communist party membership, if he proves to be a serious misfit within the party. If the applicant has been a member of the Communist youth league, of which there will be discussion later, he may substitute for one of these recommendations that of a district committee of the Communist youth league.

When an application has passed the scrutiny of the primary party organization to which it is delivered, it is reviewed by the district committee of the county or big-city Communist party conference to which the primary party organization concerned sends a delegate. If this superior, and presumably more reliable, body approves the recommendation of admission made by the primary party organization, the applicant has passed the first barrier. He is not yet a member of the party, for he must prove his worth during a period of trial.

During a candidate's period of trial, which is currently established at one year, he is subjected to rigid tests in the form of duties such as propagandizing with party doctrine groups among whom he circulates. If he shows himself to be well disciplined and effective, he is admitted to full membership by the primary party organization in which he has been a candidate. If, after one year, discussion within the primary party organization concludes that a candidate has not yet proved himself worthy of membership but can be expected to do so in time, a year's extension is voted. If a candidate is clearly undesirable, he is dropped from candidacy and returns to the ranks of non-party people from which he came.

During World War II, this selection system was ignored in an effort to bring into the party men with proved leadership qualities. Refugees from the U.S.S.R. have since reported that desirable soldiers were pressed to accept membership and that recommendations were arranged for them by the party secretaries. The same procedure has sometimes been applied to men and women in industry or in agriculture who catch the eye of party secretaries as potential leaders. Nevertheless, the principle of careful scrutiny of membership applications has been maintained by subjecting persons admitted through exceptional procedure to a subsequent review. If the new member indicates after admission that he is below standard, he is expelled. Many soldiers admitted on the field of battle during the war were expelled in later years when they showed themselves lacking in desire or capacity to make the theoretical studies required of party members.

Reports of refugees also indicate that careerists have sometimes slipped through the selection process for new members. With the passing of the years and with the increasing favoritism shown party members in the allocation to them of positions of power and prestige, the desirability of party membership has been enhanced. It no longer attracts persecution as it did in prerevolutionary times nor does it require self-denial as it did during the 1920's. In consequence, ambitious opportunists have crept into the party, with the result that members are not today always as dedicated as party rules would have them appear. This is especially so of the more youthful ones.

In its formalized selection of members the Communist party reveals one of the primary distinctions between itself and the mass political parties familiar to the student of politics in the United States and in many other countries. In the West, parties other than the Communist party generally provide no such process for the selection of members. In most parties there is required no more than a declaration of membership, and there is no obligation to perform duties or to accept any form of discipline. Even representatives of these parties within the various parliaments or congresses of the West generally consider themselves free to oppose their leaders if they think that a decision has been unwise.

Limitations on Expression of Opinion

The extent to which opinion may be expressed on matters of policy has come to be a measure of a democratic system of government, and the designers of the Communist party have found it necessary to provide a semblance of honor of this measure both to hold the loyalty of party members and to attract outsiders into the ranks. Again, however, there seems to have been a problem of providing a means for popular expression of opinion and at the same time of devising a counterweight. The party leaders seem to want to be sure that expressions of opinion will never result in the adoption of a policy before the highest officers of the Communist party have had an opportunity to consider its prospective influence upon the course of events.

In defining democratic centralism, the rules drawn up by the Communist party leaders and adopted formally by The All-Union Communist Party Congress establish the outlines of the control mechanism. Every party member is given the formal right to express his opinion within the group to which he belongs, whether it be his primary party organization or a higher-level conference to which he is a delegate. This right is widely advertised by the Communist party press as indicative of the democratic character of the Communist party.

Having given the formal right of free speech to party members within their organizations, the draftsmen of the party rules provided a counterweight. The rules declare that members shall not be permitted to form a voting bloc, known in party parlance as a "faction," within the organization to which they belong. This restriction means that while a member is permitted to rise in his place and speak his mind at a party meeting, he may not have consulted with friends in advance to solicit their support of his view so that his speech will not be the solitary one on the subject he espouses. Nor may he have bargained with others to vote for his project in exchange for his subsequent vote in favor of some project dear to their hearts.

The effectiveness of this counterweight to free speech will be obvious to any American who contemplates the working of any organization to which he belongs. It will quickly be evident in any group that a single voice carries no weight, unless it be that of an unusually persuasive speaker or of one with political power within the organization. Even the persuasive speaker will be voted down if his colleagues are in no mood to listen. Minorities have been effective in tempering policies only when they could organize into groups which threatened to grow and become majorities, or if they were able to manipulate themselves with such skill that they held positions of balance of power, promising support to one or the other side of an argument in accordance with the willingness of the one or the other to support their causes. Soviet politicians seem to have put their finger on the key to a minority's strength and to have locked the door and thrown away the key. They can champion democratic forms within the Communist party without fear that any minority will become unmanageable.

There is yet another formal counterweight to the democratic right of free speech guaranteed to individual members within the party. It lies in the obligation established by the rules that when a decision has been taken, it is binding upon all those who shared in it, even if they voted against it on the floor. They are not permitted to argue for its reversal until it has been tried to the satisfaction of the leaders. The decision is binding upon them until opened again for discussion.

Discipline for Party Members

Discipline within the Communist party is enforced in two principal ways, by persuasion and by punishment of violators. Persuasion plays a part greater than is often appreciated outside the U.S.S.R., for though the Communist party is a relatively small core of persons guiding the destinies of the entire country and thus attracts people who enjoy the perquisites of power, there are here, as among any group of leaders, not only those who enjoy a sense of power but also those who have a sense of mission. It is upon those individuals who seek admission to, and continue within, the party because they have a sense of mission that persuasion especially acts as a means of enforcing discipline. These have joined voluntarily, and they remain voluntarily. To be sure, if they resigned they would be considered "quitters" and would lose favor both with those whom they left behind in the party and also with millions more who have not desired or could not gain membership but who accept party values. But while such social opprobrium is to be reckoned with before resigning, there is a still stronger force for those who feel a sense of mission—the force created by a consuming interest, without which life would not be worth living.

To those who have entered the Communist party with a sense of mission, the party leaders who seek to win them to a point of view have only to explain policy in terms of improving conditions within the U.S.S.R. and even, eventually, throughout the world—the declared mission of the party. If the explanation is well phrased and convincing, it will be seized upon and incorporated as a design for living without serious question. For such persons, persuasion is a mighty instrument of control, and the training of Communist party secretaries, on whom the primary burden of persuasion rests, includes a very extensive portion on the art of effective public speaking.

Punishment awaits those party members who feel less or no sense of mission and are not persuaded by argument to accept the orders of their superiors within the party. It takes several forms. There are the moderate forms of admonition, reprimand, and censure, the order of censure being made known within the party by publication. There are the harsher forms of temporary removal from party work or recall from a position in a government agency. The most severe form consists of expulsion from the party: for the disillusioned party member who has compelling personal reasons for remaining within the party while disliking official policy, the threat of expulsion is a strong incentive to conform. Each of these forms of punishment is designed to attach to the culprit a measure of social stigma in the eyes of fellow party members.

Members of the Central Committee of the party, and of the executive committees at each lower level within the party hierarchy, are protected against disciplinary action by the primary party organization to which they belong. Under the rules, penalties may be

exacted of such persons only if approved at a full meeting of the
Central Committee or of the executive committee concerned, and
then only when a two-thirds majority consents. The leadership has
thus assured itself of no surprises from below.

Internationalism within the Party

Group organization on the basis of ethnic origin has been opposed
within the Communist party from the outset. Lenin insisted, even
against serious opposition from fellow members belonging to ethnic
minorities within the Russian Empire, that the party was not to be a
federation of ethnically organized groups. He opposed any suggestion that Jews have a party organization that would bring together
Jews wherever they might live and that would co-operate with a
Russian or Ukrainian or Lithuanian organization similarly constituted. He demanded that the party structure be centralized without
regard to the ethnic origin of its members.

Due to historical migrations, the population of the U.S.S.R. contains many ethnic groups living in relatively compact communities
in various parts of the U.S.S.R. Thus, the Ukrainian minority lives
in one corner, the Georgian and Armenian minorities in another, the
Finnish minority in another, the Latvian, Estonian, and Lithuanian
minorities in still others. Under the system of organization based
upon broad geographic areas, in which all party members within a
republic are represented through their provincial delegates in the
party congress of that republic, it may appear to an outsider as if
there were separate Ukrainian and Armenian and Latvian party
units. Communist party leaders have always emphasized, however,
that there is no basis for ethnic representation within the party.
Consequently, the unit named the "Ukrainian Communist party" is
not conceived as an ethnic unit comprising all Ukrainians wherever
they may live but rather comprises Communist party members of
whatever ethnic group who happen to be living at the time within
the borders established for the Ukrainian Republic. It includes Russians and Jews and Armenians and Georgians who live within the
Ukrainian Republic's borders. Even its head, bearing the title of
"Secretary of the Central Committee of the Ukrainian Communist
Party," may be, and has been, a man of Russian rather than Ukrainian ethnic origin. Usually the party secretaries are chosen from the
ethnic unit that has the largest representation within a given area,
but this need not be so. In consequence, the way is open to substitute a secretary of another ethnic group if there should appear

among the Communist party members within any republic a sense of conflict of interest between the ethnic unit from which most of them come and the whole party.

This concept of "internationalism" of party structure, as contrasted with "nationalism" or structure based upon ethnic groups, aided Stalin, a member of the Georgian ethnic minority, to maintain his position among the very much more numerous Russian ethnic element within the Communist party. He could claim to represent the Russian element as well as all other ethnic elements because he was to be thought of not as a Georgian but as an internationalist—as a member of the working class, which is supposed, in Communist theory, to have no ethnic loyalties cutting across its class line.

In spite of the theory of internationalism within the party, it was common gossip in the U.S.S.R. before Stalin's death that to please the people his successor would have to be a Russian. Lip-service was given to internationalism, but political wisdom suggested that attention be paid to the sentiments of the majority ethnic group in selecting the party boss.

Funds to maintain the Communist party are obtained through a system of party dues levied upon each party member. There is collected from each candidate member a small initiation fee of 2 per cent of one month's wages. Thereafter all candidates and full members pay monthly dues graduated on the basis of monthly wages. The tax begins at ½ of 1 per cent of wages under 500 rubles and increases to 3 per cent of wages exceeding 2,000 rubles a month.

It is remarkable that the Communist party, with its control over the finances of the entire Soviet state, has chosen to continue a system of party dues. One might expect the party to dip into the state treasury for its maintenance and to abandon the payment of dues as an outmoded heritage from prerevolutionary days when its political campaign against the government of the Russian Empire could be financed in no other way. Nevertheless, the dues are still collected, although it may be that expenses beyond those covered by dues are hidden in some item of the state budget. Such subsidization by the state treasury, if any exists, is not, however, reported specifically in any line of the state budget devoted to Communist party administration expenses. Presumably the Communist party's leaders have concluded that there is an additional emotional bond established between a member and his party if he is made to feel that he is sacrificing the satisfaction of some personal need to maintain his party, or it may be that relations with the non-party public are facilitated if there is no published support for an argument that the public is taxed to fatten the Communist party apparatus.

In spite of the various control features built into the Communist party's system of democratic centralism, party bosses have often found it expedient to go beyond even them. The most notable violation of the Communist party's own rules is the infrequency with which meetings of the representative party groups at the various levels of the party structure have occurred, and local party secretaries are occasionally criticized openly in the Communist party press for failing to call the required meetings of their county or city conference. But these local party leaders have not been set a good example, for The All-Union Communist Party congresses were called during Stalin's lifetime only at rare intervals, in spite of the requirement of the rules. The Congress held in 1952 should have been held in 1942, had the then existing requirement of a congress every three years been fulfilled. The Congress of 1939 took place at an interval of five years after the preceding Congress of 1934. To be sure, the Second World War intervened between the 1939 and the 1952 congresses, and few party members could have been expected to resent postponement in the light of war conditions. Yet the war ended, and still no congress was held for six years after its end. Only since Stalin's death have the leaders seemed to be prepared to follow the rules. The twentieth party congress was held within the prescribed four-year period after the nineteenth party congress. The twenty-first was called as an extraordinary congress only three years after its predecessor.

The Focus of Party Power

Power within the Communist party is presently centralized in the Presidium of the Central Committee. This body was established in 1952 to absorb the Political Buro, which had previously formulated party policy, and the Organizational Buro, which had devised plans for executing policy up to that time. Each of the absorbed bodies had contained a small number of members, usually fifteen, during the years shortly prior to the amalgamation. The All-Union Communist Party Congress set up the Presidium as a body of 36 persons, 25 of whom were classed as members and 11 of whom were classed as candidates.

Many commentators outside the U.S.S.R. who compared the number of men in the Presidium with the smaller number that had sat in the Political Buro and the Organizational Buro thought that the aging Stalin was increasing the circle of leaders to distribute power. The increase in numbers looked like a step toward satisfying what many believed to be a growing desire on the part of the party leaders just below the summit for a greater share in the determination of policy. Other foreign students thought the enlargement was Stalin's way of diluting the power of his potential opposition and thus strengthening his dictatorial position. Khrushchev gave credence to this interpretation in a secret speech to the twentieth party congress.

Of the two theories, the one that stresses Stalin's recognition of the new intelligentsia's desire for representation at the top seems the more plausible, in spite of Krushchev's explanation. Various bits of evidence support such a conclusion. For example, Stalin did not limit his policy of increasing numbers to the Presidium as the potentially most powerful party agency. He sponsored at the same time an increase in the size of the Central Committee of the party from 139 persons to 236, of whom 125 were members and 111 were candidates, and he increased the number of party secretaries attached to the Central Committee from 5 to 10. These increases seem to bear no relation to a desire to dilute power, for little existed at these points. They seem to be part of a general pattern of enlargement of participation in party bodies to satisfy a growing desire for participation by more than an extremely limited few.

With Stalin's death, his heirs seem to have been frightened of possible unrest within the Communist party, and they took a step to reverse the policy developed by Stalin and to reduce the circle of those with power. The Central Committee of the party was left unchanged in size, but the number of Presidium members was reduced to 14, of whom 10 were classified as members and 4 as candidates, and the number of secretaries of the Central Committee was lowered to 5. By these measures the inner circle of the Communist party became again about what it had been prior to the innovations introduced by Stalin in October, 1952.

By reversing Stalin's policy of enlargement of party agencies the new rulers provided powerful evidence that the enlargement policy had not made it easier to rule. Stalin's heirs reaffirmed a lack of faith in the bulk of the Communist party members—an unwillingness to permit even limited participation in policy-making by more than a handful of leaders, most of whom had served with Stalin on the old Political Buro. But the limitations were not to last. In July, 1955, 2 secretaries were added to the party structure, to bring the total to 7, and 2 new men joined the members of the Presidium of the Central Committee of the party. In February, 1959, a Presidium of 24 was named, of whom 14 were full members and 10 were candidates. The secretaries were increased to 10.

The passing of Stalin from the political scene naturally changed the power structure, for his had been a powerful personality. Stalin had never established for himself a titular position of party "chairman," but for many years he had, in fact, ruled the party with a strong hand from his position as General Secretary of the Party. Although nominally, at least, looking to the Political Buro for advice, he apparently took less and less of it as he advanced in age until he stood alone as supreme boss of the party, demanding absolute loyalty. Under such conditions, no one had been able to prepare himself to assume the mantle of party boss—not even G. M. Malenkov, who had frequently been mentioned as Stalin's choice for heir. Those who survived Stalin came forth quickly to report to the nation that Stalin had been succeeded by a "committee," and they denounced one-man rule of the party. No one was named immediately as General Secretary, although Malenkov was assumed to have become the first among the secretaries. While many believed that he would use this post to establish himself as sole successor to Stalin, just as Stalin had used it in 1924 to snatch power from the triumvirate that had been constituted within the party at the time of Lenin's last illness, his resignation from his party secretaryship was announced within a few weeks after Stalin's death. Nikita Krushchev moved into his place, although he did not assume the title of "First Secretary" until September, 1953, and has not yet assumed the title of "General Secretary of the Party." Even without Stalin's title, Khrushchev was able to use his secretarial position to terminate collective leadership. In four years he methodically placed men loyal to him in the key posts of party secretaryship of republic and provincial committees. When some veterans of Stalin's time sought to oust him from the Presidium before he had perfected monopoly power, he succeeded in postponing decision until the Central Committee could be called. In unprecedented rejection of Presidium guidance, its majority supported Khrushchev as their patron, and the way was clear for his assumption of power. Once again the position of First Secretary had proved to be the key to power.

There has been no change since Stalin's death in the structure or in the disciplinary requirements of the Communist party. Party members may not oppose decisions or develop factions. While those at the top seem to feel greater freedom to express publicly their differences of opinion, such public expressions of differences have been few. It appears that rigid discipline, and unqualified acceptance of decisions made by the majority within the Presidium of the Central Committee, are required in practice, as well as by rule, of all Communist party members. Centralism and discipline remain the basic characteristics of the party and distinguish it from political parties in other lands. Only in the rare circumstance of Khrushchev's challenge to Presidium control in 1957 has discipline been exposed as vulnerable, and then only to the skilful assault of a First Secretary.

A Challenge to Party Centralism

A challenge to the policy of limiting the exercise of democracy within the Communist party arose during World War II. A Soviet general named Andrei Vlasov, having been captured by German troops, gathered together under his leadership an army of former Soviet soldiers, some of whom claimed for some time after capture to be Communists but prepared to fight against Stalin to establish the right of party members to share in party decisions. While this group was unsuccessful and its leader executed when he was returned to the Soviet high command after the war, its existence dramatized a change that has been occurring in the character of Communist party membership. Educated people are becoming the majority of Communist party members.

There has been in recent years a marked change in the composition of party membership with respect to educational level and professional occupation. Earlier, the rank and file was composed primarily of bench workmen, and only a handful of leaders had formal education. Lenin had preferred it that way. He had always argued that the bench workmen were the most trustworthy element from which to choose party members. He was suspicious of the peasantry, and even more suspicious of those with education, whom he called "intellectuals."

Lenin declared that the workmen required the support of the peasants to win a revolution, but he felt that peasants were inclined toward individual exploitation of the land rather than toward community exploitation. The peasants' attitude seemed to Lenin to be in contrast with that forced upon the factory workman by the circumstances of his job. The factory workman could see in his daily toil that co-operation was necessary to achieve results, for no machine in a factory was of any use unless it was operated in concert with the other machines in the factory. The workmen seemed to

Lenin certain to accept the socialist form of production that he had in mind, with its heavy emphasis on state operation of production rather than on the individualism of private enterprise. The peasant could not be counted upon to accept the discipline of socialism, and so Lenin assigned him a subordinate place in the power structure.

The intellectuals were the most doubtful people, in Lenin's opinion. He declared that they had no rooting in a production process, as did the workmen or the peasants. They had skills required by the party leadership, but they took positions based upon intellectual reasoning, and one could not anticipate which way they would turn as ideas crossed their minds. They made poor followers, for each thought his mind as good as the next man's. In short, intellectuals in the aggregate could be useful and were to be tolerated so long as they accepted leadership from Lenin and his small group of colleagues, but they were to be watched lest they turn against the party leaders.

Stalin inherited Lenin's distrust of the intellectuals. Like Lenin, he had to use the skilled men and women of the old regime to develop the country and, in particular, to perform the technical operations of government offices, but he let very few of them into the ranks of the Communist party. He established a hierarchy of categories of persons seeking admission to the party, according to a descending order of prospective loyalty, and required persons in the successively lower categories to produce correspondingly more recommendations for admission to membership and to serve longer in the period of candidacy. The intellectuals were at the bottom of the list, in the least-favored position.

Under the system of selection of party members, which left unchallenged within the party the few men who had education and experience in leadership, the Communist party was molded by degrees into the disciplined group that it had become by the late 1930's. Those of the small circle of intellectuals who had been members of the party in its early years were purged when they questioned Stalin's position as party boss. The statistics show that in 1945 party members with education fell into the following categories: 400,000 with a university education, 2,750,000 with an incomplete or complete high-school education, and nearly 2,900,000 with a grammar-school education or less.

The Influence of Intellectuals

In spite of his attitude toward intellectuals, Stalin found himself forced, by the necessities of the complex industrial society that he was establishing, to train citizens in the skills of the intellectuals. These trainees were drawn from the ranks of the workmen, some of them from the ranks of the peasants. By the late 1930's there had emerged a large category of people who had education but who were yesterday workmen or peasants. Stalin had to presume them loyal if he was to claim convincingly before his people that his system was a success. While many of the newly educated people remained outside the party as technical directors of factories and of government offices, the ambitious among them sought admission to the Communist party. By degrees the ranks of the membership filled with these new intellectuals, and statistics reflect the change.

In 1952 the credentials committee of the nineteenth party congress reported that, of the 1,192 delegates, 709 had university degrees, 84 had an incomplete university education, 223 had completed high school, and only 176 had nothing more than a grammar-school, or an incomplete high-school, education. The same movement in the direction of college education is seen in the educational qualifications of the entire party membership. Statistics published in 1956 show that, of the party's more than 7,000,000 members and candidates, those with a college education number 801,000, an additional 257,000 have attended college but have not completed the course, and a further 1,593,000 have benefited from a secondary-school education either in whole or in part.

In 1939 the party rules had been changed to eliminate the unequal requirements for membership based upon presumed prospective loyalty to the regime, and intellectuals had been placed on a par with workmen and peasants. The gates had been opened for heavy admissions, and they followed, particularly in the period after the war. This influx of educated persons into the ranks of the party has prepared the way for the greatest challenge yet faced by the small group of party leaders presently sitting in the Presidium of the Central Committee. The new group of educated persons in the lower and intermediate levels of the party hierarchy seem to feel that they have a right to share in the formulation of policy. In their daily professional activity they bear the great burden of the administration of the state government, of industry, and of the collective and state farms. They are better paid than the bench workmen, and they are more often recognized in the lists of honors announced from time to time on anniversaries of their own or of their places of employment. They feel themselves completely loyal to the principles of the Communist party to which they have been admitted and for whom they work, and the leaders of the party are compelled to cater to them by the necessity of holding their support in directing the economic life of the country.

Khrushchev has recognized the peril created by the increasing number of intellectuals for a regime based upon the acceptance of rigid and unreasoning discipline. He has taken precautions to dilute the intellectuals by providing that two-thirds of the 1,023,000 new members admitted to the party between 1956 and 1959 be bench workmen and dirt farmers. In emphasizing the importance of admissions primarily from the working ranks, he has shown his desire to reverse the trend of the first postwar decade and given credence to the conclusion of outsiders that the enlarging group of intellectuals might demand an increasing share in policy determination and resist leadership of Stalin's type.

Re-emphasis upon the importance of the rank and file has not stopped intellectualism within the party, nor could it do so in a modern world requiring intellectuals as specialists to guide the complex economic machine. Those who have fled the U.S.S.R. confirm that intellectuals provide the major threat to preservation of rigid discipline of the type Stalin demanded. A second point of challenge may eventually be complete centralization of party structure.

Up to the present the second challenge has not come into the open, for the Communist party remains structured like an army, although it provides within its framework a system that could be expanded to permit local bosses to share in the selection of leaders and determination of policy if the counterweights were removed. Khrushchev announced from the tribune of the twentieth party congress in 1956 that collective leadership must be recognized not only at the top but in every party body right down to the bottom. Within little more than a year he had abolished collective leadership at the top, but the place of the party secretary at lower levels is not as dictatorial as it was under Stalin.

Communist party intellectuals may hope that Stalin's type of dictatorship, enforced as it was by the execution of opponents, has been ended forever. It is notable that, when Khrushchev ousted three of his colleagues from the collective leadership created at Stalin's death, he staged no "treason trials." The offenders were humiliated and transferred to distant and inferior positions, but they lived. Such treatment of political opponents, while shocking to Westerners accustomed to parliamentary procedures of respect for the opposition, cannot be overlooked in attempting to assess the influence of intellectuals who find no place today for the blood bath that had become routine as an instrument of policy under Stalin.

CHAPTER 3

RADIATING INFLUENCE

Communist party leaders have heralded as the role of the Communist party official the guidance of others in their performance of the many functions required in a complex modern society. Officials have been called upon to step into operating positions in times of crisis, but generally they are expected to attend to party affairs. A party secretary at any level is not supposed to manage a factory or preside over a collective farm or head a ministry. Until the war crisis of 1939 the General Secretary of the Party, Stalin, was kept aloof from administrative tasks relating to the economy of the country as a whole. At that time Stalin stepped into the chairmanship of the Council of Ministers, where he remained until his death. When his many functions were divided, after his death, the role of party secretary was again separated from that of chief of the administration of the country, but not for long. In 1958, when Nikolai Bulganin was demoted in delayed revenge for the support given Khrushchev's opponents in 1957, Khrushchev as First Secretary assumed the post of Chairman of the Council of Ministers as well. The emergency required union of Communist party and state power in the same individual just as it had under Stalin, and in this emergency the established policy of separating policy-making and executive functions was departed from at the top.

The rank and file of the party is in a different position. An individual's election to party membership has not meant alteration in his employment: a steel worker admitted into the party remains in the steel mill, a government clerk in a ministry remains at his ministerial desk, a brigade leader on a collective farm continues to be responsible for the operations of the dairy or of the chicken house. A distinction is made between the role of the party professional, who is paid for full-time work as a party secretary or as a member of an executive committee of a county or city party conference, on the one hand, and that of the rank-and-file party member, on the other.

While the professionals within the party are relatively few, the rank-and-file members are many and are scattered throughout every branch of activity within the U.S.S.R. The reason for this scatter lies in the party leaders' desire to facilitate the radiation of party influence throughout all the nation's activities. Party members are located nearly everywhere, and they know personally what is happening so that they do not have to ask for reports. They provide a skilled network of observers to collect the information that the party leaders need to formulate policy.

The rank-and-file party members in industry, on the farm, and in the office perform an additional function. They are at the right and left hands of the non-party millions, situated to propagate party policy in a thousand subtle ways under instructions from the party secretary of the primary party organization to which they belong. They are given every two weeks little printed pocket books for "agitators," containing themes to put forward not only in the general shop meetings but in daily conversation in the factory canteen. Their task is to win by intelligent argument unanimous approval of all party policies.

Whenever there is a meeting of persons interested in any specialized activity, such as the improvement of the courts or the writing of poetry or the feeding of pigs, the Communist party members who are present because of personal expertness in the matter under discussion are required by party rules to gather in caucus to determine what should be the decisions of the entire interested group, and to work for the general adoption of those decisions by skilful use of the opportunities available. If the meeting is of very great national importance, as when it brings together all the principal writers of the country in a writers' congress, the party members present will receive instructions from the Presidium of the party itself regarding the policy to develop. In less important meetings, decisions of the party caucus at the affair are sufficient, perhaps excepting the assistance of the secretary of the nearest big city or county party conference. It is presumed that party members read the daily party newspaper, *Pravda,* and the bimonthly party journals, *Kommunist* and *Partiinaya Zhizn,* as well as the journal specializing on the subject matter of their professional training, whether it be agriculture, or industry, or the writing of belles-lettres, for these journals provide an idea of the positions which the top party leaders, and the top party experts in the subject under discussion, expect to have taken.

A Communist Organization for Youth

The Communist party increases its influence by enlisting young age groups under its banner through the *Komsomols* and the *Pioneers*. These two organizations interlock with one another and with the Communist party itself to provide a core of Communist-indoctrinated youth down to the age of nine. They bring close to the Communist party millions of the young boys and girls on whom the party relies for its future.

It is the task of the Komsomols to organize the most politically minded and active of the country's youth into a centralized disciplined community second only to the Communist party itself. Membership is open to individuals between the ages of fifteen and twenty-six, but those who are elected to high office within the organization may continue to be members so long as they hold that office. Until 1954 any member was permitted to continue his membership beyond the age of twenty-six for as long as he liked, with the result that the supposedly "youth" organization became heavily weighted with older brothers and sisters. This was probably not without the intent of the party leadership, for the older heads assured conformity within the youth group to the policies of the party. From the early years of the Komsomols up to the late 1920's, the young members had often protested against policies forced upon them by the party—especially against the tightening of discipline and the restraints on the choice of leaders and determination of policy, which were eventually made the same as for the party itself—but this vocal insubordination had been silenced, and the Komsomols in their public meetings had for twenty-five years followed without question the policy established for them by the party.

However, at The All-Union Congress of the Komsomols in 1954, it was proposed that the custom of continuing membership in the organization beyond the age of twenty-six be modified. It was suggested that ordinary members, on reaching the age of twenty-six, have the option of filing with their Komsomol primary organization their wish to continue as members until the age of twenty-eight, after which time they would have to withdraw unless elected to official position within the organization. In this move, which must be regarded as a concession to growing discontent on the part of the youth with the domination of their elders, there was evidenced the readiness of Stalin's heirs to relax some measure of the strict control that the party had been exercising through these elders. Yet the relaxation of control was not complete. There was no proposal to exclude the older members from positions as officers in the organization, and thus the party retained a means of direct influence upon the youth at the control point.

The structure of the Komsomols parallels that of the Communist party. Individuals apply to primary organizations for admission, and these are located in places of employment. Each primary organization elects its secretary and its delegates to a higher level in the structure until The All-Union Congress of the Komsomols is reached. This, like its counterpart within the Communist party, chooses its Central Committee. The congress itself meets only once every three years. The Central Committee meets only semiannually, leaving the conduct of daily affairs to the Presidium.

At each level of the structure the Komsomol unit must, according to the rules, accept direction and control from the Communist party organization at the same level, whether it be of the republic, the province, the county, or the big city. Since Komsomols work in the same places as Communist party members, there is constant interchange of ideas in personal relationships between them at the factory, in the school, or on the farm. When Communist party members are too few to provide the basis for a primary party organization in any such unit, they join the Komsomol organization to carry out programs. This makes for broader Communist party influence in organizations in which youth predominates, such as the professional schools and the universities.

Membership in the Komsomols is achieved more easily than in the Communist party—for example, there is no period of candidacy—but it is still granted on an individual basis. There are no blanket admissions of an entire school class. An application must be supported by recommendations from two members of at least one year's standing or from one Communist party member, and those who recommend are held accountable with their own membership just as in the party. Dues are exacted of members.

In contrast to the analogous policy governing the Communist party, there is no restriction placed upon the number of Komsomol members. While the Communist party has permitted only slightly more than 8,200,000 persons to join its ranks, out of the entire population of adults throughout the country, the Komsomols had 18,500,-000 members in February of 1959. This was a high percentage of those potentially qualified to join, for the youth group on which the Komsomols can draw for members is obviously smaller than the adult group on which the party can draw. The policy of the party seems to be to open wide the gates to Komsomol membership, so as to use this large body of youths both to radiate party influence throughout organizations and communities which the party cannot reach because of its age level or limited numbers and also to prepare a large group of tested men and women from which to skim the cream for party purposes at a later date.

Examples of the types of community into which the Komsomols have been sent to radiate party policy are numerous. In the late 1920's Komsomols were sent in large numbers to the city of Komsomolsk in the Far East, in a dramatic gesture to excite Soviet citizens to leave European Russia and pioneer in the unopened areas of Siberia. In the mid- and late 1930's the Komsomols worked as the rank-and-file tunnelers on the Moscow subway project, to dramatize the duty of every citizen to aid in the industrial development of the country. Today 100,000 Komsomols have been assigned to the "virgin lands program" in the marginal farming areas of Central Asia and Siberia, to dramatize the party's desire for more food production and to instil enthusiasm into the project. Each such program is selected for its political value in developing an aspect of the nation's economy. There is for the Komsomols, in addition to these dramatic programs, the day-to-day work of aiding teachers to establish and maintain discipline in the schools. In this work they come into direct relationship with the next youngest youth group, the Pioneers.

A Communist Organization for Children

Almost every school child is a member of the Pioneers. No membership statistics have been published for some years, but it can be presumed that membership corresponds almost exactly to city populations between the ages of ten and fifteen and probably includes as well a high percentage of the children on the farms. This is the only age group that has a distinctive uniform for, unlike the Nazis, the Communists have adopted no uniform or arm band for party or Komsomol members. The Pioneers are the exception probably because boys and girls of the age enlisted in this organization find a uniform appealing. Simple, and much like that of the boy and girl scout organizations of the Western countries and of the United States, it consists of a white blouse and blue skirt or trousers, and a red kerchief held around the neck by a metal ring on which is stamped the Pioneer motto *Vsegda Gotov*, "Always Ready"—or even "Be Prepared," in emulation of the motto of our Boy Scouts.

The Pioneers have no hierarchy of national organizations. They exist only in "brigades," to each of which a Komsomol is assigned as leader. There are no requirements for admission and no recommendations expected, although a child must serve as a candidate for two months to show his capabilities and to impress upon him or her the seriousness of membership. Programs include camping, bird watching, and all the many activities for which youth groups in other lands give badges, but they also include extensive political education prepared for young people of this age. In contrast to the thoroughly mature official journal of the Komsomols, *Molodoi Kommunist*, and to the Komsomol daily newspaper, *Komsomolskaya Pravda*, the Pioneers have a journal, *Pioner*, profusely illustrated in color and containing many simple children's stories and poems, and a daily newspaper, *Pionerskaya Pravda*, written in easy fashion so that the children themselves can read it.

The Communist party seems to hope that this group of young children will radiate influence not only among the youngsters of the country but also in the parents' circles and into the family itself. In the early years following the Revolution, Pioneers were encouraged to report political deviation in their parents' attitudes, and a statue was erected in honor of one young Pioneer, Pavel Morozov, who was alleged to have been persecuted by an enraged parent for political reporting of this nature.

For small children below the age of ten there was re-created in 1957 the organization called the Little Octobrists to provide politically directed recreation, under Komsomol supervision, for children prior to entry into the Pioneers. This organization had been abolished during World War II when preschool education was disrupted. Its functions were then absorbed by reducing the entering age of Pioneers by one year and by intensifying political work among preschool teachers.

While the interlocking Komsomol and Pioneer organizations would seem to be effective instruments for spreading Communist party influence throughout the land, they are often criticized in the Soviet press for their lack of vitality. For example, Komsomols have been accused of failing to take on leadership of Pioneer brigades. It is evident that in spite of the efforts that have been made to excite youth to join these organizations because of the stimulating programs which they offer, there is some apathy among the members. Soviet youth is much more indoctrinated and disciplined than that of Western countries, but it is still human. Homework is drudgery in many cases, even though it is sugar-coated with promises of political preferment and accompanied by the explanation that it must be performed in loyalty to the regime. The system of enlisting youth to spread Communist doctrine is effective, but not completely so.

The Soviets as the State Apparatus

The Communist party's greatest sphere of activity lies in policy-making for, and administration of, the state. Here it has performed its major function, and here it is that the organization called the Communist party has established a position that, in its view, permits it to lay claim to being a political party.

The mechanism called the "state" has been adapted from one inherited from the period of revolutionary opposition to the Tsarist government of the Russian Empire. This was created in the year 1905, when a first attempt was made to conduct a general strike and even to seize power in local municipalities, with the result that the Tsar established a limited form of parliament called the "Duma." It was utilized again to organize the radical left of the revolutionary movement that forced the abdication of the Tsar in March, 1917. Upon the Tsar's abdication, the Duma created a provisional government representative of all elements in the Russian populace and, simultaneously, the parties of the left in the Duma re-created the mechanism with which they had promoted the revolutionary riots of 1905. The left-wing parties called this apparatus a "soviet," because it was based upon the concept of committee organization rather than upon one-man responsibility.

During the spring of 1917 this "soviet" type of organization spread throughout the countryside as a rallying point and co-ordinating mechanism for the parties of the left, until by June it was sufficiently widely organized to permit creation of a national organization. To establish such an organization there was called in Moscow what became known as the "First Congress of Soviets." At that time the political group that was eventually to take the name "Communist," but was still using the title of "bolshevik wing of the Russian Social Democratic Labor party," claimed the loyalty of only a small minority of the delegates. Control over the majority of delegates to the First Congress of Soviets was in the hands of the more moderate elements of the left, of which the Socialist Revolutionary party represented the most people.

When in the autumn of 1917 the provisional government established by the Duma, and presided over by Alexander Kerensky as prime minister, split sharply with General Kornilov, its commander-in-chief, the various soviets were ready to exploit the dissension. The bolsheviks had utilized the summer to strengthen their apparatus and, establishing a "military-revolutionary committee" in Petrograd, which was then the capital of the country, they were able to bring to a final stage the movement of the left-wing parties for the overthrow of the provisional government. The weakening of the Kerensky regime had thrown Kerensky himself into the arms of the

Petrograd soviet to maintain his power, and the military-revolutionary committee saw that a coup was now possible. The Congress of Soviets was convened for a second meeting, and troops and armed workers were put into the streets to capture the city's key spots, including the Winter Palace in which the provisional government was maintaining its existence. The coup was crowned with success, and the leader of the bolsheviks, Lenin, chose to use the Congress of Soviets to succeed the provisional government.

Lenin may have had no other choice, for the ranks of his bolshevik party were still very small. The revolutionary peoples of Russia, and particularly the peasants, were inclined toward a program less radical than that of the bolsheviks. The peasants supported the Socialist Revolutionary party, and many of the moderate intellectuals and some of the trade unions supported the "menshevik" wing of the Social Democratic party. To bring unity into this variegated revolutionary mass, the Congress of Soviets provided the only possible effective instrument for action. Certainly the bolsheviks could not have governed alone. As it was, the mensheviks, except for a small group calling themselves the "internationalists," and the main part of the Socialist Revolutionary party withdrew from the Second Congress of Soviets after the provisional government was seized. There was left as ally to Lenin's bolsheviks only the left wing of the Socialist Revolutionary party.

The Congress of Soviets provided Lenin with a valuable instrument for maintaining the power which had been seized, and he turned to it immediately. He asked it to "legislate" a program implementing the principal slogans with which the revolutionaries had won popularity, namely, peace with Germany and socialization of the land. Lenin used the congress also as a convenient and relatively representative body from which to obtain some mandate of authority for a small group of his henchmen. To clarify the mandate, the congress called this group a "Council of Peoples' Commissars" and divided among the members of it the portfolios of the former Council of Ministers of the provisional government. Having achieved his aim, Lenin sent the Second Congress of Soviets home. It was not to be reconvened until the end of January, 1918, when power had been more firmly established in the hands of the bolsheviks. By that time Lenin had eliminated competition from the constituent assembly. This body, which had been promised at the time of the Tsar's abdication as a means of choosing the form of the new government of Russia and to which many people still looked for salvation, was prevented in mid-January from making a decision by the armed intervention of guards loyal to the bolsheviks.

Having his working committee in the form of a provisional Council of Peoples' Commissars, Lenin next convened the Third Congress of Soviets and obtained from it complete approval of the provisional system as the permanent government. To solidify their gains, the bolsheviks prepared for the drafting of a constitution.

The history of the origin of the soviets has had much to do with their character and with the relation of the Communist party to them. The left-wing Socialist Revolutionaries attempted to moderate the actions of the Council of Peoples' Commissars and of the Congress of Soviets but met with very little success, and the Socialist Revolutionary commissars finally withdrew from the government in protest, in the spring of 1918, leaving the bolsheviks in control of the soviet system. In effect, the bolsheviks, who adopted the name "Communist" in 1919, became the sole effective political party in the new Russia. Jealous of this position, the leaders kept alert to potential opposition, and any indication of a rise in strength of the remnants of either the mensheviks or the Socialist Revolutionaries precipitated violent suppression. In 1936 the factual monopoly of the Communist party was incorporated into the constitution as a principle of law.

With a hindsight of over forty-two years, it is thought-provoking to ask why Lenin and his colleagues did not abolish the soviets after victory in the Revolution and establish a system of public administration through the executive committees of the various levels in the hierarchy of the Communist party. The party might have become the state apparatus, and its Presidium might have been today the Council of Ministers of the U.S.S.R. The question is all the more intriguing at the present time, when several of the same individuals sit both as members of the Presidium of the Central Committee of the Communist party and as member of the inner cabinet of the state apparatus, which is composed of the Chairman and the First Vice-Chairmen of the Council of Ministers of the U.S.S.R.

To answer the thought-provoking question as to why there has been no amalgamation of the Communist party and state but rather a development of interlocking directorates in two separate instrumentalities, an examination of the apparatus which still uses the name "soviet" is necessary.

Structure of the State Apparatus

Under the second Constitution of the U.S.S.R., adopted in 1936 and presently in effect, the soviets have both policy-making and administrative functions. At levels above the local one, they are structured in the same way as is the Communist party. There is, therefore, a Supreme Soviet of the U.S.S.R. which corresponds to The All-Union Congress of the Communist Party. The Supreme Soviet is authorized to choose a presidium as its alter ego to make policy decisions in the form of legislation during intervals between its meetings, these intervals being usually almost an entire year, for the Supreme Soviet has been meeting only for from four to six days a year under normal circumstances. The Supreme Soviet also chooses formally a council of ministers to be the executive branch of government.

Below the level of the Supreme Soviet of the U.S.S.R., there are supreme soviets in each of the fifteen republics which are federated in the U.S.S.R. Each such supreme soviet has its own presidium and its own council of ministers. Below the republic level there is a provincial soviet, and below that a soviet in each big city and in every county. Each has its executive committee. The various soviets in the republics are elected, formally and directly by the people, every four years, while deputies to the lesser soviets are named in direct election for two-year terms. In these elections, all adult citizens of the geographical area defined as under the jurisdiction of the soviet may vote and be represented, regardless of their place of work. There is no system of indirect elections, such as in the Communist party conferences functioning at the level of the county, the big city, the province, the republic, and the union, according to which delegates to higher levels of the party system come from the party conference immediately below.

At the local level there is a marked difference between the soviet apparatus and the party apparatus. While the party apparatus comprises all party members of the local employment group at a given level of the organizational hierarchy, the soviet apparatus is composed of only a selected group of persons, nominally elected every two years, and thus bears some formal structural resemblance to the town or city council, or board of selectmen, of many an American village or city. In substance, however, it is very different, as will be indicated below.

The soviet at each level of the hierarchy is not in permanent session but is called together by its executive committee at intervals specified in the Constitution. In practice, the intervals are often longer than those specified, as indicated by complaints in the Moscow press that executive committee chairmen are not doing their duty in calling the required meetings of local soviets. Since meetings of the soviet are called only infrequently, the opportunity is afforded the local party bosses to prepare its business in small, easily controlled committees. Thus in each soviet there is created a group of "permanent committees" to which are assigned those of the deputies who have special knowledge of the subject matter to be discussed. Schoolteachers and parents are assigned to the permanent committee on education; doctors, nurses, and sanitary workers are assigned to the permanent committee on public health; engineers and bench workmen are assigned to the permanent committee on local industry; and so on.

A meeting of a soviet, when it is called, brings together a rather large number of people. While the usual number of deputies in a rural community is not more than 35, this number increases in the large cities such that after elections in 1955 there were 1,813 in Moscow. The total number of people elected to sit as deputies in all of the soviets of the U.S.S.R. is correspondingly large. Statistics indicate that in the elections of 1959 some 1,800,000 persons were named to sit in the soviets below the republic level. The elections of 1958 seated 1,378 deputies in the two chambers of the Supreme Soviet of the U.S.S.R.

Party Influence on the Soviets

By no means all of the deputies in the various soviets are members of the Communist party. In 1958 the percentage of Communist party members and candidates among the deputies elected to the Supreme Soviet of the U.S.S.R. was 75.8 in one chamber and 76.3 in the other. The Ukrainian Republic's Supreme Soviet reported party representation of 68.3 per cent following the 1959 elections. The Russian Republic showed 67.4 per cent party membership, while the highest level was reached in the Azerbaidjanian Republic with 80 per cent.

At lower levels the number is much smaller. The statistics reveal for 1957 a range from 59.6 per cent Communist party members in the provincial and lower soviets of the Armenian Republic to 32.14 per cent in the same-level soviets of the Lithuanian Republic. The other republics fall between, the correlation seemingly being established on a basis of number of years during which a republic's territory has been part of the U.S.S.R.

These statistics suggest that the Communist party is able, through the soviets, to spread the influence of its limited membership among a large number of people. More important, it is thus able to bring many of the most active non-party people into an apparatus which makes some policy decisions, even though these decisions are limited in character, and, in so doing, develop in them a sense of participation and, presumably, a corollary sense of loyalty to the regime.

Reports from the soviets indicate the subjects of their policy debates. A school milk program is one such subject. The manner of distribution of schoolbooks, whether to be through kiosks in the schools or through regular bookstores throughout the city, is another. The distribution of natural gas to consumers for their cooking stoves is studied and a policy established. Those few party members who are deputies can, through their caucus, prevent an undesirable conclusion to the debate, and meanwhile they may learn from an irate mother or from an angry housewife what needs to be done to improve the distribution of schoolbooks or milk or cooking gas. The end result is that the party need not spend the time of all its members on such details.

In the Supreme Soviet of the U.S.S.R., to which matters of greater national concern are presented, the pattern of Communist party membership is, as we have seen, different. Every election prior to that of 1954 named to the office of deputy to the Supreme Soviet of the U.S.S.R. a higher percentage of party members than to the preceding Supreme Soviet. One can conclude either that the matters presented are of such great concern that the party has felt increasingly that its members must be present in mass or that almost all politically active citizens have already been made members of the party.

Such crowding of the Supreme Soviet of the U.S.S.R. with party members may have defeated the purpose for which it was established as the peak of the state apparatus, for at the present time it brings very few people in touch with policy matters who would not ordinarily be close to them anyway by virtue of their Communist party membership. Such an approach may have been that of the Communist party leadership for two years after Stalin's death. A suggestion that party thinking was along these lines is to be found in the manner in which important changes in the national economic plan were made. A decision to introduce a greater quantity of consumers' goods into production was made by the Central Committee of the party and issued over the signatures of the Central Committee, together with the signatures of the officers of the Presidium of the Supreme Soviet and the Council of Ministers. The same was done with a program of agricultural expansion into virgin lands that was adopted in 1953. Both these very important matters would in earlier years have been brought before the Supreme Soviet or discussed at a meeting of the Supreme Soviet following adoption by the Supreme Soviet's Presidium. Yet neither program was brought before the Supreme Soviet for discussion in any form, except in so far as the programs were reflected in the annual budget approved by the Supreme Soviet at its annual sessions of 1954 and 1955. Perhaps the Supreme Soviet was being permitted to lose even the limited importance it had had in the past in bringing a group of the most active of the non-party citizens into close relationship with the economic policies of the government.

If the tendency of Communist party leaders was to ignore the Supreme Soviet on important economic issues immediately after Stalin's death, that policy began to change in 1955. The Supreme Soviet has usually met since then at least twice a year. It has received reports about and stamped with formal approval all actions of its Presidium and major actions of the Council of Ministers. Its committees, which under Stalin worked in secret, if at all, have reported to the Supreme Soviet the substance of deliberations. The budget committees of both chambers have held hearings prior to plenary sessions of the Supreme Soviet and have questioned ministers on the justification for requested appropriations. The legislative committees have reviewed over long periods drafts of codes of law proposed by the Council of Ministers. Some drafts have even been returned to the Council for revision, and some points have been vetoed on the spot. Foreign policy matters, in contrast, have been presented by Khrushchev or his Foreign Minister in reports offered only for concurrence by a show of hands without dissent.

The Supreme Soviet has provided the Communist party increasingly since Stalin's death with a medium through which policies might be ratified and with a tribune for publicizing programs in the political field. In economic and code-drafting activities, however, the Supreme Soviet through its committees has become more of a forum than in Stalin's time for discussion, within a select circle of administrators from the republics and provinces, of administrative shortcomings and legislative proposals affecting the personal life of large bodies of citizens.

From an examination of the facts, the conclusion seems justified that the state apparatus is preserved separately from that of the Communist party primarily to provide a mechanism through which party influence can be radiated throughout the whole population. Secondarily, and up to the present only at the level of the Supreme Soviet, its role since Stalin has become one of review by administrative specialists of government proposals of an economic and social character designed to implement Communist party aims.

CHAPTER 4

CONTROLLED MASS PARTICIPATION

Democracy is on the lips of the peoples of the world. Even with strict limitation on receipt within the U.S.S.R. of ideas from abroad, Soviet citizens know that mankind now measures good government in terms of the opportunity afforded a people to choose its leaders and to influence policy. The U.S.S.R. would increase its problem of keeping order internally if it did not offer to its citizens some institutions associated in the public mind with democracy. It would certainly stand little chance of gaining the support of peoples in the West for its policies, and eventually for the adoption of the Soviet system of government, if there were to be indications that the Communist party stood opposed to the ultimate development of democratic state institutions.

The Soviet state apparatus has been retained by the Communist party probably not only because it facilitates the radiation of party influence throughout large groups of the active non-party masses but also because it makes possible an argument, however ineffective from the point of view of the Westerner, that democratic institutions exist within the U.S.S.R. If in 1917 or later the Communist party had become the sole policy-making and administrative agency within the U.S.S.R., while maintaining itself as an elite group rather than as an organization to which all adult citizens might belong, it could not have obtained from much of the world acceptance of its claim that it provided a democratic system of government. It would have had to admit that there was no democracy, when the right to participate in the choice of a parliament and to formulate policy was limited to one-seventeenth of the adult population.

Elections and the One-Party System

To make a case that the U.S.S.R. is moving toward democracy, Soviet leadership argues that within the Soviet state apparatus it has become possible to open elections to all and that since 1936 they have been so opened. The restrictions existing until 1936, under which only those could vote who hired no labor, did not serve as priests or monks, or had not been members of the former Imperial Police or royal family, have been abolished. Elections are now open to every person of eighteen years of age and over, regardless of social origin, occupation, race, or creed.

It is argued further that since 1936 the elections to all levels of soviets have been direct. There is no longer the indirect system of election, still maintained within the Communist party, under which delegates to all higher levels within the party are chosen not by the rank and file of party members but by the next lower party body. Further, since 1936 all elections to the various soviets have been secret. Printed ballots are used, and curtained booths are provided for the voter to scrutinize and mark the ballot. Herewith, the U.S.S.R. is able to offer to its citizens and to the world a picture of general, direct, and secret elections, and to claim that it has established institutions that are the cornerstones of democracy.

To understand how little risk is really being taken by the Communist party in reforming the electoral procedure, the Westerner must note the counterweights that have been set up to prevent popular selection of state functionaries who might be unwilling to accept the guidance of the party. The most important of these counterweights is the constitutional provision establishing the Communist party as the sole political party within the U.S.S.R. No other political party may be organized in competition for votes.

While Western peoples do not consider one-party systems compatible with the processes of democracy, it must be admitted that there are parts of the world that are accepted as democratically governed and in which there is only one effective party because the competing party is traditionally too weak to make the slightest challenge to its rule. It is possible, therefore, for a system to merit attribution of the democratic label if there be only one effective party, but, in such cases, there must be a choice of candidates within that party. In many places this choice is provided through a party primary, in which the citizen can select the candidate he prefers. If he belongs to the traditional minority party, he may even declare membership in the perpetual majority party, so as to have an opportunity to vote in its primary and thus share in the selection of candidates.

Opportunity for such choice of candidates is denied in the

U.S.S.R. The Communist party holds no primaries, nor does it permit the placing of more than one name per office on a ballot. Nothing in the law prevents a multiple-candidate election. On the contrary, the new constitutional provisions applied in elections for the Supreme Soviet in 1937 provided for a ballot on which was printed the instruction to the voter to cross out all but one name. This same form of ballot is still in use. There is nothing in the regulations to show that there is no choice.

The nominating procedure provided by law appears to make possible the naming of more than one candidate for each office of deputy. Under this procedure, public organizations, such as sports clubs, trade unions, and co-operative associations, may propose candidates in addition to those named by the Communist party. However, none of these organizations may be a political party or conceal the mechanism of a political party under a mask, so it is clear that its basic program must conform to that of the party. It can be imagined that one organization would propose a candidate who would emphasize local school improvement, another might enter a candidate who favored building branch libraries or sports fields. All would have to favor basic party policies such as progression toward communism. None could seek to retrace steps from state-owned enterprise to private enterprise, but candidates could differ in emphasis and, easily, in ability.

In spite of the legal possibility of a choice of candidates in the elections of 1937, the first held under the new rules, there was no choice. On the day the ballots were printed, there appeared on each ballot only one name for each position. The individuals who had been nominated by different organizations within each district had been reduced to one, presumably after the executive committee of the party conference at the county or big-city level had made its selection from among the nominees. To this day, there has appeared on the ballot only one name for each place.

Since the Second World War, the variety of nominations has been reduced so that only one real candidate is nominated within each district by all the nominating groups in factories, in universities, in sports organizations, and in trade unions. The other nominees are nationally known members of the government who are nominated in all but their customary constituency for honorary reasons alone. This very fact—that the established leaders of the party are nominated in many precincts but ultimately have their names withdrawn from all but their customary constituency, leaving only one real candidate for election in each district—indicates that the nominating agencies have been advised whom they are to nominate. If they were not advised, withdrawal of the names of national figures might leave two, or no, candidates. Such pat results can be achieved only when there has been some planning at party headquarters.

Soviet defenders of the claim that the soviet system of government is democratic often point to the fact that citizens may cross out the name of the sole candidate appearing upon the ballot. The voter may even write in a name, so the defenders say. Soon after each election the electoral commission in each voting district publishes statistics on the number of scratches, and on each occasion a considerable number are reported. For example, in the 1958 elections for the Supreme Soviet, the scratches were said to have totaled 580,641 for deputies to one chamber of the Supreme Soviet and 363,736 for deputies to the other chamber. In spite of these scratches all candidates were elected, for in no instance did the scratches exceed the number of affirmative ballots for a candidate.

For local elections there have been reported, each time, cases in which the single candidate for the position of deputy to a village or city soviet has failed of election because the total number of scratches constituted a majority of the votes cast. These failures have not been many, however, totaling only 65 candidates in the Russian Republic in 1950. In 1948 the number of candidates who failed of election to local soviets throughout the whole of the U.S.S.R. was 102—less than 2 per cent of the total seats filled.

Controls over Voting Procedure

Foreign correspondents who have visited U.S.S.R. polling booths since World War II report that there has developed another practice which yet further reduces the possibility of dissent. Although curtained booths are always provided for the marking of ballots, voters are not required on pain of punishment to enter the booths whether or not they wish to mark the ballot, and zealous citizens are permitted to stand ostentatiously in the open room, fold their ballot without marking it, and then move to the urn and deposit it. Such a practice illustrates the possibilities open to leaders who want to control the vote: folding the ballot unmarked, in plain view of the poll watchers, can and probably has become a sign of loyalty to the regime, which timorous persons dare not fail to give.

It is clear that even though the elections for soviets at all levels are now open to all and are also secret and direct, they are subject to various strict controls so that they cannot result in a serious surprise to the Communist party leaders who guide them. The laws provide the formal framework of democratic institutions, but the counterweights prevent their operation toward an unhindered expression of opinion.

Notwithstanding this, Soviet leaders make much of full participation in elections. It is impossible for foreigners to verify the attendance, but it is annually reported to be in the neighborhood of 98.8 per cent of the eligible voters. It may be that the attendance indeed approaches this percentage, for by all accounts nearly everyone votes, if need be in the ballot boxes that are carried into the hospitals and the homes of the sick, onto Soviet ships at sea, or to Soviet troops abroad. Communist party pressure to vote is so great that it results in an even higher percentage of participation than is found in those democratic countries where the law itself requires a citizen to vote and provides a penalty if he does not.

Voting by deputies within the soviets is controlled by the simple procedural expedient of voting by show of hands. It may be that a deputy would always choose to vote for the party's program out of gratitude for the prestige brought him by election to the soviets, for prestige obviously accrues to being a deputy. Yet, even if he wished to vote against some measure, he would probably think twice lest he lose the confidence of the party and the seat he holds. He might even fall under the observation of the repressive agencies, of which more will be said later. That there are no such public dissenters—at least in the Supreme Soviet, to which foreign diplomats and correspondents are invited as observers—is proved by the fact that there has never yet been a vote, on any subject, which has not been unanimous. This was so even on the dramatic occasion when in 1955 Malenkov was replaced as Prime Minister by Bulganin. Although the move came as an obvious surprise to some of those in the room, not a voice was raised against it. Everyone must have assumed that the change had been arranged by the Presidium of the Central Committee of the Communist party, and, with such sponsorship, there was no likelihood of opposition from the floor.

Given the system that evolved during Stalin's time for the election of deputies to soviets and their participation in meetings, the representative function was that of a rubber stamp on a program prepared by the Communist party. Still the drama of deputy participation in budget-making was presented in realistic form. After the

Minister of Finance had read the budget proposals, the two chambers of the Supreme Soviet met separately to hear the reports of their respective budget committees. These reports made detailed suggestions for changes in the government's proposals, recommending items to be added to the revenue and expense sides of the budget. When the draft was resubmitted for action by the deputies, the committees' proposals were always incorporated.

The drama was too well acted in Stalin's time to have substance, particularly for those with knowledge of the planning of the Communist party for each Supreme Soviet meeting. For the Communist party there could be no surprises, and it seemed obvious that the drama had been planned in advance.

Since 1955 the emergence of committee hearings well before the Supreme Soviet sessions to which reference has been made in the preceding chapter may be preparing the way for a change. The Communist party under Khrushchev's secretaryship gives evidence of having decided that it is to its advantage to utilize the committee structure to seek to improve efficiency through consultation with the republic and provincial experts who sit on committees. Such consultation would, of course, be possible within party circles alone, but it is being sought through Supreme Soviet committees as well.

Explanation of the increasing importance of budget committees suggests that the drama of committee consideration without the substance of real participation may have seemed undignified to those who participated in it, especially in light of the exposure of its lack of substance by critics abroad. The value the drama may have had in winning friends for the U.S.S.R. among peoples who really did not know that it was being staged may have been reduced as explanations of competent observers of the Soviet scene reached their ears through advanced media of mass information.

Whatever the explanation, a report on activity within the Supreme Soviet cannot omit consideration of increasing committee activity. Yet, the conclusion is still justified that the forum provided by the Supreme Soviet is still a highly controlled forum. It provides nothing like the place provided by parliaments in Western lands for the introduction of ideas unexpected by a party in power and for the possible rejection in totality of a scheme introduced by that party.

Limitations on Freedom of Expression

Democracy is measured in the public mind by more than parliamentary representation. Before the Russian Revolution, Communist party leaders claimed for their adherents the right to speak their minds, and the first Soviet Constitution included this as a right to a free press and to free speech, but a qualification was added. In this qualification the policy-makers of the new state showed their concern with a counterweight to complete freedom of expression. They provided that the constitutional freedoms be extended to the general public for a limited purpose. They might be exercised solely in the interest of the socialist revolution, and, if exercised contrary to that interest, the responsible person might be deprived of them.

Limitations upon freedom of the press and of speech have been stated less clearly in subsequent Soviet constitutions but they seem still to exist. The 1936 Constitution retains the limitation mentioned above, in the form of a declaration that the right of free speech is granted "in accordance with the interests of the toilers and for the purpose of strengthening the socialist structure" of the U.S.S.R. The Criminal Code states that it is for the courts to determine whether speech is contrary to the interests of the toilers and whether it is exercised with the intention of harming the Soviet state.

Probably few among those who supported the Soviet regime in the early years thought that the limitations on the right to free speech and press would prevent a significant part of the citizens from expressing their views. None of the revolutionaries felt sorry about constitutional limitations on their enemies. The opponents of the regime were thought to be relatively few and all to be members of classes that had supported Tsarism or the provisional government that followed it. These classes were thought to have failed to provide the masses with economic benefits, and Marxist supporters of the new regime felt them to be outright traitors to the Russian people in opposing a development that was an outgrowth of a scientific analysis of the course of history. As political failures or even as traitors who would prey with their ideas upon the uninformed millions who had not yet come to understand the program of the revolutionaries, these opposition elements had to be silenced, at least until the new regime had established its own power. Writers of the time indicated that the restraints which they espoused were to be operative solely upon the enemies of the regime. They did not anticipate that any but the obviously capitalist elements would be denied the exercise of democratic rights, and they cared nothing for these elements. They trusted the new state apparatus to preserve the rights inviolate for their own purpose.

History has proved the peril of thinking that democracy can be preserved if any group is deprived of the right to a free press and to freedom of speech unless it is established beyond reasonable doubt that a clear and present danger to the state is threatened by persons attempting to exercise the constitutional freedom of speech and press. The Soviet authorities began with a limitation which seemed to them to be beyond question a reasonable measure for preserving power over their enemies. They have since turned it, again and again, against citizens who have no desire to upset the regime but who have wanted to grumble against some detail immensely important to them.

Early judicial decisions interpreting the constitutional guarantees in the course of application of the criminal code's ban on speech designed to overthrow the regime exemplify the type of extreme action that was taken by local officials to silence the opposition. A man was convicted for opposing the plan for spring sowing in his village by speaking up in the meeting of the village soviet in which he was a deputy. His opposition was in no sense an effort to overthrow the regime; he simply wanted to discuss a very concrete problem, since it affected his personal life, and was doing no more than many an American farmer who opposes his government's plan for agricultural subsidies. Yet the local soviet judge, on motion of the local prosecutor, found the soviet peasant guilty of violating the criminal law. Only on appeal to the Supreme Court of the Russian Republic was the peasant successful in having his conviction quashed, and then it was not because his words were not deemed seditious. It was concluded that he could not have intended to overthrow the regime since he "was a workman, he had been at the front in the civil war, he was an invalid, and he was not a class enemy." In short, the Supreme Court felt that the speaker had been one of those who were presumed to support the regime, and his criticism of the sowing plan must therefore have been intended by him to be a proper, rather than an improper, exercise of the constitutional guarantee of free speech.

A class enemy in the form of a well-to-do peasant also was convicted of counterrevolutionary speech, in opposing a plan of self-taxation introduced for approval of the village soviet. His conviction was appealed, and the Supreme Court of the Republic freed him because it found that no harm had come from his opposition to the plan since it had been adopted by an overwhelming majority. The peasant was, however, convicted of criminal defamation because he had cursed the officials of the Soviet in "unprintable words" while registering his opposition to the proposal.

The Supreme Court of the Russian Republic reveals in these two decisions of the early 1930's that it was trying to establish some yardstick which would remove from the ban against seditious speech grumbling against proposals introduced into soviets, even when those proposals were deemed necessary by local party bosses to the success of a program. The court, in establishing its yardstick, examined the class origin of the speaker to see if he could be presumed to be a class enemy and also looked to the result of the speech. The court seems to have felt that the local authorities needed correction for reading revolutionary intent into speech of a limited critical character.

Examination of class origin to determine the real intent of a critic continued into the 1940's. For example, a Soviet army sergeant training recruits on the drill field during World War II was heard to make derogatory remarks about the rights granted by the Soviet Constitution. In a trial for counterrevolutionary speech in violation of the criminal code, he was acquitted because the court could not believe that he meant to harm the regime. He was found to have served most of his life in exemplary fashion in the army, had been a member of the Communist party for twenty-three years, and had always conducted himself in a manner which suggested that he was devoted to the motherland.

By these court decisions top Soviet authorities are obviously trying to make a good impression upon the public. They are hoping to put a popular meaning into their constitution's guarantee of free speech. They have built an official record designed to show that while the guarantee is not unlimited, it will be held to be meaningful in circumstances when no real harm is caused, or when the speaker can be presumed loyal because of his record of loyalty or class origin. Testimony of émigrés indicates that lower Soviet officials are not so careful and that here the guarantee provides very little restraint on repressive action against the vocal dissenter, even when his dissent is expressed on a subject of local concern having no connection with the stability of the regime.

Practical Restrictions on Printing and Meetings

Limitation upon the constitutional guarantee of freedom of the press is even more clearly defined by Soviet law and regulation. Because of a constitutional ban on the employment of labor by a private individual for any commercial purpose, no private individual may own a printing establishment in which labor is employed. In consequence, operation of a mass-circulation daily paper or even of a less frequent periodical is impossible, unless it were to be by a co-operative association of printers. But even this is forbidden, because the licensing instructions under which private enterprise without employed labor may be conducted, within limits, excludes specifically the operation of any reproductive apparatus. A citizen may not, therefore, so much as operate a mimeograph or duplicating machine for the publication of handbills. He may not use the printed word to spread his ideas, except through channels provided by the state.

Even state-operated printshops are censored under a law requiring submission prior to publication, of all matter prepared for reproduction. On some notable occasions a book or drama has been licensed by the censor only later to fall afoul of the highest party leaders. In such cases it is withdrawn, and all copies available for public distribution are destroyed. The private citizen hesitates to keep the book in his library lest its possession be taken by his guests as an indication of his lack of support for the regime and subject him to suspicion and surveillance.

The right of assembly as a popular democratic right is also guaranteed by the Soviet constitution, but a statute requires that all public meetings be licensed, whether to be held indoors or out of doors. No meeting to which representatives from all parts of the country are to be invited may be licensed without the consent of the Council of Ministers of the U.S.S.R. If the meeting is to bring together only people from within a single republic, the consent of the council of ministers of that republic is required. If the gathering is to include only members of a single ministry, the minister must consent. When the people to be invited are only from within a single province or smaller unit, the Provincial Soviet's Executive Committee has discretion to determine what shall be permitted.

The right of association is also guaranteed by the Constitution, but, again, is subject to limitation. Any association must be licensed, regardless of the purpose for which it is to be formed, and each republic is authorized to establish a procedure under which such associations may receive a charter.

By virtue of these licensing provisions, public opinion can be effectively expressed only through a licensed agency. This is not to say that the Communist party wants to hear no public opinion. The contrary is true. The party has always been attentive to restlessness among the masses, for such restlessness can spell difficulties for the leadership. If there were no way short of violent revolution for dissent to find expression, the Communist party would not only have little chance of convincing anyone at home, much less abroad, that a democratic system existed within the U.S.S.R., but would find out about the unrest so late that it would have to apply expensive measures of repression, causing perhaps even greater unrest.

The state-owned and -licensed press is therefore thrown open to letters to the editor. Analysis of great numbers of these letters has indicated that their subject matter is far different from that which might be found in any American newspaper. For one thing it is limited to complaints about public administration, and never refers to a basic matter of policy. Further, criticism of administrators is limited to those only slightly higher in the administrative hierarchy than the writer. Thus no bench operator would write in criticism of the minister under whose supervision his factory might be but rather of his foreman or, at most, of his factory manager. No one has ever had published a criticism of the Presidium of the Central Committee of the Communist party, or even of the Presidium of the Supreme Soviet. The highest position to be criticized seems to be that of minister, and such criticism is usually made by a deputy to the Supreme Soviet either in a letter to the editor of the local newspaper or in a speech from the floor of the Supreme Soviet.

All letters to the editor are obviously subject to clearance in the editorial office of the party-controlled newspaper, just as any proposed speeches in the Supreme Soviet must clear the office of those who plan the agenda. It can be presumed that censorship, or anticipation of censorship, causes the exclusion of those letters and speeches which touch upon matters too sensitive to air. Still, many criticisms are aired, and a letter to the editor is usually followed some days later by an article in which the editor reports on action taken to set right the administrative shortcoming in question. It is quite possible that many Soviet citizens interpret such action as proof that the public can influence administration and that the Soviet system is democratic.

Soviet citizens with little knowledge of the extent of public criticism in Western countries and of the influence brought to bear upon major policies by associations of irate citizens cannot measure their success against anything but the experience of their own limited past. Although Soviet youths sometimes think out for themselves the political shortcomings of the Soviet system, it has been more usual to find the defectors from the Soviet system among those who are sufficiently old to remember accounts of the freedoms of Western democracies read in their childhood or who have been brought into touch with Western practices through capture during the war, visits outside the U.S.S.R., or Western broadcasts.

Limitations on Trade-Union Organization

Trade unions represent the largest non-governmental system of organizations in the U.S.S.R. and, as such, have probably presented Soviet leaders with their most difficult problem in controlling freedom of association. During Tsarist times the workmen had come to associate trade unionism with the democratic goals for which they were struggling, and after victory the bolsheviks had to permit trade unions to function if they wished to retain the loyalty of these working masses in the factories. Moreover, since these were the people to whom the leaders turned for maintenance of their leadership, trade unions were given wide powers. At the outset they could do no harm to the Soviet leadership, and indeed, since they helped to eliminate the remaining private owners of industry, in accordance with the bolshevik policy of nationalization of resources, they were not only a necessary evil to humor the laboring masses but also a useful tool.

With the progress of events following the turbulent revolutionary years, private industry became extinct in all but its artisan form. Of this category of industry, only the self-employed artisan, or the closely controlled co-operative of artisans, was allowed to produce goods. Since the great factories and mines were state owned, producing in accordance with a national economic plan, the question was raised, in the Communist party's Central Committee in 1928, as to whether trade unions still had a place.

The issue was made quite clear, because the leader of the trade-union movement, who had been placed in his position by the Communist party, had been won over to the cause of his charges, the workmen. He saw in state-owned industry very little less opportunity for arbitrary direction by management than the Communist party as a whole saw in a private enterprise system. He thought that the workmen would now have to be protected against overly ambitious state managers seeking to enhance their own reputations within the administrative hierarchy by cutting costs of wages, lengthening hours, and being inattentive to workers' grievances. The Central Committee concluded that it could not support the position of the man it had placed in charge of the trade unions, and it ousted him. It declared that there could be no antagonism between state managers and the workmen because the manager was representative of the state, and the state was the creature of the workmen. This was clearly not the case, as the state was the creature of the Communist party which ruled in the name of the workmen, and the workmen were by no means admitted to the Communist party in such numbers that it could be said to be directly responsive to their demands. Nevertheless, the party had to find a solution to its problem of keeping the trade unions as the most important institution through which the democratic right of association could be exercised and, at the same time, holding these multimillion-member organizations in check.

To be sure, party members had permeated the trade-union organization as they had permeated all organizations within the U.S.S.R., and these members had tried in their caucuses to influence all its decisions. But this seems to have been an inadequate form of control for such a body. One of the strong men of the inner party circle, Lazar Kaganovich, was therefore put in the position of the ousted trade-union chief, and the task of the trade unions was finally defined clearly. It was not to combat management but to assist management in increasing production.

New Functions for Trade Unions

To popularize the trade unions in their new role, the Communist party leaders sought a dramatic function for them. They achieved their aim by abolishing the Ministry of Labor in 1933—then called a Peoples' Commissariat—and transferring its labor-inspection service to the trade unions. This meant that the trade unions were placed in control over safety devices and could require management to meet the safety rules established by law. Further, the trade unions were given the task of administering those provisions of the social insurance system requiring payment to workmen incapacitated on the job and believed by the doctors to be able to return to work after a temporary absence.

With these new functions, the trade unions could again appeal to the masses. This appeal was enhanced by a provision in the social-insurance law which doubled for trade-union members the payments made to non-members. Finally, the trade unions were provided with supervision over a grievance procedure under which workmen who tangled with foremen or with managers over details relating to the performance of their job might express their grievance and obtain a decision as to its merits.

No mass pressure was to be brought upon management through strikes, nor was the trade-union system to be permitted to influence, through collective bargaining with management, the level of wages or the number of working hours. These came to be set by statute, and for a time collective bargaining ceased. It was resumed only after World War II, when it seems to have been found useful in providing an occasion for arousing enthusiasm among workmen for greater production, and in providing a dramatic *quid pro quo* in allocation, to projects chosen by the trade-union members, of funds set aside by law from the receipts of the enterprise.

To preserve the popularity of the trade unions in the face of legal restrictions and narrowly defined functions, the trade-union chief was given honors. In 1946, on the death of the long-time chairman of the Presidium of the Supreme Soviet, Mikhail Kalinin, the trade-union chief, Nikolai M. Shvernik, was placed in the post. His successor as trade-union chief, V. V. Kuznetsov, was made a member of the Soviet delegation in the first General Assembly of the United Nations, to argue for inclusion of the World Federation of Trade Unions within the framework of the United Nations. By this act the Soviet leadership sought to win friends among the trade-union membership of the world.

Following a period of apparent reduction in prestige after Stalin's death, the trade unions have been given a more important place than at any time since 1937, when Stalin forbade trade-union interference with management at the plant level by abolishing the formal structure of the "triangle" of management, trade union, and Communist party representative, through which major plant decisions had passed.

While the "triangle" has not been restored in name, the role of the trade-union shop committee has been enlarged by the Central Committee of the Communist party in its decision of December, 1957, instituting "permanent production meetings" to consult with management on matters of output and efficiency. Although this institution is not to be permitted to upset the principle of managerial responsibility for conduct of factory affairs, its existence serves as more of a check on managerial predominance than has been evident since before the war. It is far from the "workers' council" lauded by Marshal Tito in Yugoslavia and demanded by Hungarian workers during their short-lived revolt of 1956, but it appears to be the Soviet answer to an ill-formulated desire of Soviet workmen to obtain some measure of participation in the operating decisions in the plants in which they work, particularly those decisions regarding dismissals for incompetence and unfitness, as well as holiday arrangements and pay.

Trade-Union Structure

Trade unions in the U.S.S.R. are structurally organized so that control by top state agencies is relatively easy. They do not take the form of craft unions, such as has been traditional in the United States, and thus there are no unions of bricklayers, carpenters, or longshoremen. Instead, employees in all the agencies falling within a given branch of economic activity are brought together into one union comprising the craftsmen and the charwomen of the industry. Under such a system there can be no coming together in defense of a common professional or craft interest. Management has to deal with only one union, instead of with several as is still frequent in the United States. In the plant there is a factory trade-union committee, which works with the factory management. At the county level there is a trade-union committee, for each union, to coordinate the work of the various factory committees of that union within the county. There is a similar co-ordinating committee for each union at the provincial and republic levels and an all-Union committee for each trade union in Moscow. Since 1957 with the creation of economic councils in small republics and in provinces of large republics, it is the co-ordinating committee of the unions at the same level that has become the most active instrument in the conduct of trade-union affairs.

To facilitate interchange of ideas among trade unions, and presumably also a measure of centralized control, there is at each level a committee to which each union operating within a given county, big city, province, or republic sends its representatives, and at the all-Union level there is a congress of trade-union delegates. This congress—which in 1959 brought together 1,322 delegates from 23 industrial trade unions—chooses its Central Council, its chairman, and its Presidium. It is through this Presidium of 21 members that the Council of Ministers exercises its influence over the entire trade-union hierarchy. In addition, the chairman of the executive committee was, until the 1952 Communist party congress, a member of the Organizational Buro of the Central Committee of the Communist party. Through this tie the trade unions could be fitted into any plan of action designed to mobilize the production process for a given party program.

The trade unions have regained some of the prestige lost during Stalin's declining years. Still the chairman of the Central Council of the all-Union congress of trade-union delegates has not been recognized with advancement in prestige by appointment to the Presidium of the Central Committee of the Communist party as were his predecessors in the early years and again for three years after Stalin's death, when the post was held by a close confidant of the group that formed the collective leadership.

Creation of the "permanent production committees" to co-ordinate employment matters with the managers of the factories has increased trade-union prestige at that level, but soon after the Communist party's organizations in the same places were given new powers to audit all managerial decisions, so that the trade unions are held in their accustomed secondary place.

Trade unions do not perform the function normally associated with the right to trade unionism in a democracy. They are an instrument of state policy, rather than a pressure group through which interested citizens may formulate a program beneficial to their special interests and press for its adoption over programs presented by similarly organized associations of citizens with other interests. An instrument which has become, in democratic countries, a vehicle for expressing the will of an important segment of the population has been subjected in the U.S.S.R., together with other popular institutions, to controls at vital points.

CHAPTER 5

TERROR AND ITS RATIONALIZATION

Terror has always been an instrument of government in the Soviet system. From the earliest days of 1917, members of classes that owned productive property, as well as priests, monks, policemen of the Tsarist government, and members of the royal family, were considered to be enemies of the government and were terrorized accordingly. In a sense they were outlaws, although no formal law declared them subject to arrest and execution if apprehended. Punishment was to be meted out to citizens only when there was crime, yet in practice the "class enemy" could expect no leniency if he aroused the hostility of anyone in authority.

The exclusion of a part of the population from participation in government was formally accomplished by the Third Congress of Soviets in a resolution of January, 1918. The first Constitution of the Russian Republic, adopted in July, 1918, made the rule specific by listing in detail the classes of people who could not vote or hold office. They were, in effect, second-class citizens, subject to all the obligations of citizenship but denied any share in the determination of policy or in the administration of the state.

The first law establishing a Soviet court system to replace the courts of the Tsar created a special bench called a "revolutionary tribunal" to try allegations of opposition to the bolshevik regime. Contemporary accounts indicate that although these tribunals were supposed to act with some semblance of legal procedure, they reached quick decisions on limited evidence whenever they had before them a member of the enemy classes. There appeared two yardsticks of criminality, one for the worker and peasant, and another for the property owner and the priest.

As if this double standard of justice were not enough to protect the regime, there was created an "Extraordinary Committee" called the *Cheka*, with power to ferret out conspiracies against the state and with authorization to take immediate action, even to the point of execution, to prevent a new revolution. During the winter of 1917–18 the Minister of Justice opposed the extensive powers granted to the *Cheka*, because he, as a member of the Socialist Revolutionary party, anticipated that the apparatus would turn eventually against the leaders of the state itself. But his voice went unheeded. Ardent supporters of the new regime seemed to feel that the *Cheka* could be kept within bounds and directed solely against the class enemy. The records of the time show no signs that any definable group within the government except the Socialist Revolutionaries anticipated what was eventually to come. Only the Socialist Revolutionaries feared that the *Cheka* would turn upon some of its masters.

As the day loomed, and *Cheka* agents infiltrated into the activities of workers and peasants, and finally into the ranks of the Communist party itself, the bolshevik commissar of justice who had succeeded the Socialist Revolutionary incumbent began to appreciate the danger and to struggle for the supremacy of his own commissariat in maintaining order. By December, 1921, hostility to the lawlessness of the *Cheka* even in dealing with supporters of the regime had gone so far that the Ninth Congress of Soviets voted its abolition and the assumption of most of its duties by the revolutionary tribunals and the regular courts. Only its investigatory functions were to be left, and these were given in February, 1922, to a newly created State Political Administration known as the G.P.U.

The terrorizing apparatus did not keep its place. The G.P.U. arrogated to itself greater authority than it had been given, and it was soon trying people in its own tribunals without publicity or benefit of counsel.

Stalin seems to have found this terrorizing apparatus a convenient instrument. Although the people became so restless under the lash of the G.P.U. that he found it necessary in 1934 to abolish it and transfer its functions in limited form to the Ministry of Internal Affairs, this Ministry was rarely restrained in performing its task. Even today, its role is important in the Soviet system of government, although its power has been reduced considerably since Stalin's death.

The Terrorizing Apparatus

From an examination of evidence brought to light by those who have escaped from the U.S.S.R., the pattern of terrorizing and its part in the system of government have become clear. The instruments are the Ministry of Internal Affairs and a companion agency that has sometimes been within the Ministry and sometimes outside it as a Ministry of State Security. The Ministry of State Security has had the task of ferreting out potential threats to the stability of the regime and investigating them. These investigations have been exposed by the Soviet authorities themselves, since Stalin's death, as characterized by the practice of physical and psychological torture to obtain confessions of guilt. With such confessions, or even without them, the Ministry of State Security has made a report, and a decision has then been made, presumably by the Prosecutor General of the U.S.S.R. or his representative, either to prosecute before a court or to permit the case to be handled by a special board of the Ministry of Internal Affairs.

The special boards in the Ministry of Internal Affairs were created by statute. They were not required to hold their proceedings in public, nor to provide any of the procedural guarantees of the constitution such as right to counsel, nor to follow the procedural provisions of the criminal code. According to the testimony of some whose fate has been settled by one or another of them, they often heard cases in the absence of the accused. Under a 1934 statute, they were permitted to sentence persons found to be "socially dangerous" to five-year terms in remote places in the U.S.S.R. or in concentration camps. No definition of social danger was set in the statute, and, from what is known from refugees, the provisions and definitions of the criminal code did not bind the special boards to prove a charge. On the contrary, their primary task was to apply terrorizing methods when there was no specific crime involved. They had no function if crime could be proved, for in such circumstances the case was tried by a criminal court in accordance with the code of criminal procedure and the constitutional guarantee of counsel.

Documents stolen from files of the Ministry of Internal Affairs in the Baltic states indicate that the terrorizing process has been applied to frighten into submission communities in which opposition to the regime was of serious proportion. To arrive at this effect, local representatives of the Ministry were instructed to arrest and deport to camps in the Russian Republic specified numbers of persons of given categories, but no specific individuals were named. The categories were those of prospective enemies, such as army officers of the former Latvian army, estate owners, factory owners, and merchants. The local official determined which persons within the given categories were the most likely enemies and proceeded to arrest them under conditions as mysterious and dramatic as possible. The entire operation was designed to strike fear into the hearts of those who remained and thus to silence them, lest they be next. Some of the effectiveness of the system would be lost if it were not arbitrary, that is, if one could predict where its hand would fall. Apparently, it is in popular insecurity that the regime's security has been thought to lie.

The Ministry of Internal Affairs and its security police, sometimes organized as a separate security agency, were given a privileged position under Stalin. Although the central office operated through ministries in each of the republics, its chain of command was completely centralized below that level in that the on-the-spot officials were free from any influence of local soviets. These officials were appointed or dismissed by the Ministry in Moscow, and they were beyond the reach even of local Communist politicians. Only the Prosecutor-General of the U.S.S.R. had administrative authority over the Ministry of Internal Affairs and its security agents.

As an element of post-Stalin reform, the privileged position of the Ministry of Internal Affairs was abolished, in part, in that its officials at the province level were made department chiefs in the executive committees of the provincial soviets, thus having to answer to provincial officials as well as to the Ministers in the republic capitals and in Moscow. The security police, however, retained their independence of provincial officials. This was done by separating them from the Ministry and placing them under a Committee for State Security, known as the KGB, created in the Council of Ministers of the U.S.S.R., and in the Council of Ministers in each of the Republics. By this move there was re-emphasized the desirability of separating the investigative function from any possibility of local interference.

Instances in which the Ministry has exceeded its authority have been disclosed in the past. The Minister of Internal Affairs, Henry Yagoda, was purged by Stalin in 1938 because he seems to have tried to make himself a threat to the inner circle of Stalin's associates. His successor then overdid his assignment by pressing the purge begun by Stalin into every corner of the industrial and state apparatus, and he himself was purged. Finally, after Stalin's death, his friend Lavrenti Beria, who had been for many years supervisor of the security apparatus, was arrested and executed as a traitor under circumstances said by those who have fled his Ministry to havens abroad to have been related to his desire to seize power.

To facilitate its work the Ministry of Internal Affairs has found it desirable to enlist large numbers of informers from the rank and file of the population. Through them, much information is obtained about unwary neighbors, and the expectable presence of such informers in every group enhances the terror of those who have reason to fear the hand of the state.

Terrorizing is obviously a weapon that was designed by the Soviet leadership to maintain itself in power, but events since Stalin's death suggest that it may be losing value in the eyes of the new leaders. Fearing that the structure of their power might disintegrate in a wave of mass opposition to the severity of the regime during Stalin's declining years, Stalin's heirs promised to redraft the criminal code, to make it less severe, and they amnestied many prisoners. Also, they declared false the allegations brought against the Kremlin doctors during Stalin's final weeks of life. These doctors had been indicted only a short while before on the strength of their alleged confessions to composing a revolutionary band planning to kill the Kremlin leaders by malpractice, and the new leaders branded the confessions as untrue because they had been obtained through torture.

Stalin's heirs promised that in the post-Stalin era enemies of the state would be tried in accordance with the rules of Soviet law and that "justice" would be done in the administration of the state. This series of events has been read by foreign observers as evidence that terrorizing is not now conceived by Soviet leaders as a desirable weapon. Yet it is noteworthy that at the very time that new general principles for criminal law and criminal procedure were adopted in December, 1958, there was emerging a new instrument of social control permitted to function outside the law. This was the "social assembly," created in a few border republics in 1957 but increased in number so that by 1959 eight of the fifteen union republics contained them.

In structure the social assembly is a gathering of citizens living together in a large apartment house, on a city street, or on a farm.

It is convened on call of the community's public order committee, composed of Communist party members and other community leaders. It hears charges leveled by the Communist Youth League, a trade union, or other public organization against a citizen of conduct showing "an anti-social, parasitic way of life." This is not defined except to indicate that it is evidenced by evading socially useful work or by living on unearned income. This covers speculators in scarce commodities on the public markets.

The vote on the charge is by a show of hands, and the penalty may be banishment for periods up to five years to a remote area within the republic. There is no appeal, although the executive committee of the local soviet must confirm the sentence and must have someone present at the hearing. No rules of procedure are specified, except that the accused be present, unless he refuses to attend.

Practice has shown that these bodies have heard charges not only against speculators but against those who listen to foreign broadcasts. It is evident that the bodies have a political function. Since gatherings of citizens bound to observe no codes and unfamiliar with legal principles can be tyrannical in any society, especially when whipped to a frenzy by able agitators such as the Communist party can provide under circumstances in the U.S.S.R., the social assembly must be categorized among the agencies suited to the terrorizing process. Insufficient time has elapsed to indicate whether they will arrogate power as arbitrarily as the *Cheka* and its successors did, but the potentiality is present.

The Rationalization of Terror

Although the written record and refugees' verbal accounts of terrorizing activities in the U.S.S.R. might lead an American to suppose that restless Soviet millions must seeth on the verge of revolt, very few students of the Soviet system believe that such a conclusion is justified. To understand this apparent paradox, one must consider the unusual phenomenon of a people who appear, in the main, to have accepted terror during Stalin's time as a necessary evil. In short, one must understand that terrorizing as a technique of government was rationalized by Stalin for most Soviet citizens. Appreciation of this fact is important for those who attempt to measure the strength of the Soviet regime, for it is likely that opposition could come only from the very leadership group to which the necessity for the policy of terror has been imparted.

In a Western democracy, where there is no "official" philosophy of government and no monopoly of the press and the public platform, it is incredible that any governmental propaganda line would have universal or nearly universal acceptance. There is always a powerful opposition newspaper to act as critic of the government and of its propaganda. As has been seen, the Soviet system has eliminated the possibility of an opposition party, and the media of information and propaganda remain completely subject to the Communist party's control. These media, augmented by compulsory study groups for all members of the population, are employed to convince the people of the correctness of certain propositions. These propositions bear examination, because it is through their acceptance that the Soviet leaders expect to reduce and in some quarters even eliminate opposition to the policies of the regime, including terrorizing.

The foundation of the Soviet government's propaganda line is that its program rests upon scientifically proved fact. To twentieth-century man in any land an aura attaches to a thesis said to rest upon scientifically proved fact, and Soviet leaders can exploit this situation by quoting Marx and Engels, who claimed to be always scientific in evolving their doctrine of revolution and the dictatorship of the proletariat. The strongest card played by these nineteenth-century writers, on whom Lenin based his own thinking, was the claim that the process of historical development had finally been analyzed correctly and the key to the process found. It could then be argued that it was now possible for man to control the future course of history.

In strengthening his thesis, Marx argued that there was no God, no inscrutible divine being who intervened in the development of human history. Only the interplay of discernible factors caused man to develop the structure of his society at any given period. The primary discernible factor was said to be the instruments of production, the tools with which man worked to obtain his food, his clothing, and his shelter. So long as the tools were primitive, man could produce no surplus. He had to share with others, each of whom did his part to keep the family alive. The structure of society was centered in the family.

By degrees man learned to domesticate animals and to improve agricultural implements, and this permitted production of a modest surplus. Engels argued that some families specialized in animal husbandry and traded their surplus for the surplus grain of a neighboring family, and with trade Engels found developing the concept of ownership, which he believed to be essential to trade. With constant improvement in tools of production, families grew in size until they became clan groupings with an increased quantity of property. At this point Engels distinguishes a very important step. He says that those who were leaders of the family by virtue of birth and age developed a lust for property, appropriated family property to themselves as individuals, and built around themselves an apparatus of force in the form of clansmen with whom they shared a portion of the property as the purchase price of support. Thus, according to Engels, there was created the first state apparatus.

Marx and Engels concluded that the first state apparatus rested upon a need to protect private ownership with brute force, and that those who owned the most productive form of property at the time became the rulers. They argued that the state was born as an instrument to be used by a rich ruling class to exploit less wealthy classes, and that in this fact lay the key to subsequent social development. As new tools were developed, new and more valuable types of property came into being, and the class which came to own the most valuable property seized the state apparatus, by revolution if need be. In this way Marx and Engels attempted to explain the fall of Roman ownership of slaves and the growth of feudalism with its ownership of land. They moved on to explain the fall of the feudal kings of France by the invention of industrial machines and a consequent reverence for private ownership of factories.

For Marx and Engels, it followed from these major factors governing the course of history that private ownership of factories, and private enterprise generally, were bound eventually to be less productive than public ownership because the profit system of necessity required wages to be of less than full value for work done. They thought it self-evident that profits had to be siphoned off to the factory owners to make the profit system work. Since factory workmen thus received less than full value for their labor, they could not be expected to work as hard as if they had received full value. In Marx's opinion, factory workers were not as productive under the private enterprise system as they could be enticed to be if the factories were owned by the state and if the state itself were set up by workmen as their own. The world would eventually come to realize this truth.

Marx did not expect, however, that the workmen would be able to obtain control over the state apparatus through orderly democratic procedures. Few of the workmen would appreciate the possibility of such control, since teachers could be expected to mask it and so, also, newspapers, the owners of which were rich men and thus had a personal stake in the status quo. Moreover, when factory owners realized that eventually they must lose their own favored position, they would strengthen the police arm of the state and thereby introduce censorship and terrorizing and all the other weapons of the state designed to prevent seizure of power. Under such conditions, said Marx, the only way for workmen to achieve the economic and social system to which history pointed was violent revolution. The workmen were advised to maintain power achieved through revolution by turning the state apparatus against the former rulers, by establishing the dictatorship of the proletariat.

At this point Marx and Engels stopped, except to say that eventually society would require no formal restraints and the state would wither away. Marx and Engels were most concerned with the first step, the instigation of revolution. They left the planning of the postrevolutionary period to those who would live to see it, and it fell to Lenin to develop the Marxist thesis to meet what he believed to be the needs of this postrevolutionary period.

As was indicated in the first chapter of this book, it was Lenin who argued for the creation of a small elite group to lead the workmen in their revolutionary struggle for ultimate establishment of the dictatorship of the proletariat. He embellished Marx's thesis that the great bulk of the workmen could not be expected to understand the course of history and their own mission. He said that they would require leadership, and he set out to create it in the form of the Communist party. Later Stalin redefined this "leadership" by the Communist party to mean dictation of a program of action to the working masses, enforcible upon men and women who opposed it even if they were of workman or peasant stock.

The Effectiveness of the Rationalization

All Soviet citizens have been made to memorize the Marxian interpretation of the course of history. Those who are less tutored or incapable of grasping the detail are taught but the simple thesis: that a scientific analysis of history leads to the conclusion that the Soviet system of government is the highest type of state. It also claims to be the most democratic type of state, the logical final stage in the development of an economic and social system designed to come closer to satisfying man's wants than has any society in the past. It alone is said to make possible, through state ownership of land, factories, mines, means of communication, and means of distribution, the quantity of production necessary to meet man's needs. It alone claims to be structured in such a way that the workmen, and their allies the peasants, may determine policy and hence claim the position of masters of their own fates. It alone claims to be preparing the way for the ultimate withering away of repression, when men will perform their social duties without need of compulsion and when production will be sufficient to distribute goods to men in full accordance with their needs.

Western students can point out effectively that the Marxist thesis is oversimplified and untrue, that the Soviet state is structured so that in the name of democracy there have been eliminated the fundamentals of democracy because the general public cannot control the formulation of policy. Western economists can also prove that a workman in a private enterprise economy is much more productive and better paid than in the U.S.S.R. The iron-curtain policy of closing Soviet frontiers to the foreign press and to foreign speakers has been designed in part to prevent the foreign view, and even the facts of Western economic life, from reaching the ears of the masses of Soviet workmen and peasants.

The success of Soviet propagandists in preaching their line can now be measured by means of interviews with those who have escaped. These interviews, conducted by teams organized by Harvard University, have indicated marked success in certain fields, which is the more remarkable because they were held with people who had come to dislike the Soviet system so much that they were willing to flee, often at risks to themselves and to the families they left behind.

It is generally true of all those interviewed that they have been convinced by Soviet schooling, press, and radio that production for maximum public benefit is possible only when factories, natural resources, and means of transportation and distribution are state owned. In short, private enterprise as a way of life has been rejected even by those who hated the Stalin regime. The key to long-range prosperity has come to be for most Soviet citizens, whatever their political persuasion, state ownership of the means of production.

This acceptance of state ownership as the key to prosperity has extended even to the peasants, although among these there is divided opinion. Among the older farmers in the displaced-persons camps of Europe in which most of the interviews occurred, there was found strong opposition to state ownership and to its handmaiden, collective-farm operation of the land, on the ground that such communal use of the land was not right. The younger farmers, on the other hand, as reported by Alice C. Rossi, seemed to have accepted their Soviet education. While these younger people thought that the collective farms had been bad, their criticism was of management rather than of the system. All, both young and old, were agreed that there must never be a return to the system of estates under which large landowners owned the land and employed peasants to work it.

With mass acceptance of the basic tenet of Marxism—that there is no room in modern society for private ownership of productive resources—the Soviet leaders have scored their major victory. They do not have to worry about any serious opposition to the fundamental principle of their society. No large group of persons is likely to try to restore private enterprise in relation to the primary sources of wealth. There will be individuals who will want to make a profit on the sale of homemade products or of home-grown vegetables or meat, and there will even be individuals who want to steal state property and sell it on the open market, particularly during periods of short supply when the price is high. But there is not to be expected a demand for a basic change from the policy of state ownership of the means of production. The basic principle behind the implementation of this tenet—the principle that workmen require leadership to reach the goal of abundance—is also generally accepted. Respect for education is high, and leadership based upon superior skills, whether in operating a factory or in conducting the affairs of the state, is revered.

Here Marxist doctrine has helped the Communists especially, for it relates political parties to class interests. It teaches that in Western democracies one party will normally represent the landowners, another the peasants, a third the wealthy industrialists and their associates, a fourth the shopkeepers and small producers, and a fifth the working class; then, that class lines are clearly drawn in the differences between political parties, whence it can be argued logically that multiple political parties develop to represent the different economic interests existent in a given society. Conversely, where instead of multiple economic interests there is but a single economic interest, there need be only a single party. Soviet society is said by the Communists to have reached the stage where there is only one economic interest, that of the "toilers," whether these be workmen, clerks, or farmers. In consequence, there need be only a single political party to provide the leadership which all agree to be necessary. Since both refugees from, and recent American travelers in, the U.S.S.R. say that belief in a necessity for multiple parties has lessened there with the years, it is probable that most Soviet citizens accept this tenet of Communist doctrine.

It is probable that most accept also the idea that they can have a democratic system under conditions of state ownership when there is only one political party. What doubt there has been within the U.S.S.R. has centered on the desirability of permitting factions or organized voting blocs to exist within the single party. Stalin thought it necessary to preservation of his own power to stamp out with violence those of his colleagues who wanted to retain factions within the Communist party, but it is uncertain how successful he was in eradicating the lingering desire to form them.

Since Stalin's death factions have emerged within the party, and public notice of the fact was provided in June, 1957, when one group tried to oust Khrushchev from the Presidium, only to be answered by his successful exclusion of the group from the party's governing circle. It seems likely, as a result of this action, that the no-faction rule will not be questioned soon again. Unless the desire to influence policy through group action is stimulated again by some extreme change of policy, such as that introduced by Khrushchev in the field of industrial management and agriculture in 1957, it can be supposed that there will be no challenge in the foreseeable future to Stalin's contribution—a no-faction monopoly party—to Marxist political lore.

The Beginning of Disbelief

Having established in the public mind the Marxist tenet of the desirability of state ownership of the productive forces and the Communist tenet of the desirability of a strong and skilled leadership, it has not been hard for Soviet leaders to claim convincing reason for a policy of terror. It has been necessary only to relate the objects of the policy to a stand opposing the Marxist definition of social progress. So long as elements of the old regime remained in Soviet society, this relationship was usually established on the domestic scene. For example, middle-class farmers called "kulaks" were ordered liquidated as a class in the early 1930's for their opposition to the collectivization of agriculture. In the propaganda line, emphasis was placed on the fact that these farmers were natural enemies: they had employed labor on their farms, they favored private ownership of land, and, in short, they had been capitalists. It must have been expected that this was sufficient indictment in peasant eyes to justify terrorizing the rich as enemies of social progress.

When the remnants of the private enterprisers of pre-Soviet days were no more, or almost no more, it became necessary to relate those marked for imprisonment to the capitalists of other lands. First, the opposition was linked with the French, as the archcapitalists of Europe, and then with the British. Before the war with Hitler, the purge trials linked Stalin's opposition with Hitler and with his efforts to march to the Urals. Since the war, persons marked for execution in the U.S.S.R. have been called "American spies" and have been linked with "capitalist powers" generally, as was the case with Beria.

Only since Stalin's death has there begun to appear some hostility toward the argument that terrorizing is justified as an instrument of government. The opposition seems to come from the newly educated workmen and peasants forming the ranks of the technical and managerial class. It has already been suggested in an earlier chapter that these new intellectuals are probably exerting pressure on the Communist party leaders to expand the circle of policy-makers at the very top of the party hierarchy. While they probably support wholeheartedly the economic system of state ownership and the idea of one-party government, it may well be that they now oppose terrorizing because it threatens predictability of tenure of office among members of the technical and managerial class. The managers of today witnessed the prewar purge, when those who were then their superiors were blacklisted as capitalist agents and placed in concentration camps or executed. They do not want this to happen to them. They are sufficiently well educated to question the accuracy of the "capitalist" label placed by Stalin upon their former colleagues. It may be that this group is now pressing for a relaxation of terrorizing, in the interest of greater personal stability, and that for them, at least, the Stalinist rationalization is wearing thin.

Such an explanation may lie at the base of the seeming reduction in importance of the Ministry of Internal Affairs since Stalin's death and, in particular, since Beria's execution. The regular army is said to have absorbed the border patrol troops of the Ministry of Internal Affairs. The special boards of the Ministry of Internal Affairs are reported to have been abolished in September, 1953, and their field of jurisdiction transferred to the military tribunals under the supervision of the Supreme Court of the U.S.S.R. Such a change is of some importance because the military courts are required on pain of Supreme Court reversal to observe procedural codes and constitutional guarantees.

Some of the instability of life seems to be slipping away for the managerial class, but it is still too early to say whether it has gone for good for the population as a whole. The social assemblies created in 1957 are ominous reminders that Communist party officials are not yet prepared to tie their hands with legal procedures from which they cannot depart.

While the changes in policy relating to terrorizing are beginning to be impressive, the end is not yet. Khrushchev used the twentieth party congress to denounce the excesses of Stalin's terrorizing apparatus, but he told his fellow party members at the same time that the agents of the Ministry of Internal Affairs were still necessary. The terrorizing apparatus is to remain, although there seems to be a desire to make its presence less evident.

CHAPTER 6

THE FEDERAL SYSTEM

Democratic institutions have sometimes been said to depend upon a federal system of government. The experience of the United States has made its impress upon the world, and federations have appeared in countries such as Brazil, Mexico, Argentina, Venezuela, Canada, Australia, India, Indonesia, Burma, and Yugoslavia. The reorganized German Federal Republic was consciously shaped in the form of a federation so as to improve its chances for the development of firm democratic institutions. It was thought that its *länder* might provide grass-roots democracy that would restrain any trend toward authoritarianism at the center. To many people who shared in the planning for Germany, a centralized government spelled potential dictatorship, even though the history of France, with her great centralization, had indicated that a centralized state could also be democratic.

The Soviet leaders have made much of the fact that the U.S.S.R. is also a federation. They have claimed that through the federal form the various peoples of the U.S.S.R. have obtained control over their own affairs, and that they have more privileges than states in other federations. The status of the various Soviet republics that make up the U.S.S.R. is said to be further proof of the democratic base upon which the Soviet system rests.

In spite of the familiar terminology used to describe the relationship among the various peoples of the U.S.S.R., the Soviet federation has some special characteristics. It is not as loose a federation as that of the United States, and by no means as decentralized as Canada or Australia. The Soviet leaders have characterized their system as being a federation that is "national in form but socialist in substance." An examination of its details will indicate what is meant.

The federal structure of the U.S.S.R. grew out of the efforts of the bolsheviks to win friends to their revolutionary plans. The Tsarist empire, unlike the United States, had been a territory in which large numbers of persons of different races, religions, languages, and cultures lived in self-contained pockets rather than diffused throughout the empire. In addition to the Great Russians, representing the most numerous of the Slavic branch of mankind, there were large numbers of Ukrainians and Byelorussians, who were also within the Slavic group but had cultures and languages differing from the Russian. There were the Latvians, Lithuanians, Estonians, and Finns, who had quite different cultures and religions from those of the Slavs. In the areas south of the Caucasus there were the ancient Armenians and Georgians, and in Central Asia and Siberia the numerous Turkic peoples and some Mongol peoples.

Tsarist practice had been to give the underdeveloped peoples of the non-Slavic groups in Central Asia and Siberia considerable cultural autonomy, but for all peoples the official language of the empire had been Russian, the positions of prestige were given primarily to Russians, and the empire had been administered in a completely centralized manner, except for the Grand Duchy of Finland. Even Finland had been closer to union with the Russians than the Finns had been willing to admit. Because of the policy of centralized government and what seemed to the minority peoples to be a policy of "Russification" of culture as well, considerable hostility toward Russian domination had developed by the turn of the twentieth century. Lenin decided to play upon this hostility in winning friends for his program. In 1912 he set Stalin to work to write a program for the national minorities that would enlist them in bolshevik ranks on the basis of the subject of their dreams, namely, independence. Stalin, being himself a Georgian, was well fitted to dramatize the willingness of the Russian Lenin to accede to the wish for independence expressed by the national minority groups.

Stalin's Concept of Self-determination

In Stalin's book, which subsequently became the bolshevik propaganda manual for dealing with the minority peoples, the position is taken that ethnic groups have the right to self-determination, that is, they have the right to determine their own political future. Stalin knew that all of them had but one desire, and that was to be independent. He knew that in taking his position he was inciting revolution against the Tsar and dismemberment of the empire.

Stalin anticipated the trouble which might befall his bolshevik party in the event of ultimate victory in the revolution. The newly independent national minority peoples might go their own ways and become splinter groups so weak as to be absorbed by another empire. He argued, therefore, that while each people had the indubitable right of self-determination, the party for which he was writing would oppose the exercise of self-determination if it did not represent a step toward what the Marxists called "progress," namely, communism. Stalin warned that his party would not agree to the passing over of the minority peoples, once they were free from the bonds of the Russian Empire, to a capitalist camp hostile to what was to be the new Russia.

When the Revolution had been won in the capital of the Russian Empire, Petrograd, the bolsheviks found themselves tested in their policy toward the peoples who had been the national minorities of the old empire. The right of self-determination had been promised, and it had to be offered, at least to the peoples who were sufficiently numerous to present a problem in control if it were denied. In some cases, as with the Finns, it meant losing them for the Soviet system, yet they, and the Ukrainians, the Byelorussians, the Armenians, Azerbaidjanians, Georgians, and Baltic peoples, were permitted to break away. The Central Asian principalities that had been in close union with, but not a part of, the empire were likewise permitted to establish their own states. Yet, for the peoples of Buryat Mongol, Yakut, Bashkir, and Tatar stock, no such privileges were granted. They were kept within the new Russian state, although it was called a "federation" to indicate that they were to have at least token autonomy.

Lenin could not afford to fail to fulfil his party's promises of self-determination to the really vocal minorities. He probably thought that in fulfilling these promises he was gaining more in good will than he was risking in ultimate loss of these peoples and of the territories they controlled. Lenin had two reasons to expect that the newly emancipated peoples would eventually return to his fold. One reason was the Communist party, and the other was force of circumstances.

The Communist party had been organized as a unitary body soon after its permanent creation in 1903. The minority peoples who had asked that they be permitted to create their own party organizations and to federate them with the Russian organization had been denied that privilege. In consequence, the members of the Communist party who lived in the territories of what had become the new

Ukrainian and Byelorussian and other republics were under orders from the highly centralized headquarters of the Communist party. Their task was to bring back into close association with Lenin's new Russian Republic the peoples with whom they lived. Their ideal was "internationalism" of the working class, and not nationalism. They knew full well that their party had bowed to the demand for self-determination in order to win friends and that it was their task to bring back the various new republics into the fold as soon as possible. In most cases they proved themselves competent to the task.

Force of circumstances greatly aided the Communists in their effort to reunify the republics. The Revolution had taken place in November, 1917, a year before the Germans, Austro-Hungarians, Bulgarians, and Turks were finally defeated by the allied and associated powers in the First World War. The German army was still a very powerful force on the Russian front, and it continued to press its advantage as the Russian troops disintegrated. The republics on the fringes of what had been the Russian Empire were being overrun. The peace of Brest Litovsk in the spring of 1918 brought only a respite, for there soon began a merciless civil war in which those who remained loyal to the past sought to unseat the bolsheviks. This civil war raged most prominently in the Ukraine, and the forces hostile to the bolsheviks finally captured all but a small part of it in mid-1919. Various foreign powers participated in the civil war, the most effective being the Poles, who marched into the Ukraine and captured its capital in 1920. It was a time when the Ukraine and the other fringe areas could conclude with reason that their future as independent states depended upon military and economic support from the Russians.

The lesson that unity was necessary for survival in war was reinforced by the lesson that unity was necessary for economic development in peace. The empire, quite naturally, had developed its economy without thought of ethnic boundaries. Railroads ran where the terrain was best, crossing and recrossing what had now become the new ethnic frontiers. Raw materials from one province had been used to supply industry in another. After the Revolution, these provinces were often separated by what was in law an "international" boundary. It was clear that if the boundaries were not to be eradicated, a very difficult economic readjustment would become necessary, and in this readjustment productive capacity would be reduced. Unification within one state was the obvious solution to the problem.

Creating a Soviet Federation

Playing upon the growing realization of most of the minority peoples, fanned by the Communist party in each republic, that there must be a new unity within what had been the Russian Empire, Lenin and Stalin planned a federation. Communist party delegates from the various republics that had adopted the Soviet system of government, frequently under the pressure of military operations, met during the late summer of 1922 and evolved a draft constitution that called for a federation of four republics. Three of these already existed as the Russian, Byelorussian, and Ukrainian republics. The fourth was created by bringing together in a new Transcaucasian Republic the three existing republics of Azerbaidjan, Armenia, and Georgia.

While each of the latter was to retain its own republic structure, it was to be within a federation which, in turn, would join the larger federation of the U.S.S.R. The reason given later for the subfederation of the Transcaucasian Republic was that the peoples south of the Caucasus had to be forced into a mold of co-operation because of their long history of conflict with one another. Presumably it was easier to do so with them than with the more numerous Ukrainians and the Byelorussians. One can speculate that if the Ukrainians had been more pliable and less nationalistic in outlook, they also might have been brought closer to the Russians than was done in 1922.

Having secured agreement among the Communist party members living in the various republics, the Russian party leaders had to take only a step to obtain formal agreement among representatives of the four republics that were to join in federation. A constitutional congress was held in Moscow at the end of December, 1922, and the delegates from the four republics accepted the treaty of union that had been drafted. They then declared themselves the new All-Union Congress of Soviets, which was to be the body bringing together delegates from the whole territory of the new U.S.S.R. A constitution was ordered prepared; it was completed and adopted provisionally in July, 1923, and when the Congress of Soviets of the U.S.S.R. met in a second session in January, 1924, the Constitution was ratified.

Where was the federal principle to be found in the governmental structure of the new Union? As in all federal constitutions, there were clauses allocating powers to the federal government and clauses reserving powers to the states that had come together to form the federation. Those who know the history of the Constitutional Convention in the United States know of the struggles between those who wished to reserve to the states significant powers and those who urged greater federal powers. There is no indication that such a struggle occurred in the Communist party group that formulated the first draft of the Constitution, nor in the drafting committee of the Congress of Soviets which prepared the formal document for adoption. The Communist party seems already to have become sufficiently sure of its power and of the acceptance of its leadership by the minority peoples to plan for much more centralism than was acceptable to the Founding Fathers in Philadelphia.

The federal government in the U.S.S.R. was granted by the Constitution some powers familiar to the system in the United States. The federal government alone could coin money, maintain a postal service, establish standards of weights and measures, regulate citizenship in the Union, and settle disputes among republics. The federal government also had sole power to declare war, conclude treaties, and conduct diplomatic relations. At this point similarity ends, for the Soviet Constitution gives additional powers to the federal government, of which the Founding Fathers in the United States had not even heard.

This grant of additional powers stems from the Marxist doctrine of what is necessary to achieve maximum production. As has been seen, the Marxists deny that private enterprise can produce as much as state-owned enterprise. One of their professed reasons for such a belief is that the workman will labor harder when he anticipates payment in full for his work rather than payment of only that part which is left from the value he produces after the private enterpriser's profit has been siphoned off. Another reason, one which has been elaborated by the Soviet leadership on the basis of limited implication by Marx, is that economic planning will save waste and duplication. In a planned economy there should be no surpluses seeking customers.

For both these reasons, economic planning has become one of the major tenets of present-day Soviet leadership, and the reflection of this view is to be found in the first federal Constitution of 1923. The first Constitution empowered the federal government to develop a general plan for the entire national economy; to establish general principles for the development and use of the soil, mineral deposits, forests, and waters; to direct transport and telegraph services; and to conduct trade.

Special Features of the Soviet Federation

While the Soviet federal Constitution transferred far more economic power to the federal government than did the United States Constitutional Convention in 1787, there were some notable omissions in other areas. The Soviet federal Constitution included no bill of rights, such as did the United States Constitution in its first group of amendments. The Soviet bills of rights, such as they were, existed in the constitutions of the republics that had formed the Union, and it was decided, apparently, to leave them in these constitutions alone. It was also left to the republics to develop their own electoral law. No federal provisions declared who might vote and who might not vote. Finally, the federal Constitution left unmolested the civil, criminal, family, land, and labor codes, and the codes of criminal and civil procedure, as these had developed in the republics before federation. While some of these codes might be affected by such general principles for the use of the soil, mineral deposits, forests, and waters as the federal government might adopt, the Communist party seems to have preferred to rely upon the unifying influence of its members in the various republic legislatures rather than to require the republics to accept a system of federal codes.

The concept of federation found reflection in the structure of the Central Executive Committee of the U.S.S.R., which, under constitutional provision, was to be elected by the Congress of Soviets to legislate and generally to supervise the administrative and judicial arms of government during the year-long intervals between meetings of the Congress of Soviets. The Central Executive Committee was made bicameral: one chamber was to be chosen on the basis of population representation alone, while the other chamber was to be chosen on the basis of representation from each national minority group within the U.S.S.R.

The chamber in which each national minority group was to be represented seems to have been the major concession made to the minority peoples in the federation. It may also have been introduced into the Soviet system of government to appeal to other peoples outside the U.S.S.R. In 1922 it was still anticipated that revolution of the Soviet type would occur in Europe and in Asia in the foreseeable future. It was equally anticipated that German and other Western European Communists, who were by this time sending delegations to a Communist International with its seat in Moscow and having as its goal world revolution, might be sufficiently proud to

want a share, in any future union, equal to that of the very numerous Russians. The bicameral Central Executive Committee could
serve as proof to national groups outside the U.S.S.R. that they
would not be submerged in a sea of Slavs.

The second chamber of the Central Executive Committee was to
contain representatives not only from the constituent republics that
had formed the Union in December, 1922, but also from other
national minority groups as well. The Communists had to think of
the sensibilities of the Azerbaidjanians, the Armenians, and the
Georgians, who had started as independent states after the revolutions organized in each and thus had been of equal status with the
Russians, Ukrainians, and Byelorussians. While these three peoples
south of the Caucasus had been brought into the federation as a subfederation, they were proud, and each was therefore given the same
number of seats in the chamber of nationalities as each of the three
larger republics, rather than only a one-third share of the seats
which might have been given to their subfederation. Then there
were the Buryat Mongolians, the Yakuts, the Tatars, the Bashkirs,
and the Volga Germans, as well as some less numerous peoples
who had been, since the Revolution, given the title of republics
within the Russian Republic. These peoples had, apparently, expressed through party channels in 1922 the feeling that if the
Byelorussians and Ukrainians were to be brought into the Union
on an equal basis with the Russians, there was no reason why they
should be one step removed from the top level and required to
channel their relations with the federal government through the
Russian Republic.

A Place for Small Minorities

Stalin reported at the constitutional convention of 1922 that some
thought had been given to the status of the small ethnic groups
within the Russian Republic. He said that he believed that their
relationship with the Russian Republic had been established on a
satisfactory basis and that to put them on the level of a constituent
republic would be to take a step backward and to loosen a bond
which had been tightened. In making this remark, Stalin indicated
the direction in which he intended to move and clarified the reason
why the federal rather than the unitary form of state was being
adopted. The reason was simply that no closer bond than that provided by federation was politically possible at the time.

As a concession to the pride of the Tatars and of the other peoples within the Russian Republic who had cultural minority status as "Autonomous Republics" but not the higher political status of a constituent republic, the Communists offered them a number of seats equal to that of the Russians and of the constituent republics in the chamber of nationalities of the Central Executive Committee. With this provision there appeared the curious form of representation that has become a peculiarity of the Soviet federal system: subordinate parts of the republics that comprise the Union send representatives to the highest body of the federation, somewhat as if the Pennsylvania Dutch had a representative in the United States Senate alongside the senators from the Commonwealth of Pennsylvania. Even the Eskimos and other very small national minority groups were given seats in the chamber of nationalities, though not in the same number as the larger groups. In consequence, the chamber of nationalities contained a large number of representatives of non-Russian peoples. To the minority groups, and to the world at large, it looked as if the Russians were prepared to share power with their small neighbors in the U.S.S.R.

Yet, in assessing this situation, the role of the Communist party must be kept in mind. Throughout each national group there were Communists, required to think of themselves as internationalists and subject to strict discipline originating at the center. These might even be nationals of groups other than the one in which they were ordered to make their home. Further, they had been trained in the party to propose only those programs which central party officials favored. Under their influence, the representatives of the national minority groups have never expressed a special interest in any but very limited local policy matters, such as the allocation of funds for irrigation in Central Asia or for housing in Georgia. The minority representatives have always voted unanimously for any program presented by the party, and it has never been necessary to reconcile through reconciliation procedure any contrary views of the chamber of nationalities and the chamber composed of representatives selected on the basis of population alone, although the Constitution provides for such an eventuality. The very real contrast between the Soviet legislature and those of Western democracies is indicated by the fact that there has never been a public difference of opinion between the chambers.

The Influence of the Years

With the passage of time, the local nationalism of the minorities seems to have been reduced, although events in Georgia in 1956 suggest that it may still be aroused by signs of discrimination against a minority people. Soviet text writers declare that a lessening of local patriotism is inevitable, since these minority groups have found that no "Russification" of their cultures is occurring. However, such a declaration does not accord with the facts. It is true that Soviet law does not require that Russian be the sole language spoken in schools, government offices, and courts. On the contrary, the law guarantees that both schools and government business will be conducted in the language of the local ethnic community. Nevertheless, Russian is compulsory as a second language, and any young man or woman who wants to achieve a position of prominence in the U.S.S.R. learns Russian to the best of his or her ability because it is a key to social and geographic mobility. Knowledge of Russian opens doors to the highest professional schools, where it is the language of instruction. Knowledge of Russian enables a man to communicate both in any part of the country to which the party orders him and also on the international scene. The Russian language has become a political and social asset, and the ambitious Ukrainian, Georgian, or other minority representative cultivates the use of it. Thus, today, anyone who visits the U.S.S.R. will find that Russian is commonly used throughout the land, although it is often noted that in outlying districts, and even on Ukrainian farms, no one but the farm officials speaks it with facility.

While minority cultures are fostered, if need be through Russian subsidization of their opera, drama, and literature, local authors are admonished not to be "chauvinistic" in their art. Some of them have even been criticized and disgraced within the Communist party for alleged preaching of national pride and of hostility toward the Russian culture. Since Stalin's death, insufficient respect for national minority susceptibilities has been declared to have been one of his shortcomings, and his heirs, setting out early to rectify the balance, assigned Beria to the job. This assignment has complicated the situation, however, for on Beria's arrest he was accused, among other things, of fostering national animosities, and it may be that he went farther than the rest of Stalin's heirs were willing to go in placating minority restlessness following upon Stalin's glorification of the Great Russians for their major part in winning the Second World War.

Federal Changes in the 1936 Constitution

In the second federal Constitution, adopted in 1936, the powers reserved to the republics were somewhat reduced. A federal bill of rights and electoral law were introduced, and it was also provided that civil and criminal codes, and codes of civil and criminal procedure, should be established by the federal government rather than by the republics. No federal codes were completed in Stalin's time, although the existing codes were brought into increasing uniformity by federal acts made compulsory for the republics.

The second federal Constitution also changed the state structure, which had been headed by the Congress of Soviets of the U.S.S.R. and its Central Executive Committee. The unicameral Congress of Soviets was abolished and the former Central Executive Committee was made into the new bicameral Supreme Soviet to which reference was made in chapter three. The general powers of this body have already been discussed, but it remains to indicate the extent to which it reflects the principle of federation.

The Supreme Soviet of the U.S.S.R., like the preceding Central Executive Committee established by the first federal Constitution, has two chambers, one representing the population generally and called the "Soviet of the Union," the other representing the national minority groups and called the "Soviet of Nationalities." This latter body is not composed in precisely the same manner as was its predecessor, for now only the constituent republics have the same number of delegates as the Russian Republic, that is, twenty-five. The lesser minority peoples organized in what are known as "Autonomous Republics"—the Tatars, Yakuts, Bashkirs, and Buryat Mongolians—now have only eleven delegates and, thus, a relatively lesser position, as measured by number of deputies, than before. The still smaller ethnic groups, those organized into "Autonomous Regions," have five deputies, and the even smaller ethnic groups, those organized into "National Districts," only one. Thus all peoples who number more than a handful and who can claim to be of unique ethnic stock have representation, but in quantity graduated according to population.

The varying levels of representation and of prestige that resulted from the provisions of the federal Constitution of 1936 gave rise, apparently, to new criticism from the Tatars and Bashkirs, if not from other national minority groups. When Stalin was explaining the state structure to the constitutional congress called to adopt the 1936 Constitution, he dwelt at some length on the reason for placing some of the national minority groups into what appeared to be the favored category of "union" republic while others, just as numerous and as culturally mature, were left out. In so doing, he stressed that the distinction between republics in the "union" and "autonomous" categories was based not only on size and on maturity of cultural development but also, and in some cases more importantly, on location. He argued that location was crucial because the Constitution gave only "union" republics the right to secede from the U.S.S.R., and, if secession were to be more than a paper right, a people exercising this right should not find themselves completely surrounded by the U.S.S.R. from which they had seceded and, therefore, would have to be situated on a border of the U.S.S.R. in the first place.

To foreign students of Stalin's writings, such an explanation sounds strained. The right of secession had been guaranteed since the first federal Constitution, presumably to placate the last diehards among the minority groups that were not yet sufficiently under Communist party control to accept permanent federation. The right of secession may even have been included in the Constitution to please Germans and other non-Soviet peoples who would have been reluctant to enter a permanent union. Whatever the reason for making the right of secession part of the Constitution, in the view of foreign students the right lacked reality.

Limitations on the Rights of Republics

Both in his 1912 manual and in subsequent statements, Stalin had made it clear that he felt that the Communist party should oppose any movement for secession if it meant that a people would return to the capitalist form of economy, for, in Marxist terms, a return to capitalism was a retrogressive step and, by definition, should be opposed by Communists. With Communist opposition assured against any effort to secede, it seemed to foreigners inconceivable that any republic could exercise the right successfully.

Stalin's argument for categorizing peoples in "union" or "autonomous" republics seems especially empty in the light of his writings on secession. The argument can have been thought to have value only for propagandizing the peoples who live on the frontiers of the U.S.S.R., such as the Iranians, the Afghans, the Latvians, the Poles, and others. At the time of his utterance, Stalin probably had not anticipated that some of these territories could be brought within the Soviet orbit so soon by military action rather than by the subversion to which his argument might be said to have appealed.

The limited nature of the powers reserved to the republics in the Soviet federal system is most clearly demonstrated in the law governing the budget of the U.S.S.R. Annually, the Supreme Soviet of the U.S.S.R. adopts a budget for the entire Union that is broken down republic by republic in its totals. No republic has its own source of revenue subject to its own control, and no republic can spend on its institutions any funds except those allocated by the federal budget. Only after the Supreme Soviet has adopted the budget for the entire country do the supreme soviets of each of the union republics meet in annual session to adopt their budgets. The total for a republic has to be the total established by the federal budget for that republic, but the republic may divide that total among its various provinces as it thinks fit. Obviously, the federal planners have drafted the federal budget with knowledge of the needs and possibilities of each province in each republic, but a republic's government can provide some variation. It can, through the budget debate, give to the deputies from the various provinces and from the various "autonomous republics," "autonomous regions," and "national districts" within the republic some sense of participation in the process of government. As has been seen, this sense of participation is probably one of the primary reasons why the Communist party has maintained the system of soviets alongside its own institutions.

To the outsider who knows the jealousy with which the states in the United States have guarded their budgets from federal encroachment, it is evident that one of the bases on which the autonomy that is still maintained by the American states rests is the power of the purse. In relinquishing this power to their federal government, the republics of the U.S.S.R. have given away the key to much of the independence possible within a federal system.

Of recent years, Soviet leaders have sought to enhance the appearance of independence in their republics by amending the clause in their federal Constitution that relates to the division of powers between federal and republic governments. In 1944 the Supreme Soviet of the U.S.S.R. extended to each of the then existing sixteen union republics the power to conduct its foreign relations, within the limits of policy established by the federal government, and to establish military formations of its own, within limits established by the federal government. The republics were permitted to organize ministries of foreign affairs and of defense to administer their affairs in these areas, but federal ministries of the same names were retained to co-ordinate policy. Further, the federal government was charged with "the representation of the Union in international relations, conclusion and ratification of treaties with other states, and the establishment of the general procedure in the mutual relations between the Union Republics."

Various reasons have been suggested for the changes of 1944. The most cogent is that Stalin was preparing to ask for sixteen seats in the United Nations, which was then being planned. He made such a request of the planning group at Dumbarton Oaks and, again, at the Yalta Conference. The world now knows the compromise that was accepted by Franklin D. Roosevelt and by Winston Churchill, under which the Byelorussian and Ukrainian republics received membership in the United Nations along with the U.S.S.R. while the other fourteen republics received no international recognition. The voting and debating records of these two Soviet republics in the United Nations since that time indicate that the federal government of the U.S.S.R. sets policy on all matters, as its Constitution requires it to do.

An additional reason for the 1944 amendments may lie in their possible appeal to the U.S.S.R.'s neighbors in Asia. For example, the Afghan government could deal directly with the governments of the Central Asian republics on border matters, though, when any cession of territory is made, as was the case in 1955 when territory was ceded to Iran, the treaty is made with the U.S.S.R. The republics concerned indicated their formal consent to the Presidium of the Supreme Soviet of the U.S.S.R. There was no negotiation between Iran and the two republics whose territory was affected.

After Stalin's death the trend toward centralization was accentuated by the reduction of the Karelo-Finnish Republic's status from that of a union republic to that of an autonomous republic within the Russian Republic. This event of mid-1956, which marked the first occasion in Soviet history of reduction of a union republic's status, provides a possible explanation of the real criteria used in 1936 and subsequently to determine which ethnic groups shall have union republic status within the federation. Stalin may have conceded union republic status to the minority peoples on the federation's frontiers not for the reasons he gave publicly but to improve the power of each people to entice their blood brothers across the frontiers in Poland, Rumania, Turkey, Iran, Afghanistan, China, and Finland to withdraw in revolt from the states in which they lived and to join the Soviet federation.

The reduction in status of Karelo-Finland in 1956 may have occurred because Stalin's heirs no longer shared the expectation which Stalin had evidenced as late as the war with Finland in 1940 that the citizens of Finland would join the Soviet federation as a part of the Karelo-Finnish Republic if given an opportunity. Stalin's heirs may have decided that it was time to be realistic and to incorporate the Karelo-Finnish minority within the Russian Republic to which they were already closely bound economically. Efficient administration may be easier when all matters can be handled through the apparatus of an autonomous republic rather than channeled through the relatively more cumbersome procedures of a union republic.

The Karelo-Finnish case was shown to be an exception to the plans of Stalin's heirs for the federation as a whole by events of 1957. At that time constitutional amendments were introduced into the federal and republic constitutions, returning to the republics some of the authority of which they had been deprived by Stalin. Notably, the drafting of codes of law became again the task of the republics, as it had been prior to 1936. The federal government returned to its former position of guide in that it dictated the general principles to be followed by the draftsmen. The republics were also authorized to draw the administrative boundaries of their internal subdivisions, their provinces and counties. Previously these had been dictated from the center in accordance with directions of the planning authorities.

Changes in the relationship between federal authority and that of the republics occurred in the administration of industry within a few months of the constitutional amendments, and the administrative apparatus of secondary and higher education followed suit in 1958. Industrial and educational reorganization had to do primarily with public administration where operations and not policy were concerned. To assess the political importance of the new approach, the administrative apparatus of the Soviet state will be examined.

CHAPTER 7

POPULARIZING ADMINISTRATION

"Bring the housewife into administration!" This was one of the slogans by which Lenin hoped to dramatize a popularization of public administration. He declared that the new Russia was to depart from the system of the past under which a highly skilled and conservative group of professional employees manned the offices of the state. His plan was to simplify management procedures and to discard the red tape that is characteristic of all large-scale administrative machines. This he expected to be able to do if he could put the housewife and her husband into the local soviets, which were the administrative bureaus of the new regime, for short periods of time. To effect his plan, he provided in the first Constitution of the Russian Republic that the term of deputies to the local soviets should be but three months.

While espousing the popularization of administration at the local level, Lenin held no brief for the decentralization of policy-making. He wanted citizens to take turns at local offices performing the tasks of the state, but he wanted the principles on which the tasks rested to be established by the central government. He and his party opposed vigorously a January, 1918, attempt by the left wing of the Socialist Revolutionary party, with which the bolsheviks were still in coalition government, to place policy-making as well as operating functions in the local soviets. Just as he had opposed any decentralization of policy-making within the Communist party, Lenin opposed decentralization of authority in the state apparatus.

Lenin had his way. The left-wing Socialist Revolutionaries finally withdrew from the coalition government in the spring of 1918, and with them went the last effective challenge to Lenin's favored principle of centralization of policy-making. Lenin adhered for some

91

years, however, to his program for the popularization of administration. It was not until December, 1921, that the terms of deputies to local soviets were extended from the original three months to one year. The change coincided with the abandonment of many other early policies, in order to establish a mechanism capable of administering the modified system of capitalist economy introduced in late 1921 to restore the economy after the devastation of the civil-war period. Lenin found it necessary at the time to sacrifice some of his precious principles to the needs of the people for food, clothes, housing, and industrial goods. Among the sacrifices was the concept of a non-professional civil service.

The principle of popularization of the administration not only was applied at the local government level but was set as an ideal for the central government of the Russian Republic as well. Yet here there was less opportunity to place the housewife in government. Administration of a central government in a huge state could not be simplified, and it was necessary to maintain an apparatus at headquarters composed of professionals. Many of these had to be held over from the offices of the old regime, for few of the bolsheviks could cope with the details of complex operations such as those of the Ministry of Finance or of the Ministry of Communications. Thus the old ministries were bound to influence the structure of the new commissariats, even though Lenin hoped to avoid such influence by eliminating the Tsarist bureaucrats as fast as new personnel could be trained to replace them. Meanwhile he could do nothing more than place his own supporters at the head of each commissariat and sprinkle throughout the ranks a few "commissars" who would have the task of watching the professionals and stopping sabotage on their part. The policy of utilizing such political commissars was even extended to the new army, in which the old officers had to be retained because they alone knew the skills of war.

Mass Psychology Requires Attention

Public opinion was always a matter of grave concern to Lenin. He had gained the mass support necessary for his revolution from workmen and peasants, to whom much had been promised. Lenin knew that these largely uneducated people would lose interest in his regime, and even become hostile, unless he carried out his promises of democratization of the state administrative apparatus. He had to be careful lest the masses conclude that they had supported no real revolution but had only changed one authoritarian state for another.

Lenin discussed the council of heads of administrative departments with his colleague Trotsky, who recorded their conversation. Lenin asked Trotsky what might be done to indicate to the public that the new Council of Ministers would differ from the old. Trotsky said that he recommended a new name for the body, "commissar," because this term had become popular in its application to the watchdogs of the new regime scattered throughout the old apparatus. Trotsky further proposed that, to indicate superior rank, the men who would perform the function of ministers be called "Peoples' Commissars," and their government or "cabinet" the "Council of Peoples' Commissars." Lenin is reported to have been delighted with the suggestion. He said, "That is splendid. That smells of revolution."

The title "Council of Peoples' Commissars" was retained until 1946, when the name was restored to the traditional "Council of Ministers." The government gave little explanation for the reversion, except to say that the old name was more conventional and that there was no longer need to emphasize the new character of the council in this way since its special character had been established by the practice of the preceding nineteen years.

The scheme of administration established in the Russian Republic in 1917, and subsequently in the other soviet-type republics that emerged within what had been the Russian Empire, accorded with Lenin's concept of centralized policy-making and localized operations. The new "Peoples' Commissariats" in the capital were to establish policy, while the executive committees of the provincial, county, village, or city soviets were to execute policy. Thus, the Peoples' Commissariat of Justice enunciated the policy to be followed in establishing the courts, but the actual establishment was the work of the county bureaus of justice within the executive committees of the county soviets, and these were co-ordinated within each province by the department of justice within the executive committee of each provincial soviet.

The local soviets were so sure of themselves in the early months that they often determined their own policy instead of waiting for the decisions of the Peoples' Commissariats in Moscow. In the early days, local policemen were recruited and put to work by local soviets, and it was some months before the Peoples' Commissariat of Internal Affairs was able to establish its policy direction over the police function of the local soviets. It was a time when the men and women who had fought the Revolution were drinking the heady wine of power, and they were slow to relinquish any part of it, even to a central government to which they had pledged allegiance and in which they were supposed to have confidence.

Only in a few matters, such as the conduct of foreign affairs, did the local soviets play no part. In such realms the central government both determined policy and conducted operations. In the great bulk of administrative matters touching the people, the conduct of affairs was otherwise. The people were given the authority to decide questions of local concern subject only to the policy set by headquarters. In fact, they often usurped even the policy-making function. It was not until 1919 that the Moscow commissariats began to pull the reins into their own hands and not until late in 1920 that a strong centralized policy-making authority was clearly apparent. It is hard to tell whether the men around Lenin during this period were being forced to centralize because of the inefficiencies caused by decentralization of policy-making or whether their political philosophy dictated centralization while mass resistance against it compelled them to compromise. Most students of the period incline toward the latter view that Lenin and his colleagues were in favor of centralization from the start but had to move slowly lest they unseat themselves.

The Effect of Federation on Administration

Federation of the republics in the U.S.S.R., at the very end of 1922, raised again the question of administrative structure. As has been seen, the federal rather than the unitary form of government had been thought necessary by Lenin and Stalin to win the confidence of the national minority peoples, who were suspicious of highly centralized government after their experience with the unitary system of the Russian Empire. This concession to the sensibilities of the minority peoples found further practical reflection in the structure of the new federal administrative apparatus. It was impossible, under the circumstances of the time, to give policy-making authority in all fields exclusively to the federal government while leaving only operating authority in the hands of the republics.

The division of powers between the federal government and the governments of the republics had given the federal government certain monopolies, such as the conduct of foreign affairs and foreign trade, the conduct of defense, and the preparation of economic plans and basic rules for the use of the land, but nothing had been said on such a vital matter as education. Education was obviously closely

linked to the preservation of culture, and culture was a touchy subject. The fear of "Russification" had been one of the primary reasons
why the minority peoples had wanted to separate from the Russian
Republic immediately after the Revolution. Culture was a field into
which the federal government could not intrude without stirring up
old hatreds and losing mass support from the minorities whom it
was trying to woo.

Those who drafted the first federal Constitution prescribed an
administrative structure suited to their purposes. In the economic
areas whose development seemed essential to the materialist Marxist,
the emphasis was upon centralization. Most of the state factories
were placed under an agency like a commissariat but called "The
All-Union Council of National Economy," which was charged with
centralization of policy and sometimes of operations as well. For the
cultural areas such as education and judicial administration, no commissariat was established in the federal government. Both policy-
making and operations in the form of the conduct of schools and
courts were left solely to the republics comprising the federation.

Because of the policy of nationalization of factories and of other
instruments of production, the U.S.S.R. had at its inception in late
1922 an unusual administrative problem. Although very few cabinet
members in countries such as the United States devote even part of
their time to the administration of natural resources and of industry,
this had become the U.S.S.R.'s principal administrative burden. This
weighting on the industrial side was evident in the first federal
Council of Peoples' Commissars, of which The All-Union Council of
National Economy was one major member. Within the offices of this
specialized agency sat the men who supervised and sometimes
operated the nationalized industries. The All-Union Council was still
a relatively small body at the time, but it was destined to grow in
importance until its administrators became so numerous that it was
split into many parts, each given the rank of a Peoples' Commissariat
dealing with a specific and limited branch of industry, such as steel,
chemicals, textiles, machine-building, coal-mining, petroleum, or
copper.

For the industrial plant there was thought to be no problem of
hostility on the part of the national minorities toward centralization.
The sole consideration for those who established Soviet administrative policy in this sphere of industry was, therefore, efficiency. The
question asked at headquarters was whether the operation of a
given industry would be better if it were turned over to the republics

or if it were retained by the commissariat in the federal government. In some fields, such as textiles, the Russian Empire had achieved a reputation for production, and there were already numerous textile mills that had been nationalized by early decrees following the Revolution. In other areas, such as metallurgy, the Russian Empire had been less developed, and the new regime, with its desire for self-sufficiency in the field of heavy industry, called for rapid metallurgical development as a matter of defensive necessity.

New Forms of Ministries To Aid Efficiency

As events have proved, the policy decision taken at the time of federation or soon after seems to have been to retain in the federal government's hands complete authority to plan and operate the various heavy industries of the land, while passing on to the republic governments the authority to operate the consumers' goods industries within a framework of policy established by the federal government. Two distinctive types of commissariats were designed to administer these two kinds of industry: the type that planned and operated heavy industry was called the "All-Union type," while the type that did the planning but left operations to the republics was called the "Union-Republic type."

Although these two types of ministry, with roots in the federal government, seemed peculiarly fitted to administer industry, they were expanded to other fields as well. Foreign trade is still planned and conducted by a ministry of All-Union type. Until 1944, foreign affairs and defense were planned and conducted by ministries of All-Union type. Until 1955, communications (telephone and telegraph) were planned and operated by the federal government through a ministry of All-Union type.

The All-Union type of ministry is to be found only in the federal government at the federal capital. Thus, a Ministry of Power Plant Construction exists only at Moscow, and its chief sits in the Council of Ministers of the U.S.S.R. To construct the plants on the Angara River in faraway Siberia, the minister in Moscow acts through agents responsible directly to him. Although such agents are supposed to be considerate of local sensibilities in performing their functions, they often are not. For example, Soviet newspapers once complained that men from the Ministry of Communications cut down the prized boulevard trees in a provincial town to make room for the wires they were stringing. Although the local state officials could complain in the newspaper or by telegram, they had no administrative channel through which they could require consideration of their views, for the Ministry of Communications was at the time and until 1955 an All-Union type of ministry, responsible to Moscow alone.

The Union-Republic type of ministry is different. In the federal capital there is a Ministry of Communications, and there is a ministry of the same name also in the capital of each of the fifteen republics. If Ukrainian officials and citizens with authoritative voices have a complaint against the local employees of such a ministry, they have more than an opportunity to write letters to Moscow. The Minister of the Ukrainian Ministry of Communications sits in the Council of Ministers of the Ukrainian Republic in Kiev. He is responsible to the ministry of the same name in the federal government in Moscow, but he is responsible also to the government of the Ukrainian Republic. He is not remote and unapproachable for the Ukrainians he serves.

As the trend toward centralization of authority, to which reference was made in the last chapter, extended, the effectiveness of complaints from enraged citizens to nearby ministers of the Union-Republic type probably diminished. Nevertheless, although, under Stalin, the republics lost political power, the fact remains that the Union-Republic type of ministerial structure provided a direct channel through which the influence of local officials could be brought to bear upon operations. There was no such channel in a ministry of the All-Union type. This difference may have been of some importance under Stalin and is probably more important since his death.

The possibility of local influence upon operations is enhanced by the manner in which ministries of the Union-Republic type usually conduct their affairs locally. Unlike the linesmen of the Ministry of Communications, who were responsible only to the head office in the federal government at the time of the tree-cutting episode, the managers of public health clinics in a given province or city are not responsible solely to a distant ministry. This ministry decentralizes its operating functions by channeling them through the executive committees of the provincial, county, and city soviets. Within each executive committee at these levels, there is a "department" charged with the duty of serving as the administrative arm of the ministry of Union-Republic type in connection with operations in the province, county, or city of the kind controlled by that ministry. It is these departments that employ the civil servants who co-ordinate relevant activities in the territory over which the soviet has jurisdiction.

Facts and figures on public health in a given locality are gathered by these departments of local soviets. Also, administrative orders containing policy directives pass through the hands of these departments for distribution within the territory over which they have jurisdiction. Thus, the Ministry of Public Health in the Ukraine will not transmit its orders directly to the heads of public health clinics throughout the Ukraine but will channel them through the department of public health in each province of the Ukrainian Republic, whence they are fanned out to the many counties within each province and, finally, may be sent to various small city soviets for execution.

There are exceptions to systematic procedures in any administrative system, and the U.S.S.R. had a large share of them under Stalin. Thus the efficient operation of some units of industry subject to the control of a ministry of the Union-Republic type was deemed to be so critical for the nation as a whole that administrative authority for the unit was given directly to the ministry in the federal government. For example, a particular textile mill or shoe factory was sometimes subordinated to the then existing Ministry of Light Industry in the federal government rather than to the Ministry of Light Industry in the Latvian Republic in which it was physically situated and to which it would normally have been subordinated in accordance with the principles established generally for units of the textile or shoe industries. Shortly after World War II, when the Soviet economy was barely able to put itself on its feet, a considerable number of such key units were transferred from the administrative supervision of ministries of the Union-Republic type in the various republics to the ministry in the federal government. In mid-1956, many of these plants were returned to the operating control of the ministries in the republics, as a first step in recognition of the advantages of local direction of operations.

The transfers to centralized operation after the war and back to local operation in 1956 have suggested to foreign students that loss of skilled personnel in the war reduced the number of able administrators in the provinces and counties so greatly that the central authorities dared not trust the judgment of local men. In spite of the increased red tape to be expected from centralization, these authorities seem to have decided to risk loss of efficiency through overloading central planners with operating functions rather than to lose production because of lack of skills at the local level.

Reorganization of industrial administration in 1957 marked recognition of the failure of the policy of centralization of operations to solve managerial inadequacies. Soviet public administration was set on a new course. The character of the change will be examined after discussion of republic monopolies.

Administrative Concessions to Minority Cultures

The cultural affairs of a republic have been classed, for the reasons indicated, in a category different from that of industry. As has been indicated, there is more involved in cultural relations between the federal government and the government of each republic than efficiency of operation. There is the whole matter of "Russification" with its overtones of Tsarist days. To meet the problem raised by the sensitivities of the national minorities, the first federal Constitution left education solely to the republics. The Ukraine and the other republics were to plan for their own schools and to operate them. The same was true of the judicial system; there was no ministry of justice established in the federal government by the first federal Constitution.

Certain other activities also were left exclusively to the republic governments by the first federal Constitution. Since the first Constitution established categories, some, such as public health and agriculture, have been removed from the exclusively republic group and others have been added. Justice has moved back and forth. In mid-1956, it was restored to the republic governments, with which it began at the outset of the Soviet regime. The republic ministries in the Russian Republic in 1959 deal, respectively, with justice, social insurance, grammar-school education, automobile transport, construction, housing administration, timber industry, paper and woodworking, and water transport.

It will be seen that the Soviet leaders have found it desirable to remove from the monopoly of the republics one of the activities deemed vital to the life of the Union, namely, agriculture. This field of activity has been placed under a ministry of the Union-Republic type, so that the federal government can plan for and make policy decisions relating to the vital matter of use of the land by collective farms. Even the conduct of education, which was originally subject to the sole control of a republic type of ministry, has been much circumscribed.

A committee on higher education was established as an appendage to the federal government's Council of Ministers during World War II. This committee was given broad co-ordinating and planning authority. The authority seems to have proved inadequate, for in 1946 the committee was transformed into a Union-Republic type of ministry, but of a special character. It was authorized not only to plan for higher education but to operate directly a group of key institutions of higher learning and to guide the republics in operating the rest. Through this action the republics lost the last vestige of control over education at the higher level, although they still retained nominally sole control over the grammar schools. Yet even these schools were brought closer to conformity with a uniform policy; the federal government set minimum limits on compulsory education, and its decrees established standards for teaching and model textbooks.

The trend toward centralization of what little monopoly administrative authority had been left to the republics by federation in 1922 reached its zenith after Stalin's death, for in March, 1954, a Ministry of Higher Education of All-Union type assumed the duties of operating the universities and higher schools. The central authorities seem to have overstepped the bounds of national minority sentiment by this latter decree, for in December, 1954, a cautious step was taken in reversal of policy: higher education was restored to the jurisdiction of a ministry of Union-Republic type. But it was not to be a ministry of the usual kind, for there was to be a republic Ministry of Higher Education only in the Ukrainian Republic. In all other republics the higher schools and universities were to be operated by the federal government. The trend toward restoration of republic authority was advanced in 1959 with transfer of all institutions of higher and specialized secondary education to ministries newly created in all republics. The ministry in the federal government, however, retained important powers: control over certification of faculty members, approval of textbooks, and the giving of assistance in the organization of teaching, methodology, and research. The reservation of these powers was clear evidence of the limits within which the republics might operate.

Experiments with Widened Local Autonomy

The year 1957 marked a sharp reversal of the trend toward ever increasing centralization of industrial management to cope with the failure of industry to achieve the levels set in the economic plans. The reversal had not come entirely without warning. There had been the cautious step with education, but that was linked with cultural sensibilities. More important had been a partial return to republic operation of two heavy industries, coal and petroleum. In 1954 both were assigned to new ministries of the Union-Republic type, and their ministries of the All-Union type abolished. The standard pattern of the Union-Republic type of ministry was not duplicated, however, for in each instance only one republic of the federation was authorized to establish a ministry subordinate to the ministry in the federal government. Those mines and refineries located in other republics were still to be operated from the federal capital.

Khrushchev took personal charge of the implementation of the policy of decentralization of operations. The Central Committee of the Communist party accepted his proposals in February, 1957. He announced that while the centralized direction of industry had been necessary for the quick development of heavy industry in the early days, it was unsuited to postwar conditions, especially since there were being operated more than 200,000 state industrial enterprises and 100,000 construction projects. To continue the former policy of attempting to reduce burdens upon ministers in the federal government by subdividing their responsibilities and creating new ministries would, in Khrushchev's view, reduce co-operation between branches of industry, increase administrative costs by duplicating ministerial services, and separate more and more plants from the local communities in which they functioned.

The national interest had to be served, in Khrushchev's opinion, by a radically new approach: by developing local decision-making. To make his proposals concrete Khrushchev published theses in March suggesting the creation of councils of national economy, to be called *Sovnarkhozy*. Each was to be placed in a region established with regard to ease of communication with plant managers and co-operation between related industries. The All-Union ministries were to be abolished, except for a few activities transcending republic boundary lines. The planning advantages provided by the former ministries in co-operation with the co-ordinating functions of the State Planning Committee of the U.S.S.R. were to come in the future only from that Committee and the State Planning Commissions in each republic. To meet the increased burdens on the planners at headquarters in the republics and in Moscow the federal Committee was to be enlarged by the establishment of departments for groups of industries, and these were to be headed by some of the newly displaced ministers.

The scheme became law in May, 1957. *Sovnarkhozy* were established in 105 economic regions, as defined by the republics. Small republics created but one, to administer industry absorbed from the abolished ministries. Large republics created many, following generally the boundary lines of their provinces but occasionally combining two provinces within a single economic region. Relatively small industries not desired for the Sovnarkhoz systems were transferred to the long existing departments of local industry in the provinces and counties and large cities to be co-ordinated with the small brickyards, gravel pits, glass factories, and repair shops which these local soviets had long been permitted to develop as being solely of local interest.

The key to the efficient operation of the new system of industrial administration quickly became the State Planning Committee and its subordinate Commission in each republic. The chiefs of the federal Committee's major industrial departments were given seats on the Council of Ministers of the U.S.S.R. While the federal Committee was supposed to function solely as a planner, its officials soon evoked criticism from Sovnarkhoz chairmen as operators. Republic Planning Commissions demanded full reports of regional proposals and examined specific projects instead of limiting scrutiny to over-all figures.

Outsiders given the opportunity to observe the functioning of the Soviet economic system since 1957 feel that the State Planning Committee and its republic agencies have reduced the authority granted to the economic regions to attend to their own affairs. In effect they have become subcommittees of the Councils of Ministers at federal and republic level.

Assumption of power by the planners may have been inevitable, given the long experience of Soviet administrators with centralized techniques. Planning authority whets the appetite for more power. This appetite was also influenced by a tendency which emerged early among some chairmen of Sovnarkhozy to attempt to assure the success of the industries under their care by refusing to ship commodities to neighboring regions. Swift growth of industry in his own region looked attractive to a chairman whose promotion in the administrative hierarchy depended upon such growth. To combat this emerging regionalism central authorities had to intervene, and in so doing they improved their own position for a less justified assumption of operating authority.

The most desirable balance between local operators and central planners has not yet been found. In reviewing the history of Soviet experimentation with public administration, it is unlikely that a balance will never be found for long. Variations of the pattern can be expected in the future as the Communist party's chiefs seek to achieve maximum efficiency within the framework of their belief that one essential element must be state planning and another, state ownership and management.

Administration of the Industrial Plant

Administrative problems at the industrial-plant level have become entwined in Marxist countries with popular conceptions of democracy. Before the Russian Revolution, bolshevik writers had argued that nationalization of factories would take from the owners the power they had enjoyed of operating their factories without consulting the workmen. In Marxist terms, industrial management would be democratized because the workers themselves would be brought into the process of management. When the Revolution occurred, many workmen seized the opportunity to oust or even to kill the owners of the factories in which they worked. In other factories the managers were retained but were subject to the control of the workmen.

Workmen understood the operation of their own machines in a factory, but they did not comprehend the co-ordinating function performed by management. In consequence, it became necessary for workmen to form committees to manage the plants, or to check upon the decisions of managers in those plants in which managers were retained. This system became known as "workers' control," and it epitomized for the workmen the democratic plant management for which they had fought.

Difficulties developed early out of the system of workers' control. It satisfied the workmen to have managerial decisions made democratically by vote in committee, but it did not make for industrial efficiency. The new Russia needed production, especially at a time when production was hampered and even disrupted by the dislocation and destruction of the civil war. As has been indicated already, by mid-1921 Lenin found himself forced to abandon his program of complete nationalization of industry and channels of distribution. Among the measures instituted in an effort to restore the economy was the system of industrial management that had been traditional in capitalist Russia. Many factories were to be restored to the original owners or leased to other persons willing to accept managerial responsibilities. In the key industries that seemed to the bolshevik leaders too important to the retention of their own political power to be restored to private ownership or management, the pattern of industrial management was to be made like that of capitalist industry. A public corporation was to be formed, and a single man was to be placed in charge. State-owned industry was no longer to be operated as a bureau of a ministry. Factories were not to be run by a committee of workmen.

Lenin's policy for nationalized industry came to be known as the policy of the "trust." The policy of vesting responsibility in a single state manager, rather than in a committee of workmen, came to be known as "one-man management." The new approach was incorporated in a decree of 1923 that grouped all nationalized industry in related combines, to each of which was given independent economic status like that of a corporation. The state treasury allocated to each group of industries such nationalized property as was necessary to its functioning, and this property was inventoried and attached as a schedule of property to a "charter," in which the purposes for which the trust was created were enumerated. Thereafter, the trust was required to operate as best it could in competition with the newly revived private enterprise sector of the economy. It was to buy its raw materials, pay its labor, amortize the value of its buildings, and sell its products to make a profit. At the head of the trust was to be a single individual named by the ministry under which the corporation was to function. In exceptional cases the industry might be run by a committee of workmen, to be called a "college," but Lenin wanted the new principle of one-man management to apply universally as soon as possible, because he thought it made for efficiency.

The system did prove successful in improving the efficiency of operation of state-owned industry, although it was years before the managers' complete authority was accepted by the workmen. In 1927 the system was extended by reducing the size of each corporate unit. The groups of related industries were broken up, and each unit within a combination was given the status of a public corporation in its own right. This means that each unit was charged with property responsibilities and held accountable for its property through a system of cost accounting like that in use in capitalist countries. It could bring suit in courts of law, and it was, in turn, subject to suit by creditors. Judgments against it could be collected from its current assets, and it could be put through bankruptcy if these assets were insufficient for all creditors.

By 1927 the private enterprise sector was being taxed out of existence, and the first of the five-year plans for the expansion of the state-owned sector of the economy was being put into operation. A decree provided that the state corporations were no longer to buy and sell in the open market as best they could with the aim of making a profit. They were now required to help fulfil the national economic plan. They had no choice but to do their part.

Capitalist-like Techniques Serve Planning Purposes

To assure that costs would not mount, as they probably would have if all the economic controls developed for the trust in 1923 had been dropped, the system of cost accounting was retained. But now there was no free market in which the state enterprises could function. Their economic activities were to be planned by the central authorities. They were to be informed of the prices at which to buy their basic raw materials and of the prices at which to sell their finished products. Wages were set in collective bargaining agreements arranged by management with labor unions and under the eye of the Communist party so that no undue advantage would be taken of the workmen by ambitious managers. Later, even wages were set by law. The corporation was expected to make a profit between the planned costs and the planned selling price. If a profit was not made, the auditors of the Ministry of Finance could presume that management had been lax, and inspection would follow. Sometimes it would be found that the fault lay not with management but with those in the state planning commission who set prices, and a revision in the price schedule would be made.

Incentives to efficiency were created through the cost-accounting system required of each public corporation. If a manager could reduce costs by rationalization of production or the elimination of waste, he could increase the profits of his corporation over the expectation of the planners. When profits increased, the inspectors of the Ministry of Finance, upon receipt of the corporation's profit-and-loss statement, would investigate to see whether the unexpected profits were really the result of skill or rather of error in the fixing of prices. If the latter, the error would be corrected, but, if the former, the successful manager would be promoted to a larger plant or to a ministerial post.

Incentives were made even more concrete, in the form of bonuses for management, and for workmen who increased production beyond established norms. These norms were measured on a piece-work basis whenever the type of production permitted such a system, and charts kept the workmen informed of their success or failure. Through such incentives some of the more intelligent workmen developed their own schemes for rationalizing production, and some even invented new machines or combinations of existing machines. To encourage such inventiveness, there was devised a system of "authors' certificates" which entitled an inventor not only to a share in the financial saving resulting from the use of his invention over a period of one year but also to a waiver of personal income tax on his bonus and to priority in the allocation of the coveted positions in research laboratories and training schools.

Those who know the methods by which capitalism encourages management and workers alike to exert themselves will see in the adoption of these incentive methods the aping of the most successful of the schemes employed in American industry. Soviet authors admit that they have copied American industrial methods, but they claim that they use them in more democratic fashion. They can no longer claim that Soviet industry is administered by committees of workmen, but they claim that the labor unions share in setting norms of work. They claim further that the state itself, which owns the factories, is the creature of the workmen and that hence there is democracy in determining the policies of the owners.

Such arguments as this sound persuasive to those who have not investigated the character of the Soviet trade union or the counter-weights established within the Soviet political system to neutralize the influence citizens might exert through the ballot box in choosing the leaders of the state. As was indicated in earlier chapters, the controls are so inclusive that Soviet industry cannot be said to be operated more democratically than American industry. On the contrary, it can be said that throughout American industry today the labor unions, with their enormous influence upon management and the considerable pressure they have been able to exert at times at the polls, provide a more democratic instrument to the workers of American industry than do the laws of the Soviet system.

Centralized Planning Remains Paramount

In a review of developments in the Soviet administrative apparatus, centralization stands out as Stalin's remedy for inefficiency. Only with his death did another approach obtain a hearing, and its final adoption caused a major rift within the Presidium of the Communist party. Centralism as a panacea dies hard in Soviet thinking, and even with the adoption of the 1957 reform there has been a tendency to develop new instruments in the direction of centralism. Planners tend to assume operating responsibility.

Early efforts to popularize the administrative process have not developed into a new form of democratic control. Compromise has been reached with national minorities where necessary, but generally Lenin's concept of centralized policy-making, tempered by localized administration, has prevailed. Control has been retained in the federal government over the planning function since the creation of the planning mechanism in the early 1920's, and the reform of 1957 has not changed this situation.

At the level of the industrial plant, some procedures utilized in private enterprise countries have been found useful by Soviet policy-makers, but their adoption has not marked a return to the independence of action associated with the private enterpriser. The procedures have been adopted solely to improve efficiency in the interest of the state, and they can be supported as being utilized more democratically than in capitalist countries only if one argues that the Soviet state is guided by people elected through democratic procedures. The argument that the Soviet people choose their leaders democratically has already been shown to be false.

The experiment with popularization of administrative procedures with which Lenin began during the first years of the new Russia was reduced by Stalin through successive stages of centralization, until there occurred what Marshal Tito of Yugoslavia, in attacking Soviet centralization, called "the cancer of socialism." Khrushchev saw the peril, and he reversed the trend, but only in limited degree. Centralized planning remained, and its influence has been evident in the conflict of view between those who look longingly at Stalin's old methods and those who seek efficiency through extension of operating autonomy to the level of the republics and provinces.

CHAPTER 8

FOSTERING THE COMMUNITY SPIRIT

The peasants of Russia have always presented the Communist party's leaders with a problem. They have wanted to own their own land, and they have been individualists. The Russian Marxist has felt that the success of his system requires eradication of both desires. Land, together with other productive resources, has to be nationalized, and the community spirit has to be fostered. Some of the early Communists thought it unlikely that the peasant mentality could be changed, therefore the peasants would not make good partners in the revolutionary movement, and plans for revolution should be prepared without peasant participation.

Lenin foresaw the difficulties but felt that victory could be won more easily with peasant participation in the revolutionary movement than without it. He believed that the very poorest peasants, especially those who were hired hands on the farms of the well-to-do peasants, could be relied upon politically to form the farm core of the Communist party. He expected that the middle-class peasants, who owned their own farms but hired no labor, could be neutralized in the revolutionary struggle and eventually won over to the Communist cause. Only the well-to-do peasants, who hired labor, seemed to be beyond the reach of the Communists, and Lenin was prepared to leave them out of his organization and eventually to declare war upon them.

Lenin's view triumphed early in Communist party circles. Peasants were represented at meetings, but they were always considered weak partners. The workmen were expected to carry the burden of the revolution and to be its enthusiasts. The peasants were to provide the mass support in the villages, but were to be subject always to the leadership of the workmen and of those of the educated classes who had thrown in their lot with the revolutionary chiefs.

The peasants of Russia resembled the peasants of Eastern Europe generally, except that they were even less familiar with problems of government on a national scale. Until 1861 they had, in their vast majority, been serfs, tied to the land of the great landowners and sold like slaves for domestic service. They had lived in peasant villages in which the landowners left them to manage their own affairs through their own elders, but they were subject always to the control of the landlord. In cases of serious disorder, the representatives of the Tsarist state entered the scene. After liberation in 1861 by edict of Alexander II, who had come to realize with his advisers that industrial progress and military strength required a free labor market and an army of free men, the peasants were given large portions of land for their own use. The landowners from whom the land was taken were provided compensation by the state, and the peasant communities were bound, as communities, to reimburse the state over a period of forty-nine years for payments made to the landowners.

Although individual peasant families tilled the land, all the families of a community shared in the village government, and some of the village pasture was given over to common use. In this arrangement there were aspects of both individualism and joint operation. It was because of the latter aspect that some of the educated people from the cities who hoped for abolition of the Tsarist system sought to enlist the peasantry in their movement. A Populist party, called the *Narodniks,* was organized in the countryside by intellectuals who went out as schoolteachers, blacksmiths, and in other disguises. The hope of this group was to play upon the long-smoldering hostility of the peasants toward the system from which they had only recently been freed formally and to which they were still bound by the duty to make payments in redemption of the land taken from landowners.

To facilitate their economic battle for existence, the peasants liberated from serfdom fell in with the peasant co-operative movement that was sweeping Europe at the end of the nineteenth century. With the model of Western European co-operatives to guide them, the peasants joined in co-operatives to buy agricultural implements, to disseminate information on new agricultural methods, to market their products, and, finally, to finance capital development. In some cases they even formed agricultural co-operative associations to farm the land. These co-operative associations aroused the fear of Tsarist officials, lest they serve as a medium through which the peasants, in pooling their resources, might also evidence collective hostility toward the Tsar's government. In consequence, the co-operatives came under strict regulation by statute, and the consent of provincial governors was required before they might be organized. In spite of these limitations, the co-operative movement thrived, and by the early part of the twentieth century, leagues of the various types of co-operatives had been organized in each province. These leagues were composed of delegates sent forward by the various local co-operatives. The provincial leagues finally formed a national association with its seat in Moscow, thus creating a co-ordinate system with considerable economic strength and some political influence as a pressure group.

To strengthen the Tsar's hand against the mounting community sense of the peasantry, one of his prime ministers, Stolypin, had sought in 1907 to create a strong well-to-do peasant element. His legislation provided that peasants were free to leave their village communes and to divide their family property, and he made available tracts of state land for sale to such peasants. He hoped that through this process the natural individualism of the peasants might be strengthened at the expense of their community spirit, which was being fostered through the need of the peasants to combine to become successful farmers in an age of costly farm implements beyond the reach of a family purse.

Peasants and the Revolution

The early revolutionary events of 1917 brought the peasant into great prominence. Most of the soldiers in the weary Tsarist army were peasants, and they wanted to stop fighting and go home. The countryside had been disrupted by the war to such an extent that food was in short supply. Finally, the continuing peasant demand for complete expropriation of the landowners had been fanned by a slogan of the most popular peasant political party, the Socialist Revolutionary, namely, "socialization of the land." After the abdication of the Tsar in February, 1917, the provisional government sought to meet the peasant demands to the extent that it could. Yet there was strong sentiment in the provisional government for continued support to the allies against the central powers, and this sentiment was so encouraged by the leaders of the allies that no peace could be considered. The only promise that the provisional government could hold out to the peasants was ultimate socialization of the land, but this moved slowly. Many of the participants in the new regime were opposed to this; there was no clear meaning of what the slogan meant, and the country was in such chaos that it would have been difficult to organize distribution in orderly fashion even if there had been a real will to socialize and agreement upon a program. In consequence, nothing was done effectively by the central government, and peasants began to take the law into their own hands.

The bolsheviks seized upon the growing unrest and unfurled their banner of "Peace, Bread, Land." These three catchwords appealed to the peasants, and when the coup d'état was effected in October, 1917, many peasants were prepared to co-operate. But they were not in complete sympathy with the bolshevik platform: peace was wanted as was bread, but the land scheme of the bolsheviks was not acceptable. The left-wing Socialist Revolutionaries, who stayed with the bolsheviks in the Congress of Soviets after the fall of the Winter Palace, wanted all ownership of land, private and state, to be abolished and the use of the land to be passed to those who worked it. This program now seems hard to understand, but to the peasant mind it seems to have been an effort to free him from all restraint. He wanted to be free of state interference in the use of his little family plot. On that small plot of land the peasant wanted to be king, and the party that represented most of the peasants forced Lenin, in drafting his land program, to make a concession on that score. Thus the first land decree did not expropriate all land but only that of the great landowners. It was not until February, 1918, that Lenin felt strong enough to push his program to the limit and declare all land to be state-owned.

Even after the bolsheviks had found themselves strong enough to put into effect their basic idea of state ownership of all land, concessions to the peasantry still had to be made. There was yet the problem of land use. No one had thought out a system of land use that could accord with the Marxist principle of community use of resources. Lenin's colleagues, indicating that their ideas would be best, now fostered as their preferred form of land use the "commune"—a peasant society in which the component peasant families would pool their land and their tools and their cattle and their buildings and use these resources as the group decided in general meeting.

Less communized forms of land use were also offered to the peasantry. A second form would pool land, herds, and heavy agricultural implements but retain private ownership of small tools, houses, and barnyard cattle. This would be called the "artel," and it followed the general pattern of an agricultural co-operative that had found favor with some peasants prior to the Revolution. The third form of land use involved co-operation in the purchase of heavy tools and in planning the use of the land, but everything was privately owned. This was called the "toz."

While the three forms of co-operative use of the land found a good many adherents, especially under the enthusiasm of the moment for communal types of economic activity, the vast majority of the peasants wanted nothing so much as to be left alone. They wanted to have their own plots of land to do with as they pleased. Though the ownership of land had been taken over by the state, the peasants had the use of the land, and to their minds the legal difference between ownership and unmolested use was small. Peasant families had lived on small plots of land for decades since liberation from serfdom, and they had no intention of moving about and buying and selling farms, such as has come to be the custom among American farmers. So long as a peasant family had the unmolested use of a plot of land, it had all that it considered vital. The Communists knew this, as a result of their close study of the peasant mentality, and they were prepared to humor the peasant for a time, even though the goal of community use of the land remained high on the priorities list of the leaders of the Communist party.

A New Soviet System of Land Use

After the civil war of 1919–1920 had been won, and the economic and political life of the country had quieted, the Communist party fostered a new land law. As put into operation in 1922, it set forth policies that had become the rule during the early years of experimentation. It reaffirmed the first rule of the Communists that the land would be state-owned. The use of the land would be distributed to peasants by their local land committees in accordance with the peasants' desires. Peasants might apply for land family by family or as communities. Though the code declared that communities be given preference in the allocation of land use, families could apply singly. In fact, most peasants decided to apply for land by family groups. Many of the existing village communities were broken up in the general swing toward individualism that came in the villages along with the evolution of limited private enterprise in the urban areas, as permitted by what Lenin called a "New Economic Policy" for the restoration of the economy.

To dramatize the rights of the peasantry, the new land law provided that, whether peasants obtained the use of the land on a family or on a community basis, they obtained it in perpetuity. This sounded almost like ownership, for a primary feature of ownership is the right to own in perpetuity. Yet the new Soviet land code revealed its special character by placing limitations upon the use in perpetuity. This right, as allocated by the village soviet's land committee, could not be sold. If a peasant family decided to give up farming and move to the city to work in a factory, it was required to return the land to the village soviet's land committee for reallocation to another family. It could not lease the land or any part of it to another family or to a community, except for short periods of time when members of the family were called into military service, or went to the city to experiment with factory work, or became ill. Moreover, it could not use the land for purposes other than those for which the land had been allocated. In short, it was not to be permitted to stop farming and to build upon the land a slaughterhouse or a sugar-beet refinery. It could not inconvenience the neighbors by committing a nuisance, and it could not use the land in such a way that its agricultural value was impaired.

Since an individual plot was allocated to a family, there was no problem of inheritance so long as the family did not die out entirely. Following long-established peasant custom, there had developed during the Imperial period rules for the passage of land and of other family property from generation to generation within the family, as well as rules for the partition of property in the event that members of the family married out of it or decided to move away. These rules were continued in force by the land code, and the village community was to settle disputes in its customary manner. Only if, as a result of division, the family became too small to work the land was reallocation considered by the land committee of the village soviet.

Stalin continued Lenin's policy of concessions to peasant sentiment on the use of land, but he seems always to have had his eye upon the goal of community use. Foreign students of the subject have thought that Stalin realized that in the peasantry he had the principal source of opposition to his rule and that this opposition was strongest when peasants were organized by families rather than as communities; so he determined to do what he could to bring about the communalizing of land use. If this was his aim, he did not have to lay it bare, because events played into his hands.

Pressures for Collectivization

As urbanization of the U.S.S.R. developed with the increase in industrialization under the first of the five-year plans in the late 1920's, the demand for agricultural products grew in the cities. The fragmentation of the land among millions of small peasant families, brought about by the swing to family use during the period of the New Economic Policy, caused agricultural production to fall. The little farms could not be operated as productively as the large-scale communes or the artels, or, at least, so Stalin could convincingly argue. He decided that the time was ripe to press for communal use. The workmen were crying for more food, and thus he had a sufficient pressure group behind him to support his plan.

In late 1929 a drive for "collectivization of agriculture" was instituted. Stalin chose as the instrument for his purpose not the commune, with its very great communalization of property, nor the "toz," with its minimal communalization, but the "artel." In 1930 his government enacted a model charter for this artel and then required all communities of peasants setting up the new artels to conform to the pattern. The charter set forth in detail the manner in which the government of the artel was to be organized, the rules for membership, and the purposes for which the artel was created. The artel's colloquial name became "kolkhoz," which is a Russian abbreviation for what has been universally translated as "collective farm."

Having established the pattern, Stalin determined to force as many peasants as possible into it. While taking a public position that formation of such collective farms should be voluntary and no family should be required to participate, Stalin allowed his officials at the village level to use violent compulsion in their recruiting tactics. Between January 20 and March 1, 1930, the number of farms was increased from 59,400 to 110,200, and the number of collectivized peasant families, from 4,000,000 to 14,000,000. Obviously no ordinary recruiting program could have produced such results among such hostile people. The violent nature of the compulsion is evident.

Strong opposition to forced collectivization took place in the only manner left open. Many of the peasants felt that in pooling their livestock in the collective-farm herd they were being asked to contribute more than a fair share, and they preferred to slaughter the cattle and sell them. The result was a large drop in livestock herds. Other peasants refused outright to enter the farms.

Stalin saw his mistake and published on March 2, 1930, a much advertised policy directive in which he accused his subordinates of being "dizzy with success" in forcing peasants onto the collective farms. He called for a relaxation of recruitment pressure, but, at the same time, he took means to see that pressure of a different kind continued. He spoke out against those who would not enter the farms, on the ground that they were wealthy peasants trying to wreck the Soviet system. He called them "kulaks," although many of them were not in fact as well-to-do as a kulak was normally supposed to be. Finally, he had his government adopt a law "liquidating the kulaks as a class." This meant adoption of a system of guilt by association. It became unnecessary for a local official to prove in court that an individual peasant had committed a crime in destroying state property or in injuring a state official trying to organize the farms. It was enough that an individual be classed in the ill-defined category of "kulak" to give cause for him to be turned over to the local officials of the Ministry of Internal Affairs for imprisonment in the Siberian hard-labor camps. Foreign experts have estimated that large numbers of peasants were imprisoned in this manner.

Even this pressure, however, was not enough to achieve the purpose of complete collectivization. Stalin therefore seized upon the opportunity of proving his point that the system of individualized farming was inadequate to the needs of the country, when the harvests of 1931 and 1932 proved to be bad in large regions of the southwest and south central parts of the U.S.S.R. Famine conditions prevailed, and over a million peasants are estimated to have died. Foreign observers who lived in the U.S.S.R. at the time felt that food could have been shipped to the famine areas from some of the less arid provinces, but it was not. The conclusion has been reached by some students of Soviet policies that Stalin let the conditions develop into famine so as to teach his lesson that collectivization was necessary to meet the food requirements of the nation. Other students have thought that famine was not planned but was the result of excessive food-collection quotas imposed on the new collective farms.

The Collective-Farm Structure

While using pressures of various kinds, Stalin was not such a fool as to miss opportunities to bring the peasants into the collective farms of their own free will. He made the organizations sound democratic and hence attractive. Under the provisions of the model charter, each farm was to be run by a general meeting of all members. As members entered the farm, they relinquished the use of the plot of land that they had been farming and pooled it with the plots brought into the farm by other members. The peasant families retained, however, private ownership of their peasant homestead, of their small agricultural tools and barnyard animals, of their furniture, clothing, and supplies of food. They were even to be assigned for personal family use a small plot of land, varying with the fertility of the soil, on which they were to be permitted to do what they pleased and from which they might sell the surplus produce in the open market.

The general meeting of the collective farm was to set the general policy for the farm, but the execution of that policy was to be in the hands of an "administration," presided over by a president, which was to be audited in its financial activities by an "auditing commission." All these officials were to be elected, on a democratic basis, although voting was to be by a show of hands rather than by secret ballot. In operation, the voting method enabled the Communist party to introduce a nominee for president to the general meeting and see that he was elected.

In theory, the members of the collective farm were like members of the co-operative agricultural societies of Europe generally. They were co-operating private owners rather then employees of a state institution. This was evidenced primarily by the system under which they were paid for their work. No one, except the bookkeeper and the agricultural expert, who were employed by the farm, received a salary. All others received their compensation in the shape of a share of the farm produce left after taxes had been paid to the state. These taxes took the form of fixed quantities of produce that had to be delivered to the state at the end of each harvest and for which a purchase price was paid. The reason why the deliveries can be considered taxes is that the price paid by the state was much less than the same goods would have brought if sold in the open markets that the state permitted in all villages and cities.

Decisions on the farm were lent a democratic flavor by making one of them the determination of each member's annual share of the farm surplus. To provide a statistical basis for payment at the end of each season, every job on the farm was rated according to its difficulty. For example, the most difficult was running a gang plow through virgin land; the least difficult was sweeping up in the dairy. The unit of measurement was called a "labor day," and for every full working day, from morning to evening, the labor of a peasant who plowed was rated in units of, let us say, one and three-quarters labor days, while the labor of a sweeper in the dairy was rated in units of three-quarters of a labor day. The bookkeeper would record the number of calendar days actually worked by a member of the farm, this figure would be multiplied by the labor-day equivalent of the calendar day, and the quotient would represent the share in the total produce of the farm, after taxes, to which the individual had a right.

At the end of the season the total number of labor days to which all members had a right would be divided into the total produce of the farm to achieve the "value" of one labor day. At one farm visited during World War II, this value was given as the following: cash, 7.50 rubles; grain, 4.4 pounds; potatoes, 6.6 pounds; cabbage, 6.6 pounds; beets, 2.2 pounds; carrots, 2.2 pounds; other vegetables, 4.4 pounds; and honey, 2 ounces. The "labor day" would then be used as a multiplier in determining the share of each member. Naturally, peasants could not wait until the end of the growing season to eat, and an advance based upon indicated earnings was given them from time to time.

While instituting on the farm what he hoped would be accepted as democratic procedures in decision-making, Stalin was not prepared to permit the process to continue without regard to the interests of the state. In 1933 he expressed the view that while it was the purpose of the collective farm to induce the peasant to accept socialism voluntarily because of its high rate of productivity, the overlaid democratic procedure could not be permitted to function if the farm became unprofitable. If it did, it was the duty of the state, in Stalin's opinion, to step in and assume the direction. This could be done by introducing to the collective, and requiring its election of, a president believed by the experts of the community or of Moscow to be capable of finding the trouble and restoring sound economy on the farm. Many such persons were imposed upon the farmers in the years before the Second World War. Even more have been imposed since Stalin's death, in Khrushchev's effort to increase production. In this practice lies one of the great differences between co-operative farming associations in the West and in the U.S.S.R. In the West, the members are left free to ruin themselves if they prove to be incompetent in administration. In the U.S.S.R., the social good, as specified by the Communist party, is used as justification for intervention by the state to prevent the members from suffering because of their incompetency, even if the intervention destroys democratic determination of policy and choice of leaders on the farm.

Further controls over the farms took the form of dictated sowing plans. Each farm was told what it must produce for the state, and until Stalin's death a farm's entire production was dictated in some areas, notably those growing cotton. Only after Stalin's death were rules established under which local authorities were to share in such decisions. Some reasonableness was exhibited, however, even under the system prior to Stalin's death, for example, in a case in which the Moscow authorities had ordered a farm to concentrate on a single breed of cattle. The local farm officials had experimented with this breed in the past, had figures to show that it did not prosper in the northerly latitude at which the farm was located, and were able to support effectively their recommendation that the order be rescinded.

Centralization of Agricultural Controls

After 1930, the collective farms were brought under other important controls. Prior to 1930, the artels provided a channel of co-operation and interchange of information by means of a pattern of relationships similar to that characterizing the co-operative associations before the Revolution, namely, a pattern composed of leagues of artels in each province and a "center" in Moscow. When the state wished to influence the artels, it had to work through the center, which passed down through the provincial leagues to the operating co-operatives the suggestions made by state agricultural experts.

In 1932, the Ministry of Agriculture of the U.S.S.R. was given the task of co-ordinating the collective farms, and the artel system of leagues and center was abolished. The ministry is of a Union-Republic type, so it does not communicate directly with each collective farm. When it wishes to institute a program, it communicates the program to the ministries of agriculture in each of the union republics. These, in turn, fan out the directive to the provincial executive committees. Where it goes from the provincial level before reaching the farm has varied. Up to the war's end it went to the county soviet, which sent it through the land department of the soviet to each village soviet. By 1950 the counties were bypassing the village soviet with agricultural orders, and in 1953 they in turn were bypassed, for the provincial soviet communicated directly with the machine tractor stations as the administrative channel to the farms. Since 1958 the county executive committee has again become the main link between the central apparatus and the farms. The reason for the variation will become evident with the explanation that follows.

To preserve the links between Moscow and the collective farms, the Ministry of Agriculture of the U.S.S.R. is divided into bureaus each of which has responsibility for the total agricultural operation of the collective farms of a given geographical region. These regions bear some relation to the boundaries of the republics, but only because the boundaries of both coincide in many cases not only with ethnic boundaries but with nature's boundaries for various types of agriculture. The basis for division of responsibility within the ministry is the type of agriculture. To assist the geographical bureaus within the ministry, there are functional bureaus specializing in animal husbandry, chicken-raising, irrigation problems, land distribution, legal problems, and other specialized questions that relate to land use. These bureaus advise the geographical bureau on techniques, and these techniques are passed down through channels to the farms. The technicians of the ministry are not in direct touch with the farms.

A major form of control over the collective farms was provided prior to 1958 by the machine tractor stations. Except on a few isolated farms in Siberia, heavy agricultural equipment was kept in tractor parks in which it was maintained by mechanics and from which it went forth each morning in the hands of expert operators. In a country in which mechanical skills were not widely distributed, there was logic in maintaining mechanical agricultural implements in such stations. On this logic the system rested, but it had wide political advantage as well. Since the farms could produce almost nothing without the machines, those who serviced and drove and therefore controlled the use of the machines could, by withholding them, enforce the will of the stations.

The Communist party saw to it that its members were strategically placed in the machine tractor stations, in greater numbers than on the farms themselves. An incipient peasant revolt could be precluded by the strategic distribution of farm machinery, and Stalin is believed to have had this in mind in setting up these stations. In addition, he may have had a reason arising out of his Marxist training. It was Marx's thesis that the ultimate success of his system required the worker and the peasant to be brought closer to each other so that the former's industrial methods and psychological acceptance of collective work would be widely diffused. Through this union of city and village, Marx expected to stamp out the individualistic approach of the peasant.

The machine tractor station represented the first step in the spreading of the industrial communal approach to the farms. Those peasants who were brought into the stations to be trained as mechanics to service or drive the machines could be expected to become shop-minded like their counterparts in the shops of the city factories. Being of the peasantry and in close contact with it, these peasant mechanics were expected to serve as a conduit of industrial attitudes and thus to hasten the day when the peasants think like workmen.

Collective Farm Reform

The year 1958 marked the reorganization of the controls over the collective farms with conversion of the machine tractor stations into repair and technical stations and transfer of the ownership of their farm equipment to the farms. On its face the change was an electrifying restoration of a measure of autonomy to the collective farms, presaging perhaps a return to the system of collective farm leagues abolished in 1932 to provide for the centralized system created by Stalin within the Ministry of Agriculture. On reflection, however, the change might have been anticipated, for the system of controls had changed, making the machine tractor station unnecessary if that was its major function.

Reorganization of the collective farm system had really begun as early as 1950 when Stalin inaugurated a program of amalgamation. Prior to his order each farm coincided in area generally with a traditional peasant village, as it had come down from the pre-revolutionary period of the empire. Under the system of division of administrative function the farm management conducted the economic life of the village, while the village soviet saw to the political and cultural life. It was the soviet that provided a link with the administrative departments of the county soviet, under whose direction the local school, clinic, store, and fire department were run. Administrative instructions to the collective farm management were funneled through the village soviet on their way down from the Ministry of Agriculture.

The large number of villages throughout the vast expanse of the U.S.S.R. required that there be a large number of collective farms; there were 254,000 farms before 1950. Stalin changed this by ordering farms combined in the interest of agricultural efficiency under modern mechanized conditions. The number of farms fell during 1950 to 123,700 and by the end of 1952 it was 97,000. The number continued to fall, and by the end of 1955 it was 87,500. Collective farms came to include several villages, and the village soviet lost importance. Some were combined as the farms had been, and the county soviet became the primary link with the administrative mechanism of the Ministry of Agriculture, although even that link was soon replaced by the machine tractor station operating under instructions from the provincial soviet.

The amalgamation resulted in the co-operation of farmers who still lived in their own familiar village but who worked together in common fields with relative strangers. More than a thousand families were counted as members of a single farm instead of the fifty or one hundred of earlier times. The general assemblies of a farm became too large for intimate discussion and policy-making. They fell, as do all large groups, to the manipulation of the skilled chairman. The Communist party was strengthened in the country-side, for there was now hardly a farm that did not contain some party members, whereas the smaller farms often had had none. The dictation of elections of chairmen and executive boards was thus facilitated, and the party provided the candidates from its own ranks of skilled agronomist-administrators.

Confidence in the administration of the newly amalgamated farms was evidenced in an order signed jointly by the Central Committee of the Communist party and the Council of Ministers of the U.S.S.R. in March, 1956, authorizing farms to depart from the rigid provisions of the Model Charter of 1935 governing farm organization. Each farm might now amend the charter to meet its own concrete problems, and specifically might alter the amount of land permitted for the private use of each peasant household. The size of such garden plots had been rigidly set in the old charter. The government indicated by the reform that it no longer feared that farmers would arrogate to private enterprise large parts of the farm, and practice showed that the zealous chairmen were prepared to move too far in the other direction. Some got their general assemblies of members to eliminate private plots, thus causing such discontent that an order had to be issued to proceed more slowly.

Chairman of the new amalgamated collective farms began to argue in the press that the machine tractor stations were impeding efficiency and duplicating what the farm could now do for itself. There was no longer need to put machines in a depot from which they could go forth on successive days to various farms. Their entire work was now for a single farm. No chairman suggested that the machine tractor stations were no longer necessary as instruments of political control, but that was the implication of the argument centered upon efficiency alone.

What the chairmen did not say about politics, the Communist party was soon to add. Following a resolution of the party's Central

Committee issued on February 28, 1958, Khrushchev declared that while the machine tractor station had previously been necessary as the state's instrument of leadership, the state could now exercise a direct effect upon the farms through the supply of machinery. In short, control could be exercised with the help of farm management alone. Efficiency needed to be the only consideration, and that dictated ownership by the farms. The task remained only of transferring the machines to farm administrations and arranging for payment, on credit terms where needed.

A month's discussion was permitted before the Supreme Soviet enacted the law, during which the major complaint came from machine tractor employees who saw their status changing from that of employees with guaranteed wages, trade-union membership, and social security benefits to collective farmers, paid labor days, with no trade-union standing and social security coverage only from the general funds of each farm and not from the state system. To silence this, it was recommended that the farms pay labor days in a guaranteed amount not less than prior wages and that social security benefits be retained, but trade-union links were to fall away. The law of March 31 left to the republic governments the task of carrying out the reorganization at their own pace and instructed the reduced repair and technical stations to assist the farms in training farmers to use and maintain the machines mechanically. The repair and technical stations were to be directed at the level of the province by soviet and Communist party agencies. Spare parts for the machines were made the personal responsibility of the *Sovnarkhoz* chairman. Inspection of the farms was restored to the county soviet as the primary link with the channel of authority leading to the Ministry of Agriculture in the republic and ultimately in the federal capital.

The State Farm Becomes Favored

Since the Revolution there has existed alongside the collective farm a different type of agricultural unit, known as the "sovkhoz," or state farm. Such farms have been primarily experiment stations and demonstration farms and, more recently, farms raising specialized crops. The sovkhoz is a form of agricultural factory operating under the same laws as industrial enterprises, and the farmers within it are employed at a wage rather than given shares of the annual farm produce as are members of a co-operative association. The management is not elected, even nominally, by the farmers themselves, but is appointed by the Ministry of Agriculture of the U.S.S.R. in the same fashion that managers of steel mills are appointed by the ministry in charge of steel mills.

Communist party leaders seem to have a predilection for the state farm as the farm of the future. After Stalin's death, his severe restraints upon the collective farms were reduced as a concession to the peasants, but the new leaders indicated that wherever they were not hampered by old customs they would introduce the state farm rather than the collective farm. Their opportunity came in developing a program for expanding agriculture in the fringe lands of the country, known as "virgin lands." In these territories, where no form of agriculture had been conducted before, there was no old-fashioned opinionated peasantry with which to deal. Great numbers of Soviet youths were organized by the Komsomols to move to these regions to begin farming, and most of these came from cities to work under agricultural specialists provided by the agricultural schools.

Most of the agricultural units operating in the "virgin lands" are state farms rather than collective farms. This represents further evidence that the leaders of the U.S.S.R. intend to use every opportunity to spread industrial forms of organization in the agricultural arena.

The Future of the Collective Farm

Increasing use of the state farm pattern of organization led many to believe before 1958 that the collective farm would soon be absorbed by it. Within the U.S.S.R. there were voices calling for such a development. Shortly before his death Stalin had hinted that this was the way of the future, for he announced a plan in the autumn of 1952 to bring the collective farms into closer relation with city industry by requiring farms to deliver all their produce to the state in exchange for industrial goods. He anticipated the abolition of money in the rural districts, which would have made the peasants completely dependent upon what they might receive from central authorities. He had no time schedule for his reform, but he praised the cotton farms as an example, saying that already they were producing in exchange for industrial goods.

Stalin expected the limited collective farm type of property ownership to be transformed into ownership by the "commonwealth of the people." This was the formula explaining the property status of state industry and state farms, and its use with regard to the collective farm suggested that it might become in substance if not in form a state farm, as soon as the hostility to this kind of organization could be eradicated from the conservative mind of the peasantry.

Khrushchev seems to have the same goal in mind with his support of Stalin's policy of amalgamation and his policy of placing all property, including the machines, within the legal entity that each farm represents. Still, he has some different methods to apply, for instead of eliminating money and exchanging farm produce for industrial goods, he has strengthened the use of money in relations between the farms and the state procurement agencies. In 1958 he abolished the long-established system of obligatory state deliveries by farms at prices well below open market levels and substituted state procurement at open market prices from the farms. This system would in his view make it important to the farms to cut production costs, since they might thereby enjoy a profit which they could never have done under the former low delivery price of crops delivered to meet compulsory quotas. The time is still too short to permit evaluation of the effect of this policy, but it is evident that it is designed to improve efficiency and not to revitalize the farm as an entering wedge to a return to capitalism. The direction still is toward the placing of agriculture on the same basis as industry so that all citizens will be employees and the difference between agricultural and industrial production will be reduced to minimum proportions. At the twenty-first Communist party congress Khrushchev restated this as the goal.

CHAPTER 9

STATE INTERVENTION IN PRIVATE AFFAIRS

Democratic currents of thought, awakened by the American and French revolutions, developed in the nineteenth-century West the concept of a minimum of state intervention in private affairs. The state was to be separated from the church, so that citizens might be free to worship as they pleased. Those laws that had to do with property and with family relationships were placed in a separate category called "private," to indicate that the state had only the instrumental function of regulating and enforcing private agreements. The state was not to utilize family and property law to achieve political ends. The spirit of the era was exemplified by the statement, "He governs best who governs least."

Marx set out to undermine this attitude in his *Communist Manifesto* of 1848. He began by attacking the society in which he lived, the society of Western Europe. He tried to show that the state was not really leaving its citizens alone. He argued that the nineteenth-century western state was the creature of that minority of its citizens who benefited most from a laissez faire policy because it left them free to exploit private property and to make profits. In short, to Marx the very absence of laws and of state intervention in private matters constituted a policy advantageous to a ruling class. Marx argued that the state was not democratic in its non-intervention because it left the economic stage free to a very small group of capitalists. He called for a state that would intervene in economic and social relationships for the benefit of the masses, and this he believed to be necessary to achieve democracy in the sense of government for the great mass of the people.

The Russian revolutionaries seized upon this principle of Marxism. They began to intervene very soon in what had been private matters of citizens. Lenin expressed the idea succinctly, when he told a friend in 1922 that all law must be considered public. He saw no possibility of developing the type of society he envisaged unless the state used every relationship, even those between citizens, to its advantage.

Controls on Religious Practices

Religion offered Lenin his greatest problem in social reorganization. He inherited Marx's view on the subject. Marx had opposed religious belief as unscientific because it could not be proved in a laboratory that there was a God. Since his interpretation of historical evolution rested upon his claim that he had found the motivating force of social development in discernible factors such as the invention of tools of production and the changing ownership of such tools, he could not accept the thought that a divine force influenced social development. It would have upset his theory and the argument for revolution which he was making. There are those who now suggest that Marx would not have been so hostile toward religion if he had not faced a practical problem presented by religious institutions.

The practical problem Marx faced when he considered religion was that the church of the nineteenth century was both very powerful in much of the West and certain to oppose him. Over the centuries it had been accustomed to associate itself with the status quo, and Marx conceived of it as a very strong instrument for preserving the structure of nineteenth-century society against which he was issuing a call to arms. Because of this fact, he opposed the institution of the church bitterly. The Russian revolutionaries had more cause than Marx to look upon the church similarly as a barrier to the success of their plans. The Russian Orthodox Church, to which the great bulk of the Russians and Ukrainians belonged, was favored as a state church under the Tsar's regime; its resources were provided in part from the state treasury; its large landholdings were protected by Tsarist laws; its bishops were named with the consent of the Tsar; and, on occasion, its priests were required to report on the political activities of members of their congregations. To oppose the Tsar often meant to oppose the church as well, and revolutionaries had difficulty, consequently, in winning converts among those who were religious and who accepted the discipline of the church.

While recognizing that hostility was to be expected from the Russian Orthodox Church and, in a measure, from the Moslems,

the Jews, and the Christian denominations with fewer communicants, Lenin could not overlook the potential danger to his regime
if he aroused fanatic hostility on the part of those who were religious. Russian history had been dotted with incidents of fanatic
opposition to state authority from religious groups. No leader could
attack the church, or religion generally, without risking ultimate
overthrow. Lenin aproached the matter cautiously.

The core group of the Communist party was small and disciplined. Within this group Lenin could, and probably had to, enforce the rule of the Communist party program that no member of
the Communist party could profess religious belief. To make certain
that his colleagues in the party did not limit themselves to lip
service, Lenin's organization carried out a vigorous program of antireligious propaganda on the theme that religion was not scientific
and that the church, its handmaiden, was a threat to the success of
the Communists' program.

For the general public, no such dogmatic approach was possible,
for violent hostility toward such an approach could be expected.
The article on religion in Lenin's first bill of rights in the Russian
Constitution of 1918 guaranteed to all the right of freedom of conscience, yet it placed the official attitude of atheism on record by
guaranteeing freedom of antireligious propaganda though also the
right to propagate religion. The constitution's article on religion, like
the others having to do with freedom of speech and of press, was
limited by the general prohibition against assertion of any right to
the detriment of the program of socialism; thus it was not an absolute guarantee of non-interference, such as that in the First Amendment to the Constitution of the United States.

Separation of Church and State

To indicate that the Orthodox Church had lost its position as a
state church, the 1918 constitution declared the separation of church
and state. This made necessary an immediate change in the mode
of keeping vital statistics and of performing marriage ceremonies
and the granting of divorces. Under the Russian Imperial laws, the
various religious communities had maintained the records on birth,
marriage, divorce, and death. There had been no records office in a
city hall run by the state, as there is everywhere in the United
States. But the early Soviet laws created a state registration bureau
at which all were required to register events having to do with
status and vital statistics. Soviet citizens might still register births

in church, but such registration had no probative value. There had to be registration also in the state bureau.

Marriages, under the first Soviet decree on the subject, might still be solemnized in church, but the parties had also to declare their intent in a civil marriage ceremony and to register in the state bureau. The ecclesiastical courts to which the Tsar had delegated sole jurisdiction over divorce were abolished. Divorces were thrown into the newly created peoples' courts, to be handled on the basis of a state law uniform for all.

The new state laws relating to vital statistics and family relationships sought to remove the necessity of going to church to contract or register these basic relationships. In this way the Communists hoped to wean the people from the church by reducing the opportunities of the priests to see citizens. The move toward secular control of marriage and divorce was revolutionary in Russia, although it had long before been completed in Western lands, where the state maintains the records of vital statistics and requires licenses for marriage. Western states even require that marriage be solemnized by a state civil servant or by a religious dignitary authorized by the state to perform marriages and thus given the status of a state official. In some Western democracies, ecclesiastical courts still pass upon the marital status of the faithful, but generally no divorce or annulment is recognized by the state unless there has also been a state divorce or unless the ecclesiastical court is given the sanction of the state to grant divorce.

Lenin's steps separating church from state were cautious. They went very little beyond what had been accepted in Western democracies years before the Russian Revolution. His other step touched a subject which he believed to be of greater importance, and it aroused more hostility. He deprived the church of its property. While churches were permitted to collect funds from parishioners, they could no longer own land and receive rents, nor could they own their buildings and the vestments and sacramental vessels necessary to the performance of religious rites.

The use of the nationalized church buildings and sacramental vestments and vessels was allocated to religious groups for the purpose of religious services, but ownership remained with the state. Under this arrangement, the state could withdraw use at its pleasure. To hamper the church further, religious communities were no longer permitted the status of a juristic person or corporation. The church building and its contents were allocated to the congregation as a partnership composed of the elders of the community. This legal form established personal responsibility for preservation of the property. Since this property was now state property, local soviets, as guardians of the state's interests, were authorized to close a church at any time in deference to the wishes of the toilers, as these wishes might be determined by the local soviet.

Local soviets were protected at the same time from expected attempts by priests and monks to influence them. This was done by depriving clerics of the right to vote in elections for the soviet or to be elected to any state office. In practice, local soviets very often decided to pre-empt the church building in a village from the elders and to turn it into a grain-storage warehouse or local club.

Forbidding Religious Education

Religious education has always been thought by believers to be essential to real freedom of religion, for without the right to propagate the faith the religious community must die out. The Mass or morning prayer has been found insufficient to win converts or to hold the allegiance of children of religious believers. Experience has shown that there must be religious instruction, as well as freedom of worship, to make meaningful a guarantee of religious freedom. The bolsheviks seem to have realized this fact, for in 1921 they put a stop to religious education of persons under eighteen years of age. The criminal code forbade the teaching of religious beliefs to children in public or private schools, which, in effect, prevented the establishment of parochial schools. Another article forbade the collection of a tax for the benefit of the church. A third forbade the conduct of ecclesiastical courts and the assumption by them of administrative functions, presumably the keeping of vital statistics for other than church purposes. Still another article forbade the exercise of religious ceremonies or the placing of religious emblems in state institutions or in places such as trade-union or co-operative-association offices.

The narrowing of the right to teach religion found its way into an amendment to the Russian Republic's bill of rights in 1929, when the right to religious propaganda was removed while the right to antireligious propaganda was allowed to remain. The amendment was soon copied by the Ukrainian, Turkmen, and Uzbek republics and was made a part of the U.S.S.R. constitution in 1936. Article 124 of that constitution now reads: "In order to ensure to citizens freedom of conscience, the church in the U.S.S.R. is separated from the State and the school from the church. Freedoms of religious worship and freedom of anti-religious propaganda is recognized for all citizens."

To carry out this guarantee, an article was inserted into the criminal code to make it a crime to interfere in the performance of a religious service, but a loophole was provided in that the article makes intervention a crime only if the service does not violate the public order and does not encroach upon the rights of citizens. The concept of public order has been broad in all European countries, and particularly so in the U.S.S.R., so that the article provides a basis only for punishing a hoodlum who breaks into a church and commits an indignity at a time not deemed wise by the state officials. The article suggests that the problem of quieting the religious people of the U.S.S.R. has been found to be a difficult one. The leaders of the U.S.S.R. apparently wish to keep in their own hands decisions as to when interference shall be encouraged and to prevent overly zealous individuals from pressing antireligious acts at the wrong times or in an undesirable manner.

The conflict between religious communities and state officials during the late 1920's and early 1930's is well illustrated by some of the judicial decisions of the times. A group of elderly peasants who caused a riot in attempting to prevent the arrest of their priest were sentenced for "mass disorder accompanied by pogrom." Their sentences were commuted by a higher court, however, on the ground that most of the peasants were old, all were working and came from poor and middle-class groups, all were ignorant, and no serious consequences resulted from what they had done. Yet, when a peasant conducted religious meetings in his home, preaching that collectivization of agriculture was an invention of the devil and that any peasant who entered a collective farm would suffer in purgatory, he was convicted of crime.

The Effectiveness of Soviet Antireligious Measures

The effectiveness of the Communists' efforts to reduce religious belief in the period prior to World War II may be gauged from interviews conducted by a research team sent by Harvard University to European camps after the war. The camps contained persons who had fled the Soviet Union or who had refused to return to it after wartime servitude to the Germans. After studying the replies and the possibility that they were not truthful, the scholars have concluded that the replies can be trusted as reliable indications of family attitudes in the U.S.S.R. in the 1930's, which was the time most of the informants left their homes.

To determine the effectiveness of the antireligious campaigns among Soviet citizens, the informants were first placed in three age groups: those under thirty-five years of age, who had been born under the Soviet regime; those between thirty-six and forty-five, who had straddled the two eras, since they were in their teens at the time of the Revolution; and those over forty-five, whose habits and beliefs had been formed during the Tsarist period. In appreciation of the fact that before the Revolution the peasants had always been predominantly religious while the educated class had included many who scoffed at religion, the three age groups of informants were again split into two groups: those who came from worker-peasant stock and those who came from white-collar and educated families.

The report on the interviews indicates the following: in the worker-peasant group, persons over forty-five numbered no "atheists" or "agnostics" but fell only into the classes of "mildly religious" or "deeply religious." Fifty-three per cent claimed to be mildly religious, while 47 per cent claimed to be deeply religious, although their deep religious feeling might be manifested by prayer at home rather than by attendance at church. Of the middle group, aged thirty-six to forty-five, there were 3 per cent atheists, no agnostics, 71 per cent mildly religious, and 26 per cent deeply religious. In the youngest group, which had been reared under the Soviet regime's influence, there were 14 per cent atheists, 2 per cent agnostics, 62 per cent mildly religious, and only 22 per cent deeply religious.

The white-collar and educated group showed even greater inroads of atheism. The group over forty-five years of age reported 6 per cent atheists, 6 per cent agnostics, 65 per cent mildly religious, and 23 per cent deeply religious. The middle group, of ages thirty-six to forty-five, showed greater response to Soviet propaganda, for 9 per cent were atheists, 15 per cent agnostics, 56 per cent mildly religious, and only 20 per cent deeply religious. The greatest effect of Soviet propaganda was found among those under thirty-five, in which category 16 per cent reported an atheist position, 11 per cent agnostic, 51 per cent mildly religious, and 22 per cent deeply religious.

The interviewers concluded that the over-all generational trend among workers and peasants has been away from the traditional "deeply religious" position toward a "mildly religious" orientation, with a total religious rejection appearing only among those who were both born and reared during the Soviet era. The conclusion on the white-collar and educated group was that the over-all trend during the Soviet era has been away from a "mildly religious" orientation toward a more complete rejection of religion.

Relaxation of Controls during World War II

The instability caused by World War II forced upon the leaders of the Soviet state the adoption of a less militant antireligious policy. In the face of threatened national disaster, the Russian Orthodox Church modified its attitude of hostility toward Stalin's regime and called upon its communicants to defend "Russia" and to contribute to the fund-raising campaigns to pay for the war. Priests fought with the armies, and the campaign funds swelled. Stalin grasped at this opportunity to strengthen his political cause at a time when military defeat was close. He relaxed the campaign against the church and against religious belief. The League of Militant Godless in which he had enlisted those prepared to fight religion, and in which 3,500,000 persons were listed as actual members in January, 1941, ceased to function. Although it was never formally abolished, the league ceased to publish periodicals in the autumn of 1941, within three months after the German attack on the Soviet frontiers began. In 1944, the government consented to the restoration of organized religious instruction for those who wished to enter the priesthood, and parents were permitted to give their children to the priest for religious training, although not in schools.

In October, 1943, a Council for Affairs of the Orthodox Church was established within the Council of Ministers, to be followed soon after by establishment of a similar council for all the other religions, including the Moslems and the Jews. These two councils provided the first formal channel through which religious communities of the Soviet Union could present their grievances and difficulties to state officials and seek redress. In the same year the Orthodox Church was also permitted to call an assembly of bishops to elect a patriarch and to form a Holy Synod to serve under him. The church was even allowed to publish a periodical for the first time since 1929.

In spite of the relaxation of pressure on the church during the war, there was a later return to many of the old positions, if not to the old fervor. During the war period, the Komsomols had been infiltrated, apparently, by persons holding religious beliefs, for after the war a question was raised in the Komsomal journal about religious members. The answer given was that no religious youths should be permitted to remain in the Komsomols or permitted to join. The organization was not to retain such persons while efforts were made to change their minds. Persons being trained in the Komsomols for Communist party membership when they reached maturity could not be permitted to hold religious beliefs.

While the League of Militant Godless was not revived, there was created in 1949 the Society for the Dissemination of Scientific and Political Knowledge, which preached the doctrine that religion and science are incompatible and that youth must be informed of this fact. Museums attempting to prove this incompatibility were opened, as they had been prior to the war, and frequent excursions to them by school children became the rule.

State opposition to religious institutions is now most noticeable toward the Roman Catholic Church. Prior to the war, the territory of the U.S.S.R. contained few Roman Catholics, but after the war, with the absorption of the Baltic republics and large numbers of Poles, the communicants of the Roman Catholic Church became numerous. To the Russians, the Roman Catholic Church seems always to have been a political threat. Even during the Russian Empire, there was a prohibition against the travel of Jesuits within Russia. To the Soviet leaders, the Roman Catholic Church represents an agency of great power because of the discipline of its organization and the faithfulness of its communicants. Because the spokesmen of the Roman Catholic Church have frequently and over the whole period of Soviet rule in Russia expressed their hostility toward communism, the Soviet leaders have, in effect, declared war on the Roman Catholic Church. To win friends among persons inside and outside the U.S.S.R., the present Soviet leaders seem to be prepared to permit Anglican bishops and American Baptist ministers to make official visits to their co-religionists in the U.S.S.R., but there are no Roman Catholic delegations.

Whenever a religion becomes associated in Soviet minds with potential political opposition to the regime, the hostility of the Soviet government against those who profess that religion seems to become intensified. This has been demonstrated in changing Soviet attitudes toward the Jews. For years after the Revolution much was done to develop Jewish culture. A Yiddish theater was subsidized. A Jewish ethnic territory was created, and friendly relations were maintained with Jewish groups abroad. With the birth of the state of Israel, and what the Soviets have thought to be its close political relations with some of the Western powers, the Soviet leaders have become extremely cautious. For a time the Israeli ambassador was not permitted to reside in Moscow. Jewish cultural media within the U.S.S.R. were greatly circumscribed, and Jews were excluded from the Soviet foreign service on the ground that they were likely to have relatives abroad and therefore could not be presumed loyal under all circumstances.

Controls over the Family

The immediate Soviet attack upon the influence of the church, exerted through the monopoly granted to religious institutions by the Tsar to keep vital statistics and to marry and divorce citizens, was interpreted by some Soviet authors in the early years as an indication that in family relationships the state was going to refrain from intervention. It was even argued that in this sphere of private affairs there should be no state intervention at all, except for the maintenance of statistics and records. People were to be permitted to marry as they wished, to beget children without responsibility or social disapproval in the absence of marriage, and to consider themselves divorced when they found themselves incompatible. Some even argued that the family as an institution was no longer necessary in Soviet society.

Lenin seems always to have opposed such sexual freedom in principle, although his political instinct persuaded him to give rein to such an approach, at least so long as the family remained the inculcator of attitudes that he associated with the old regime. He considered the mothers and fathers reared prior to the Revolution to be dangerous to his program. They taught their children religious faith, respect for the status quo, and a feeling that the days of the past provided much that should be preserved. Lenin could change the schools and separate the church from the state, but he had a very hard time entering the home. His only hope for changing social attitudes normally developed in the home was to split the family asunder.

Lenin's policies took form in encouragement to children to report on the anti-Communist teaching of their parents, to reduce parental disciplinary authority, to eliminate all but health restrictions on marriage, and to do away with all restraints on divorce. By 1927, the court was removed from the procedure required to obtain a divorce; the parties, or even one of them, could report their desire to be recorded as divorced to a state registration bureau, and the divorce became valid when the entry was made; and a new family code permitted parties to marry without the necessity of recording the marriage in a bureau. In 1929, the court recognized a factual separation as a divorce, without the prior necessity of recording it. When after this change of rule it became necessary to determine for inheritance reasons whether marriage had existed, a court heard evidence on the relationship of the parties and declared that a man or woman was considered to have been married or divorced at the time of death regardless of the state of the official record.

Social attitudes changed slowly in spite of these measures. Evidence of this fact is found in a 1935 judicial decision by a Siberian court where a mother had been indicted for the murder of her newborn child. It was proved in her defense that she had not been married and that the child's father had deserted her. Her lawyer rested her defense upon old social attitudes. He pointed out that her baby had brought great social opprobrium upon her from her family. If the lawyer's statement was true, it meant that pre-revolutionary social attitudes were persisting nearly twenty years after the Revolution. As might have been expected, the court turned a deaf ear, saying that such social attitudes had been discouraged and could not mitigate the mother's crime; yet the penalty was withheld because of the mother's poor health.

The mid-1930's brought a radical change in state attitude toward the family, for intervention of the state in all family relationships was restored. Contemporary authors indicated that new reasons of social concern were responsible for the new approach. Fathers of children born out of wedlock were deserting their offspring and leaving them penniless. The state was not in a position to care for them. In fact, statistics of the time show that children reared without the influence of a home tended to become juvenile delinquents more frequently than those with a home environment.

Measures were taken in 1936 to discourage divorce. Parents were permitted to register as divorced only when both parties had had a chance to appear and to settle the care of the child. Fees for such registration were graduated from 50 to 300 rubles, and each successive divorce cost more. Parental discipline was strengthened, because parents were fined if their child was rowdy in the streets and were responsible in a civil suit for any damage caused.

The problem of homeless children was accentuated during the war, and a divorce law of 1944 went much further in coping with the broken home than the measures taken in the mid-1930's. The law now required that parties wishing a divorce go before a court, as they had not had to do since the first years of the Soviet regime. A desire for divorce was no longer to be sufficient reason for granting the divorce. The court was required to make every effort to reconcile the parties, and it was not permitted to grant a divorce even if its effort failed. Only the next higher court was to have jurisdiction for this purpose.

No grounds for divorce were provided in the 1944 law. The second court, the one having authority to grant divorce, was required to summon both parties and to hear witnesses on the cause of the quarrel. It was then instructed to deny a divorce if it thought that there was, or ought to be, a reconciliation. Only if the home had been irrevocably broken should the divorce be granted. As with other laws that contain no precise definition of the circumstances in which they should be applied, the courts have had to develop their own rules. As judicial decisions have been published, there has emerged what might be called a "common law of divorce." Certain principles have been established in this common law: that desire of the parties is not enough reason for divorce, nor is the abandonment by a husband of a wife because of infatuation with another woman, nor is the absence of a husband in the army, nor is a husband's fight with his wife's relatives. In a general instruction of 1949, the Supreme Court ordered the lower courts to grant a divorce only if they were convinced from the circumstances of the case that divorce proceedings had been commenced for deeply considered and well-founded reasons and that continuation of the marriage would conflict with the principles of Communist morals and could not create the conditions necessary to family life and the rearing of children.

The 1944 law introduced also a second bar to divorce, for it increased the fees over the schedule established in 1936. While the 1936 law had set the filing fee at from 50 to 300 rubles, the 1944 law set the rate at from 500 to 2,000 rubles within the discretion of the court. At the same time, it relieved a man of the financial and social embarrassment to his family caused by children he might have out of wedlock. No longer was his surname to be given to such children, nor was he to be required to support them on the same basis as those born to his recorded wife. The state assumed responsibility for children born of chance relations. Although Soviet authors vigorously denied that a concept of illegitimacy had returned, this law certainly delineated a new difference between children born in wedlock and those born outside, perhaps to strengthen the position of those born to married parents and thus to encourage maintenance of a strong family unit.

Changes in Family Attitudes

The extent to which the policies of the 1920's and early 1930's influenced the thinking of Soviet citizens on the family is indicated in answers to questions directed at the same group of Soviet refugees as were interviewed by American scholars in connection with religious attitudes. The interviewers sought to determine whether Soviet parents felt that there were values that must be instilled in their children by authoritarian techniques, within the family circle if need be. As with the answers to the questions on religion, the answers on this point were classified according to age and according to worker-peasant or white-collar–intellectual stock. The results were as follows.

In the peasant-worker group, those under thirty-five who would be willing to be authoritarian in instilling in their children treasured values were only 10 per cent of those interviewed in this age group; those between thirty-six and forty-five who would use authoritarian methods were 37 per cent of those interviewed in the age group; those over forty-five who would use authoritarian methods were 48 per cent of those interviewed in the age group. In the white-collar–intellectual group, there was less variation for each age category, those under thirty-five who were prepared to be authoritarian constituting 22 per cent of those interviewed in this group, those between thirty-six and forty-five constituting 27 per cent of those interviewed in this group, and those over forty-five constituting 21 per cent of those interviewed in this group. The other parents in the main preferred to use extensively democratic, or mainly democratic, measures in persuading their children to accept their value schemes. Only a very few were indifferent to their role as parent.

The interviewers noted that in their sample the role of parent had developed before adoption of even the relatively mild laws of the mid-1930's strengthening the hands of parents, and well before the 1944 law. In consequence, their results do not reflect any trend toward parental authoritarianism that may have resulted from the 1944 legislation. Also, they caution that attitudes of parents are often a carry-over from childhood experiences with their own fathers, and not the result of law. Yet they find that "like father, like child" is a less strong pattern in the younger generation than in the older, and so they are prepared to put more emphasis on the influence of the state with youthful groups than upon the influence of childhood experience.

State Intervention in Private Law Matters

Intervention in private affairs is indicated by the Soviet leaders' attitude toward what would elsewhere be called "private law relationships" such as are normally governed by a civil or commercial code. When the New Economic Policy was established by Lenin in mid-1921, it became evident that the restorative qualities of private enterprise would not be felt on the nation's economy unless there was developed a set of laws defining civil relationships. A buyer and seller had to know what would be the expected result of a contract. A lender had to know whether he could expect to recover the principal of his loan. A property owner had to know whether his ownership would be protected not only against theft but also against damage by a careless or wilfully harmful person. No one would risk capital in private enterprise unless he could be sure of what would happen in a law court. He had to know that agreements made in good faith would be performed in most instances out of fear of the law, and that in those cases in which performance was refused by the opposing party there could be enforcement in court.

Lenin himself was trained in the law, and he had with him in his Communist party some skilled lawyers. They knew what was necessary to restore confidence in law and order in the civil-law field, but they were ardent Marxists, and they feared that if they devised rules within which citizens might make agreements that would be unenforcible in court, the way might be opened for agile capitalists employing skilled lawyers to act within the letter of the rules but to the detriment of the community.

All systems of law have to guard against misuse of the law to the disadvantage of society, and legal procedures have been developed under which persons who can establish a real interest may gain injunctions against activity which appears to be legal on its face. It is usually left, however, for the interested parties to bring the matter before a court when a smoky chimney from a neighborhood factory belches forth excessive smoke, or when a zealous municipality seeks to widen the streets at the expense of a historic tree, or when a board of directors decides to use corporation assets in a manner deemed wasteful by a stockholder. Most systems of law give no relief unless someone can prove specific damage to himself and to his legitimate interests. There is no state official who has the duty to evaluate every lawsuit in the name of the community and to file his views on the subject with a court charged with hearing the matter.

The Soviet code-makers decided to be specific and prominently so. They wrote into the civil code that they enacted in 1922 a first article denying the protection of the code to those who claimed rights under the code but in violation of the social and economic reasons for the establishment of those rights. To implement this denial, the code of civil procedure was made to include a provision permitting the state prosecutor to intervene in any civil case at any stage, or, if no case was in progress, to instigate an action to prohibit the enforcement of a right guaranteed under the code if the interests of the state or of society would be injured.

Reliance upon Article I of the civil code was frequent by courts refusing to enforce a right in litigation by a capitalist of the period of the New Economic Policy. There were also cases in which property owners were deprived of their ownership because they were not using their property in what the prosecutor believed to be the interests of the community, as when they let it fall into serious disrepair although they had funds to make repairs.

Other articles of the code provided that no contract should be enforced if one party had knowingly taken advantage of the extreme want of the other party in making the contract. Thus a sale was set aside when it was proved that a party had been starving and had sold his home for a small quantity of food.

In the articles of the code relating to suits for damages for injury, it was provided that in setting the amount of damages the court should take into consideration the relative wealth of the parties involved, so that no wealthy person might obtain a judgment against a poor person who had damaged his property and thus ruin him. It was even provided that a rich man who caused injury to a poor man's property or person might be held liable in damages although there had been no fault on the rich man's part. This doctrine of liability without fault is not unique in the Soviet system. It has become popular in many Western countries, sometimes because juries have found fault on the part of a defendant in cases in which it seems hardly to have been present. It has been suspected that juries in the West have sometimes been moved emotionally by some serious hardship situation to provide a remedy to a poor man at the expense of an insurance company or of a railroad for which they had no sympathy. What has been unusual about the Soviet system is the clear-cut espousal of the doctrine of liability without fault in the code, not only in cases of extra-hazardous activity, when even Western codes make such provision, but in all cases where a poor man suffers damage.

Social Change Requires a New Approach

A considerable change in attitude toward the preservation of loopholes in the law began to appear in the 1930's. It has been reported by Soviet authors that not since 1930 has Article 1 been applied to withhold enforcement of some provision of the code. It has also been reported that not since before World War II have judgments for damages taken into account the relative wealth of the parties involved in the dispute. The state seems to have been intervening less in the affairs of citizens as these relate to property transactions, although it has been intervening more in the family relationships of citizens.

The explanation of the change may lie in the same factor noted so often in earlier chapters, namely, the emergence of a managerial and technical class. The property owners in the U.S.S.R. of the 1950's are not those who carried over the Tsarist-day property of their parents into the Soviet regime. They are not persons receiving interest on investments, or rents on land. They are not private enterprisers making a profit in industrial activity or in a merchandise market. They have money and property because they fall within that group of persons whose will to work has been encouraged by wage incentives. They are the managers of state-owned industry, the inventors, the authors of books and poems having high propaganda value to the state, the workmen who exceed the piece-rate norms and set the pace for a factory. These are the new rich in the U.S.S.R., and they are rich because the Soviet leaders have thought it beneficial to the interests of the community to have them rich.

Under such conditions, the law that is designed to preserve the community in the image desired by Soviet leaders is not called upon to penalize the new rich, but rather to protect them. There has been no favoring of the new rich by permitting them to own land or factories or to become merchants. They are all kept in the position of wage-earner in a state institution or of manager on a collective farm. They are not permitted to own that type of property from which Marxists argue that political power springs, but they are given substantial wages, and they can buy increasing quantities of consumers' goods. They can have television sets, private automobiles, summer cottages, and private homes. All of these to be enjoyed must be protected, and so the law is enforced.

As a result of the changed social structure of Soviet society, it may be that state intervention in property relationships will be lessened with the years, but this is to be distinguished from state intervention in religious matters and in family affairs. In these two fields the Soviet leaders seem to have concluded that their system requires the intervention of the state. There is no reason to believe that there will be a change in this attitude in the foreseeable future.

CHAPTER 10

THE ARMY AND POLITICS

The army has always been related closely to domestic politics by the Marxists. It has been considered more as an instrument for a ruling class to maintain its power at home than as a tool of international combat. To the Marxist, the soldiers in any country are the second line of defense when the police are pushed to the ground. It was the army that moved into position to save the king at Versailles, and the army which was called upon to defend the regime in Petersburg, when the mob threatened the palace. Lenin said often that a revolution could not be successful under modern conditions of warfare if it did not win to its side enough of the army to neutralize the effectiveness of this strongest weapon of the rulers.

Soviet experience with the army has tended to emphasize the conclusions of the Marxists. It was because of the disaffection of large segments of the troops in the capital of the Russian Empire that the revolutionaries were able to win the day in 1917 and force the abdication of the Tsar. It was because of the abandonment of Alexander Kerensky by his commander-in-chief, Kornilov, later in the same year, that the Soviet regime, led by the Military Revolutionary Committee of the bolsheviks, was able to seize power. Only the women's battalion fired from the galleries of the Winter Palace when the mob closed in.

There followed after the Revolution a short period of liquidating the First World War's international military obligations of Russia. In concluding the peace of Brest Litovsk, Lenin had made major concessions to Germany to prevent defeat of the bolshevik regime and a German occupation of Russia. Thereafter Lenin planned a new army, not to take revenge outside of Russia by regaining what had been lost but to save the domestic situation for his party. With

142

the important help of Trotsky, he organized a "Red Army" to serve as the strongest arm of the new regime in saving itself from its domestic opponents. Within little more than a year after the successful Revolution, this new army was tested in the battles of a civil war.

Unlike the war between the states in the United States, the Russian civil war involved no massive blocks of north and south. It was not regional but universal. Some people in all parts of what had been the Russian Empire rallied to the officers of the old regime and sought to unseat the new regime. Like all military struggles, the dramatic battles were fought in a few specific regions, but less dramatic episodes occurred throughout the land. This civil war was a class war and not a regional war, and class lines cut across the social fabric of the entire country.

Because of their concept that armies are maintained to protect class interests, the new Soviet leaders built their army on class lines. They permitted only members of the working and peasant classes to enlist, and their first draft law followed the same line. Only those presumed to be loyal to the aims of the bolsheviks were to serve. To popularize the army, and probably also because they had confidence in the good sense of the natural leaders among the workers and peasants in the ranks, Lenin developed the army's organization in an unusual pattern: he attempted to make of the army a thoroughly democratic institution in which the men in the ranks would elect their own officers.

Controls within the Army

The army presented the same problem to the new leaders as did industry. War was a technical matter, like the operation of industry, and the workers and peasants who were to fight in the new army had not mastered the technique. While it was politically attractive to espouse democracy within the army in the selection of officers, it was not practical. Military commanders had to be skilled professionals, and the solution to a dearth of professionals in the army was the same as it was in industry. Those professionals of the Tsar's army who were willing to continue in the new army were retained, and some were even conscripted; together they totaled 48,000 in number, constituting 76 per cent of all officers in 1918. They were not trusted, however. They had to be watched lest they betray their units to the armies fighting under their colleagues of yesterday, who were now trying to reconquer the country from bolshevik rule.

The Provisional Government of Alexander Kerensky had introduced the institution of commissars to watch those Tsarist officers who were not trusted—and with some reason, as the Kornilov affair had disclosed. The Soviet government continued to use commissars, from the beginning, although the first order on the subject, stating that the new commissars were the direct organs of the Soviet government in the army, appeared only on April 6, 1918. These commissars were charged with the duty both of keeping the army closely knit to the Soviet system and of preventing the army from becoming a focus of conspiracies against the workers and peasants. The orders of a military commander were to have no force until countersigned by a political commissar.

With the April order, the Red Army adopted formally the system of dual control that was to plague its efficiency in later years. It was obvious that decisions in warfare had to be taken quickly and that speed was difficult to obtain if a second commander had to be convinced, before an order could be executed, that it was wise. The bolsheviks took the risk of delay and confusion inherent in their system of dual control because they thought that the risk of loss of troops by treason of the officers was greater.

The political commissars were not only to watch for treason but also to spread bolshevik ideas throughout the ranks. They were to be teachers as well as policemen. Their work was co-ordinated through an All-Russian Bureau of Military Commissars, later to become the Political Section of the Revolutionary Military Council of the Republic to which the conduct of all military operations fell. In 1919 this central control section became the Political Administration of the Republic, directly subordinate to the Central Committee of the Communist party.

Party membership increased within the army with the passage of time. The growth of party influence was facilitated at the end of the civil war by reduction of the army from the 5,500,000 that it had been at its civil-war peak to a cadre army of 562,000 men. A campaign was conducted to prepare the officers to become members of the Communist party, and by 1928 all corps commanders in the cadre army were members of the party. Those below included a large number of party men, with the end result that 55 per cent of the total officer corps belonged to the party.

Under peacetime conditions and in view of the increase in presumed loyalty of officers due to membership of so many in the party, the role of the political commissar was changed. In 1924 he was placed in secondary position and no longer required to approve the commands of the military commanders but rather to concern himself with party-political and cultural-educational work. Yet the organization of political commissars continued to be independent of the People's Commissar for Military and Naval Affairs, of the Revolutionary Military Council of the Republic, and even of local civilian Communist party organs in the territory in which the military unit was garrisoned.

The Stalin Purge within the Army

Many Soviet citizens and outside observers believed that the political loyalty of the Red Army had been assured in the mid-1930's by the increasing number of party members within the army. They did not reckon with a new factor that was not evident to the public generally—if it was to those below the highest policy-making circle of the Communist party. This was Stalin's determination to strengthen his role as dictator, not only over the masses, but over the party itself. The world, including the rank-and-file Soviet citizen, was shocked in 1936 by the first of the purge trials. On the face of them, and even allowing for distortion of evidence to prove disloyalty to Stalin, these trials indicated a new resistance to Stalin's authoritarian direction of the Communist party on the part of those of the original small groups of party leaders who had shared with Lenin in planning and directing the events of 1917 and who had opposed Stalin quite vigorously in party meetings from time to time after Lenin's death.

The purge swept through the highest party circles, marked in each of the years 1937 and 1938 with another dramatic public trial of an additional group of defendants. Forced confessions, recanted in one case on the second day of the trial only to be reaffirmed after what must have been the pressures of another night in jail, went well beyond the realm of credibility for foreigners. Yet they were dramatized so well for a people who had little factual knowledge against which to check the charges that in all probability they were believed by most Soviet citizens.

Finally the purge reached the army, with a secret trial in 1937 of the Deputy Chief of the Red Army, Marshal M. N. Tukachevsky, and of seven colleagues. The suicide of the head of all political commissars was reported at the same time. The accusation against all of these men was collaboration with the Germans, who, under the leadership of Hitler, were at the time declaring their increasing hostility toward the U.S.S.R. After Stalin's death, the army trial was denounced as a falsification, and the reputations of the executed generals were cleared.

Notwithstanding that the allegations against the accused officers were untrue, Stalin seems to have been frightened. In the face of the proved inefficiency of the military commissar system as it had existed during the civil war, he restored this system within two months after the announcement of Tukachevsky's execution. The political commissar was made equal to the commander, though not superior to him, and all orders had to be countersigned by the political commissar although they were issued to the troops only in the commander's name. The authority of the commissar extended even to approving all awards, promotions, and demotions, and to the preparation of a report on the political training and reliability of all commanding personnel in his unit.

The inefficiency of the dual command was demonstrated again in the first military operation after its reintroduction, namely, the winter war with Finland in 1940. As a result of early Soviet defeats in this war, the political commissar was again moved back to second place. He was given a new name symbolic of his position, "Deputy Commander for Political Affairs," and was charged with political propaganda.

The German attack against the U.S.S.R. on June 22, 1941, again frightened Stalin, to judge from the record on political commissars. In less than a month after the German invasion of Soviet territory, the political commissars were returned to their civil-war status and adjured to concern themselves not only with propaganda but with military decisions as well. It is now known that defections from the Red Army were numerous in the early days of World War II, before the Germans proved to the Russians that they had more than the ousting of Stalin in mind and planned complete subjugation of the Slavs as a race. The political commissar system, as it had existed during the similar peril of the first years after the Revolution, was Stalin's answer to the defections of 1941. In spite of the proved inadequacy of such a system of political control under conditions of modern warfare, the peril was deemed sufficiently great to dictate the system's restoration.

Soviet officers who have since fled to the West have written that military operations on the Soviet front necessitated constant movement and thus made the countersigning of orders by a political commissar often impossible. Military and political commanders were often widely separated, yet swift decisions were necessary. The refugee officers have pointed to the character of modern warfare as a primary reason for a decree of October, 1942, which declared that the military commanders were to be solely responsible for the conduct of the war and that the political commissars were to be reorganized and made subordinate to them. The system adopted in 1942 remains in force today.

Party Membership in the Army

Reorganization of the political commissar system, so that it became a chain of command subordinate to the military commanders, did not mean that the Communist party had relinquished its control within the army. Two factors account for the conclusion that no military caste beyond the reach of the party was being permitted to develop. One was the extension of party membership and education within the army to bring in large numbers of men and nearly all the higher officers, and the other was the expansion of a system of police officers responsible to the Ministry of Internal Affairs. Each will be considered in turn.

The extension of party membership was dramatic and in sharp contrast to the policies in force before World War II. In 1939, there had been only 1,000,000 party members in all branches of civilian and military activity. Just before the German attack in 1941, the party reported 3,876,885 members. Immediately after the war began, the requirements for admission of soldiers and officers were relaxed so that by January 1, 1945, there were 5,760,369 members. Refugee officers have reported that the required three recommendations for membership were made by the political commissar of the unit, the company commander, and the company political commissar. Soldiers were being accepted at what is said to have been the rate of 100,000 per month, and during 1942 over one million members of the armed forces were admitted. Since many were killed or captured because it was they who were required to assume the role of leader and hero, a considerable campaign of recruitment was necessary to keep the party ranks full.

Such rapid recruitment of party members from the armed forces did not give time for the careful training and disciplining characteristic of peacetime, but it did place many of the new members emotionally on the side of the regime as a part of the elite. Political commissars thus gained many men in their units on whom they could usually rely for desired political attitudes. For those who fell outside their propaganda net, there was the police net of the agents of the Ministry of Internal Affairs.

Both the political commissars and the agents of the Ministry of Internal Affairs, later transferred to the Committee on State Security, have had, and now have, organizations throughout the military apparatus. Thus, there is the Chief Political Administration of the Armed Forces, which is responsible both to the Central Committee of the Communist party and to the Ministry of Defense. It has various departments to provide educational materials, to edit military journals, to teach in military schools, and to work among the Komsomols in the army and the fleet. The Chief Political Administration works through a branch established in each of the military districts into which the country is divided and in each fleet area. These district branches channel their activities down through political sections of the corps, division, regiment, battalion, and company and through the corresponding units in the navy.

A political commissar, called *zampolit*, is appointed by, and responsible to, the next higher political commissar, but he is also subordinate to the military commander of the unit over whose political education he presides. Thus, in theory, political commissars are subject to dual subordination. They are said, in practice, to demonstrate considerable independence of the commander and even, at times, to make suggestions as to military tactics. This attitude is fostered by the requirement that they pass the usual technical examinations for any military promotion in grade, so that a major in the political corps is supposed to be as able a military leader as a major having primarily military duties.

Since all members of the Communist party within the unit in which the *zampolit* operates are expected to carry on their usual party work, there is a party organization within the unit to which they all are required to give service. This organization, as in the civilian organizations of the Communist party, elects its executive committee and its secretary. The party secretary's role is played by the *zampolit* at the level of military district, corps, and division. At the level of the regiment, and below, there is a separation of functions, in that a separate party secretary is elected, but, reportedly, he is invariably controlled by the *zampolit*, who recommends his election and who, at the regimental level, is generally one grade above this party secretary in military rank. During the war there was no pretense of democratic election of the secretaries, and they were simply appointed under a special directive, as were the members of the party executive committees for the military organizations at the various levels. In 1946 the system of elections was restored within the party apparatus of the armed services.

The schedule of activities of the *zampolit,* as reported by Soviet refugees, indicates that these political commissars are required to use every opportunity to imbue their charges with party doctrines, their major educational work being done among non-party men. Formal class discussions on political doctrine are held at regular intervals each week, if need be under trees near the front. Classes focus on basic political doctrines, but there are also current-events classes to apply these doctrines to contemporary situations. At periods which might be called "recreational," it is the political commissar's duty to see that Soviet novels, with their political messages couched in romantic terms, are read aloud. It has been reported that sometimes a *zampolit* has quarreled with a military commander because the latter called for a maneuver at the hour of political education.

The Komsomols are organized at every military level and in the same way as is the party. There is a Komsomol section in the Chief Political Administration of the Armed Forces and at each unit level a Komsomol organization that is subordinate to the *zampolit.* In theory, the secretaries of the unit organizations of the Komsomols are elected, but, in practice, they are chosen by the *zampolit.* Their work is primarily with the enlisted men, 50 per cent of whom are estimated to be members of the Komsomols. All Komsomol members are expected to be good examples to the other soldiers and to try to stimulate the interest of these men in cultural and political development.

Many of the poorly disciplined party members of wartime campaigns have been eliminated from the army since the war, for most of the rank and file has been demobilized and subsequently replaced by new draftees, who are admitted to the party only after the usual scrutiny. The officer corps also has been brought more firmly within the party. In 1952, the party congress was told that 86.4 per cent of all officers were members of the party or of the Komsomols. Under such conditions of development of disciplined party members within the armed forces, the influence of the political commissars is said to have been reduced because they can no longer claim a near monopoly on loyalty. They are surrounded by men whose loyalty is also presumed to be high.

Police Controls in the Army

No presumption of loyalty eliminates in Soviet minds the need for a security police. In all Soviet agencies, as has already been explained, there exists police supervision. It is provided by a Special Section, which appears on the organization chart of every ministry and public corporation, and even of the universities and professional schools. In keeping with the initials of the Russian words for "Special Section," these sections have been called the "OO." In the army they were designated in the same way before World War II, but during the war they became known as "SMERSH," an abbreviation of the Russian for "death to spies."

All such police sections, which exist in units parallel to those of the political commissars down to the division level, are subordinate to the Chief Administration for Counterintelligence of the Armed Forces of the U.S.S.R. This Chief Administration is today a bureau of the Committee of State Security, known as the "Third Central Administration" of the KGB. There is no simultaneous subordination to the Ministry of Defense or to the Chief of Staff, as with the political commissars. A direct line is maintained to the KGB. The Chief Administration's work is co-ordinated with that of other security agencies of the government. Below the division level, the units operate by means of informers.

The officers of the OO are said not to have had military training but only police training. They live a separate life from the army personnel and even from the party unit in which they work, for they have their own party organization within which the work of the OO is discussed. While these men are believed to exert no direct influence on the commander with respect to military decisions, they do report on the military condition of the unit and on the political morale and material and medical welfare of the troops. They exchange information with the political commissars, and they may arrange for the transfer of an informer to a unit in which they have been unable to recruit one. Clearance from them is required before any officer within the army may be promoted.

When a violation of law is found by the OO, the matter is turned over to the military courts for action. If a charge arising before 1953 was not sufficiently supported with evidence to be taken before a court, the Special Board of the Ministry of Internal Affairs might have been called upon to eliminate the suspected person from the ranks by putting him in a concentration camp as a social danger.

Since abolition of the Special Boards in 1953 this procedure has not been available.

Enhancing the Prestige of Officers

Controls such as those provided by the political commissars and the OO can be effective in eliminating the occasional dissenter from the army and in stopping plans for a mutiny or desertion before the organizers attract enough persons to be successful, but they are not enough. The long-range success of the Soviet leaders in holding the loyalty of armed forces must, and does, rest upon forces stronger than police and political commissars. To assure long-range loyalty, there must first be general emotional acceptance of the Soviet system by the great majority of the high command. Second, there must be sufficient military discipline within the armed services to permit the high command to maintain its authority over the rank and file.

The Soviet leaders have been active in both spheres. They have wooed the high command, and they have seen to the strengthening of discipline. Wooing of the high command took the form of reintroducing in 1935 military titles of the conventional type—lieutenant, captain, major, lieutenant-colonel, and colonel. Prior to this time, the commanders had been designated merely as commanding a squad, company, corps, or army. In 1940, the ranks of general and admiral were reintroduced, even though these titles, as such, had been the butt of revolutionary propaganda for so long as to make them synonymous with traitors to the bolshevik cause. The duty to salute officers, which had been abandoned in 1918, was restored, and in July, 1943, the title "officer" was reintroduced together with the epaulets of rank, which in themselves had been symbols of the old regime for all the years since the Revolution. Even the term "soldier" was reintroduced for army privates, to replace the title "Redarmyman." In 1946 the name of the whole army was changed from "Red Army" to "Soviet Army."

All these changes were intended to enhance the prestige of the officers. They could now feel that they were an elite, and the manner in which they bore themselves within the army and outside it indicated a great change in attitude toward their positions. There was also restored the Officers' Court of Honor, which resembled that of Tsarist times and was designed to guard the dignity and honor of the rank of officer by providing to the officers a means of punishing those of their own number who degraded the uniform.

Even within the officers' corps there were established notable practical distinctions. The scale of pay indicates that a sergeant receives 4.3 times as much basic pay as a private; a captain, 24.3 times as much; and a general of the army, 114.3 times as much. In addition, special privileges to buy scarce consumers' goods and to have prior right in the allocation of living quarters and in the choice of theater seats are granted the general officers.

Measures such as these are taken by the top Communist party policy-makers presumably to supplement the incentives to loyalty that they expect political indoctrination to instil in the ranks of the Communist party. If the ideological arguments do not succeed in assuring loyalty of army chiefs to the party, the favors showered upon them by the party can be expected to achieve the desired result.

Discipline has been strengthened markedly since 1940. The duty of obedience existed not at all prior to 1919, at which time soldiers were required only to execute "service" orders and "service" duties and were excused from performing commands directed against the Soviet government or obviously criminal in nature. In 1925 a new disciplinary code required performance of all orders, unless criminal in nature. The 1940 Disciplinary Code requires the execution of every order regardless of content. It allows no rejections on the basis of violation of law. To avoid a conclusion that subordinates may now have to execute illegal orders, a commentary has suggested that it will be presumed that no Soviet officer would violate the international law of war in giving an order.

To enforce discipline, the commanding officer is authorized to apply penalties ranging from personal reprimand, through extra duty, to confinement, and finally to reduction in rank. Such penalties are subject to certain procedural requirements: the penalty must be imposed within five days of the commission of the offense, it must be executed within a month, it must be proportionate to the offense, and it must not exceed the authority of the superior or he will himself be liable to disciplinary or judicial punishment. The subordinate is very much limited in his complaint on procedural grounds, for he may object to the immediate superior only on the basis of exceeded authority.

Military Crime and Its Punishment

If crime has been committed, as defined by the 1958 federal statute on military crimes, a trial is held before a military court. These courts of the federal government are organized by the Supreme Court of the U.S.S.R. in military districts, army corps, and army divisions.

The jurisdiction of each is successively determined by the rank of the person prosecuted. For the highest ranks, there is a military college within the Supreme Court of the U.S.S.R., which may also take jurisdiction over any case that in its opinion is sufficiently complex or of great political or social importance. The courts are composed of one professional judge, trained as a military lawyer, and two non-professional judges, without legal training and chosen for each case usually from the ranks of the armed services.

Appeals from a decision are permitted to the court next above the one in which the trial was held. There may be no appeal from a decision by the military college of the Supreme Court, but this does not mean that there may not be a review of the decision, for the President of the Court or the Prosecutor-General of the U.S.S.R. may always request a review by the full bench of the Supreme Court, sitting as a plenum. To provide political control over decisions in the event of need, the decision of the Plenum of the Supreme Court may be taken to the Presidium of the Supreme Soviet by the President of the Supreme Court or by the Prosecutor-General of the U.S.S.R.

The military courts are required to follow the code of criminal procedure of the republic in which they are sitting. Thus, they are not outside the regular court system with a procedure of their own. This fact is not as remarkable as it might seem, because the criminal procedure established by the code for all courts, military and civilian alike, resembles more closely the procedure used in military courts everywhere than it does the procedure of American courts of law. Discussion of the main points of the procedure will be reserved for the chapter following this one.

After reviewing the provisions and practice of Soviet military law, it has been concluded by two foreign students that Soviet criminal procedure does provide a basis for reasonable prediction by the accused of the outcome of his trial. It seems to these students, therefore, to contribute to stability within the army and to confidence that punishment will not be meted out unless it is deserved. For the officer corps, this is important to peace of mind, and it may not be chance that Marshal Georgi K. Zhukov, soon after Stalin's death, raised his glass in a toast to "justice." For the morale of the armed forces, the efficient operation of the military courts is necessary.

Army Officers' Fate since Stalin

After Stalin's death in 1953 the prestige of professional soldiers rose in the Communist party. Marshal Georgi K. Zhukov, a professional soldier, was named Minister of Defense in the first recognition of a career officer as minister. In February, 1956, he was elevated to the Presidium of the Central Committee of the Communist party as an alternate member, again an unprecedented recognition of a career officer as a political leader. In 1957 he provided what was the critical support Khrushchev needed in his power struggle with the faction seeking his ouster. By this act the Armed Forces were in a position for the first time since the days when officers were largely men inherited from the Tsar's army to challenge even the Communist party.

Zhukov in his new position manifested his desire for a strengthening of the hand of career officers to the detriment of the security police, the political commissars, and political education generally. There were many foreign observers who anticipated open conflict between Khrushchev and Zhukov, as the latter moved to separate the Armed Forces from the traditional control of party and police.

Making use of an opportunity to send Zhukov to Yugoslavia for consultations during the late summer of 1957, Khrushchev arranged Zhukov's removal during his absence. Jealousies among Zhukov's colleagues were nurtured by Khrushchev, and party discipline was reasserted among the top officers. As he stepped from the plane on his return to Moscow, Zhukov was confronted with his demotion. Shortly thereafter he was removed from the Presidium of the party and disappeared from public notice.

Political education, although left in the hands of a *zampolit* subordinate to the military commander of each unit, was reaffirmed in importance by appointing a war hero as Chief of the Political Administration to command respect for military prowess and demonstrate a concern for political education. A career officer with no past history as a first-rank hero was made Minister of Defense. He was seated on the Central Committee of the party but not on its Presidium. Matters were restored to what Khrushchev must have considered normal conditions, namely, the unquestioning subordination of the Armed Forces to the Communist party and the acceptance of a program of political education within these forces designed to assure acquiescence in such a role.

By the events of 1957 the army marshals, who had been imponderables under Zhukov's command, providing potential support to the managerial class as it emerged in industry, agriculture, and channels of distribution, were shorn of any potentiality as a source of coercion hostile to the Communist party. They sank back to the status of an interest group able to exercise pressure only through persuasion. While the army and navy and air force officers still could be expected to resist resumption of the purge policy of Stalin as it had been directed against Marshal M. N. Tukachevsky in 1937, it is unlikely that they were feared by the Communist party as a potential source of armed challenge to its program, so long as that program was enforced by measures short of a blood bath.

CHAPTER 11

ENFORCEMENT OF LAW

Justice has been claimed as a major aim by the bolsheviks since their seizure of power. They have argued that the efforts of the West to create a system of courts independent of the legislative and administrative branches of government and to provide a fair trial are designed solely to mask the injustice of the Western systems. They have quoted Marx's stricture on the courts of Western Europe as he set it forth in the *Communist Manifesto* of 1848. Marx said that the justice that was so much praised by the men of his time was really only for the limited few who ruled. In keeping with his analysis of the state as an instrument of class domination, he said that the courts were no more than instruments of a ruling class. He declared that they could not be considered impartial and that they did not administer justice in any abstract sense.

The bolsheviks have never claimed to administer justice in any abstract sense. Their claim that their courts are more democratic than any in the West rests upon their claim that the Soviet system of government represents the masses. They declare openly that their court is an instrument of state policy and by no means impartial. In the earlier years of their regime they spoke frequently and proudly of "revolutionary legality," by which they meant the maintenance of order for the benefit of the aims of their revolution. The courts were thought to have as much of a duty to maintain order of the type sought by the Communist party as did the administrative branch of the state apparatus.

The bolsheviks have not constructed their system so as to utilize the courts as a check upon the legislature or the executive. They have formally discarded the concept of separation of powers so basic to the American system. In keeping with Marx's analysis, they have said that the separation claimed in the United States is mere subterfuge and that American judges are as much subject to the pressures of the political party in power and its instrument, the executive branch of government, as are the judges in their own system. They have never appreciated the extent to which the American judiciary can and will check the authority of the executive branch, as it has done so often in history and most recently in the case testing President Harry S. Truman's power to seize the steel mills and in the various cases limiting the power of the executive to dismiss individuals from the civil service and to issue passports.

In view of the Soviet attitude toward courts and their insistence that judges be politically alert in enforcing the policies of the Communist party, one may wonder why the Soviet system includes courts at all. It is possible to imagine an official of the Soviet Ministry of Justice presiding over an office before which the police could bring charges against those whom they believed to be in need of punishment and before which persons engaged in a dispute might appear for settlement of their quarrel. Such a system was common enough in feudal times, when the feudal lord settled the disputes of his vassals and decided on the basis of his own wisdom what penalties were desirable for those who displeased him. Even in more modern times there have been many administrative tribunals, often with power of punishment. In the United States we find no difficulty in accepting administrative boards that decide the right to open a radio station or fine those who violate administrative regulations.

The U.S.S.R. has made considerable use of the administrative tribunal to keep order. The special boards within the Ministry of Internal Affairs, the heirs of the *Cheka*, have had a record of activity so vigorous as to indicate that the Soviet leaders have found them useful as instruments of terror. A chapter has been devoted to these boards and the governmental function they have performed. It might have been possible to extend the jurisdiction of these special boards to all charges of violation of law and even to disputes between citizens. This has not been done, however, and in view of the Soviet leaders' practical approach to government, there must be good reason.

Reasons for Establishing a Court System

Various reasons why Soviet leaders have preferred to establish a body that they have called a "court" rather than to utilize administrators of the Ministry of Justice can be imagined. Lenin inherited a society in which the court, in spite of Marx's criticism of its injustice, enjoyed considerable popular esteem. To have abandoned the con-

cept of a court right after the Revolution would have caused appre-
hension among the people. Perhaps that is why within a month after
the Revolution a decree established a new court system to replace
the old. Ever since that time the court has been retained, and there
has never been talk of abandoning it in favor of an administrative
official.

With their ever present concern for world public opinion, the
Communist leaders have probably also considered the effect upon
that world public opinion of their attitude toward courts. They have
not had to worry about negative reaction to their class approach, for
those who welcome a system pledged to further the cause of workers
and peasants have been ready to accept a court professing to administer class justice. A potential French Communist would not be
displeased with a system that favors the poor man over the rich,
but he could be expected to be unhappy with a system that is not
established to provide justice as he understands it to members of the
working class. Soviet Communists cannot overlook the fact that
Frenchmen have had a violent fear of administrative officials ever
since the declining days of the French monarchy. To return to arbitrary administrative determination of guilt, even though the determining official worked for a state under the domination of the Communist party, would worry a Frenchman. The Communists in the
U.S.S.R. most probably take foreign public opinion into account.

In Soviet political literature, it is possible to distinguish another
reason for maintenance of a court system rather than the institution
of an official of the Ministry of Justice to administer the law. Administrative efficiency is said to play a part in the decision. It has
been found that the judicial function is a specialized one, requiring
a greater measure of contemplation and more time to determine
facts than is customary in an administrative office. The denial of the
separability of politics and law has not meant to Soviet leaders that
the judicial function was not separable from the administrative
function. Soviet judges are admonished to study their politics carefully and to keep in constant touch with political leadership. They
are not permitted to separate themselves from the aims of the Communist party. In fact, over half of them at the lowest level, and all of
them at the highest, are members of the Communist party and subject to its usual discipline.

There can be no opposition in court to the policies of the party,
but it is accepted that a judge has a special type of task to perform
and that for this task he requires special training and special ability.

In attempting to explain the Soviet attitude, Andrei Vyshinsky has written that the Soviet system rejects the concept of separation of powers as it appears in the United States Constitution but accepts the necessity of separating functions. By this he seems to mean that the court function is considered to be a specialized one. It is to be performed by experts, but these experts are not to think of themselves, nor is anyone else to think of them, as being a check upon the executive or the legislature. All three branches of government—legislative, executive, and judicial—must be considered to be members of the same team under the guidance of the Communist party.

To indicate this fact in constitutional terms, it is provided by the constitution that the courts shall be responsible to the Supreme Soviet of the U.S.S.R. as the all-powerful authority within the U.S.S.R. In theory, the Supreme Soviet and the subordinate soviets could act as courts, but the draftsmen of the constitution preferred to have the Supreme Soviet delegate its authority to settle disputes and punish offenders to a system of courts created by it, responsible to it, and in the final decision reversible by it, if the necessities of policy require.

Political Courts in the Early Years

Acceptance of the desirability of maintaining a system of courts has not meant to the Soviet leaders that all courts need be alike. In their fear of class enemies, the revolutionary leaders of 1917 decided to create two types of court in their first decree. One was to handle the routine cases of crime and civil dispute. The other was to try the cases involving the safety of the regime itself. This latter system was called the system of "revolutionary tribunals," to indicate that its task was to make certain that the revolutionary regime was not unseated. Its judges were chosen for their political training, and they were released from the limited procedural restraints created for the new regular courts.

With the passage of years, the revolutionary tribunals came to outlive their usefulness, in the opinion of some of the officials of the Ministry of Justice. It was felt that the major dangers of the civil-war period had passed and that it had become possible to concentrate all courts within a single system. To this view, some members of the staff of the Ministry of Justice objected. They felt that the new courts, called "peoples' courts," had shown themselves to be politically innocent and too much subject to local pressures, especially when they were called upon to punish such chronic evils of the village communities as the illegal manufacture of moonshine liquor and attempts at evasion of military service. It was argued that if the revolutionary tribunals were abolished, it would be necessary to improve greatly the political quality of the judges in the peoples' courts. Improvement of the quality of judges seemed impossible to the opponents of the plan to abolish the revolutionary tribunals. It was argued that it would take time to train judges who could resist local pressures and who would understand fully the aims of the new regime. Until the time came when this process of political education was completed, the separation of the two court systems was expected to be necessary.

A compromise was adopted in 1921, under which the number of revolutionary tribunals was reduced and their jurisdiction limited. Fewer types of crime were to be brought before them, but they were not to be abolished. They were to be re-established as "military courts" and "military transport courts," subject to the control of the supreme court of each republic, through which there might be preserved the same standard of procedural protection as was to be enforced in the peoples' courts. This was thought to provide the desired unity of policy, if not unity of structure. The preservation of the revolutionary tribunal idea in its new form would make it possible to reserve for judges well trained in Communist party policies the cases involving attempts to overthrow the regime, whether committed by military personnel or civilians.

To take up the lesser cases of political importance that were being removed from the revolutionary tribunals in their new form, the political quality of the peoples' courts was to be improved. It seemed obviously impossible to the Ministry of Justice to develop enough skilled lawyers with political understanding in a sufficiently short time to staff all the courts. As a solution to their problem, the ministry officials seized upon a practice that had developed in 1920. They would establish two levels of peoples' courts, one for the routine criminal and civil cases and a second one with more experienced and politically qualified judges. The great bulk of the cases would be heard by the first court, and the fewer more complicated and more serious cases would go before the second court, which could sit in the provincial capitals rather than in the county seats close to each village community or even on circuit among the villages.

The two-stepped system of courts was carried one degree further, for the Supreme Court in each republic was given authority to try unusual cases of very great political importance. Thus there emerged a system of courts at different levels to meet the needs of different situations. At each successively higher level the political and educational requirements for the position of judge were more exacting. By the 1922 Judiciary Act, there was established a system of courts which has remained essentially the same to the present day.

The Courts in the New Federation

Federation in 1923 affected the court system in some measure. There was created a Supreme Court of the U.S.S.R., and to it were transferred the military and military transport courts that were the successors of the revolutionary tribunals. In this move, the protection of the state against acts designed to overthrow the regime became subject always to the jurisdiction of federal courts. With the passage of the years there were added to these federal military courts, with their jurisdiction over all types of revolutionary activity, whether committed by military personnel or by civilians, two other systems of federal courts. One of these had to do with crimes committed by employees of the water-transport system and by civilians whose acts affected the operation of this system. Its jurisdiction was the same as that of the transport courts concerned with railroad operations. The second new system had to do with crimes committed by inmates of the concentration camps maintained by the Ministry of Internal Affairs.

After Stalin's death all but one of the specialized federal courts were abolished and jurisdiction returned to the courts of the republics. The one survivor was the military tribunal, but even this was changed. Its jurisdiction was reduced to cases involving charges against men in the Armed Forces or charges of espionage brought against civilians.

The other courts of the republics having to do with criminal and civil cases were untouched by federation. All civil disputes between individuals were reserved for the courts of the republics. The federal courts were only criminal courts and treated only special situations. It will be seen immediately that the line dividing federal and republic jurisdiction in the U.S.S.R. is quite different from that dividing the federal and state courts in the United States. There is some similarity between the systems in the two countries as they relate to criminal law, in that federal law defines certain crimes in the United States, and offenses against such law are tried by federal courts. Such crimes in the United States include treason, just as espionage is a federal crime in the U.S.S.R., but they also include lesser crimes over which the federal government has jurisdiction because of its constitutional authority to control interstate and foreign commerce. Such lesser crimes are exemplified by the carrying of guns across state lines or by the smuggling of narcotics.

There is no similarity between American and Soviet federal courts in the civil field. While in the United States there are many civil suits brought in federal courts because the parties are citizens of different states or of different countries, in the U.S.S.R. there are no civil suits between individuals in the federal courts. Although in the U.S.S.R. there may be a suit by one republic against another, just as there may be a suit by one state against another in the United States, the similarity ends with the stating of the rule, for although states in the United States have sued each other quite often, especially over water rights, there is no public record of suits in the U.S.S.R. Supreme Court between republics of the U.S.S.R.

Soviet federal courts are subject to the same requirements as to structure of the bench and procedural rules applicable in a criminal trial as are the courts of the republics. Such difference as there is has to do with the problem raised in 1922 when the question of qualifications of judges interfered with the plan to create a unitary system of courts. The federal judges are all named by the Supreme Soviet of the U.S.S.R., not only those on the Supreme Court bench but also those on the benches of the lower courts in the federal system. The judges in each republic are named by the supreme soviet of the republic for the supreme court of the republic and by the provincial soviets for the provincial courts. The judges in the lowest courts of the republics have presented a special problem raised by the necessity of appealing to the confidence of the people.

Reaction to Democratic Pressures

Democratic pressures seem to have been felt in the judicial system as well as in the selection of deputies to the various soviets. These have been met in part by provision for the selection of judges at the various levels by the soviet at the same level. To the extent that the soviet itself was democratically elected, it could be argued that the judges represent the will of the people as expressed by their deputies. This argument is not without appeal. It is used also in the United States in support of direct election of judges. For example, public opinion polls in New York State, where judges are elected, have proved that only a very small percentage of the voters knows anything about the candidates proposed for judicial vacancies.

People are thought to vote blindly for the candidates proposed by their political party. In consequence, it is being urged by Bar Association leaders in New York that it would be better to shorten the ballot, which now has many names upon it to fill the judicial vacancies, so as to include only the candidates for the political offices of governor and mayor and for other executive and legislative offices. The governor would then name the judges. It is argued that since opinion polls have proved that the voters study the careers of those proposed as governor, they will select intelligently a man in whom they have confidence to select, in turn, the judges, while they cannot be expected to study the careers of candidates for judge sufficiently to make an informed choice. Some other states have long provided that the governor should appoint the judges, on the basis of the position now being urged in New York.

The Bar Association proposals in New York have met strong opposition from some who have claimed that the only really democratic way to choose a judge is by popular election. The fact that this argument persists suggests that there is public sentiment of this nature around the world, and it may even have reached into the U.S.S.R. Pressure for adoption of what the world accepts as a democratic choice of judges may have influenced the draftsmen of the U.S.S.R. Constitution of 1936, for it was provided therein that the judges in the lowest courts be elected directly by the voters rather than appointed by the local soviet. No change was made in the manner of appointment of judges at the higher levels, but the change was made for the lowest court.

Foreign students of the Soviet system recognized little difference between the long-established system of appointment of local judges by the local soviet and the 1936 innovation of election by the people. Since it was obvious that the Communist party had been able over the years to establish its complete control over selection of deputies to the local soviets, it was presumed that the party could control the election of judges as easily. The change in procedure seemed to be in form only, and presumably was instituted to present to the Soviet people and to the world evidence of increasing democratic practices within the U.S.S.R.

The elections to local soviets since adoption of the secret ballot in 1936 have produced few surprises, as has been indicated earlier. The Communist party has shown its skill in devising counterweights to democratic procedures so as to assure the choice of its candidates in almost all districts, regardless of democratic forms adopted for the elections. In spite of its success in controlling elections to the soviets, the Communist party seems to have been reluctant to put the choice of local judges to the vote. No judicial elections were held for thirteen years after adoption of the provision. No direct election of judges in the peoples' courts occurred until 1949. To be sure, World War II had intervened, but this cannot have been the whole explanation. When the first election of judges occurred, the pattern of elections to the various soviets was reproduced. The name of only one nominee appeared on each ballot. Voters were given no choice. Apparently, there were no large number of scratches, for all candidates were reported to have been elected for the constitutional three-year term. Similar elections have been held at the required intervals since the first election, with similar results. The elections of December, 1954, were reported to have resulted in a group of judges, 54.1 per cent of whom were members of the Communist party. In 1958 the terms of local judges were set at five years.

Popularization of the Bench

The Soviet court system has borrowed from Germany a substitute for the jury of the Anglo-American common-law court. Together with the single professional judge, chosen in the manner just indicated, there sit for each civil or criminal case two lay judges. This is the rule not only in the peoples' courts at the bottom of the judicial ladder but also for each of the higher courts, including the supreme court of the republic, when these higher courts sit as a court of original jurisdiction, i.e., when they try a case that has not been heard in any lower court. This is the rule also for the federal courts, including the Supreme Court of the U.S.S.R., when it tries a case as a court of original jurisdiction.

The lay judges are chosen differently for each court. At the bottom level, they are elected, under a 1958 reform, for two years at general meetings of colleagues at their place of work or residence. At the upper levels, they are appointed by the same soviet that appoints the professional judge. While they are, therefore, chosen to serve over a period of years, they sit for not more than ten days each year. They are not lawyers but laymen, who are supposed to add a democratic flavor to the bench. They are selected to bring to a case, whether criminal or civil, the common-sense approach of the members of the community, just as the jury contributes this element in the common-law court of the United States.

The lay judges of the Soviet courts have greater authority in a sense than the American jury, because they are permitted by law to share with the professional judge the decision of all questions, whether relating to the determination of the credibility of a witness or to the meaning of a statute. In the United States the jury is not permitted to determine the meaning of a statute. The American jury is ordered only to determine facts. Its task is usually to decide whether to believe a witness.

While he has greater formal authority than the American juror, the Soviet lay judge is subjected to more guidance than the American juror, for the Soviet professional judge sits with the lay judges to determine the court's decision. In the United States the judge may not go to the jury room with the jurors. He can tell them what law is applicable and sometimes what he thinks of the evidence, but he cannot sit with them. They are free to do as they please when they are alone, and they occasionally make a finding which is quite contrary to what the judge has suggested.

Although Soviet lay judges can under their law outvote a professional judge, the outside world has been informed of only a very few cases in which this has happened. These cases have been recounted by former Soviet lawyers who have fled to the West, and one is reported in the Soviet official reports. Generally the lay judges are believed to be quite docile in accepting the proposals of the professional judge. They rarely ask questions at the trial or show any independence of view. Nevertheless, they provide an opportunity to the general public to share in the decision, and as such they may help the Soviet leaders to maintain popular support for the regime.

It is not entirely accurate to say that the Soviet lay judges represent the general public. While very few of them are members of the Communist party, they are selected by institutions in each district, such as factories, farms, universities, retail stores, and army units. The Communist party shares in the selection by these institutions, and the nominations are unopposed. In consequence, the panels from which lay judges are called for service are not cross-sections of the entire population as are the panels from which jurors are selected in the United States. For trials in the Supreme Court of the U.S.S.R., the panel of lay judges is even less representative, for it is small and is composed of the cream of Communist party leadership to be found in the various major institutions of the country, the army, and soviets, the administrative apparatus, the trade unions, the educational institutions, and the collective farms.

Procedural Guarantees and the Exceptions

Procedure within the courts has been made to correspond in general with what the world accepts as necessary for a fair trial. The code of criminal procedure established the basic principles of orality, publicity, confrontation of witnesses, the right to introduce evidence, the right to counsel, the right to be informed of the charge, and the right to appeal. The code of civil procedure offers the same opportunities to present one's case and to rebut the position of the other party in open court with counsel.

Some of the procedural guarantees are incorporated in the U.S.S.R. Constitution, such as the right to counsel, the right to public trial, and the right to an interpreter. In spite of this fact, these guarantees are made subject to such exceptions as may be established by law, and the law has, in fact, created exceptions. One of the exceptions established by law is that public trial need not be granted when the offense involves a sex crime or when relevant military or diplomatic interests of the U.S.S.R. cannot be disclosed. Another exception which was kept until 1956 was that right to counsel did not extend to trials involving terroristic acts against Soviet officials or attempts to unseat the regime defined in that part of the criminal code devoted to "counterrevolutionary" crime. Further, there was in the law in effect until 1956 denial of the right to appeal in such cases, and in trials for terroristic acts or assassination of Soviet officials, the accused did not have to be present at the trial.

In the political exceptions to the usual rules of procedure, the Soviet policy-makers again demonstrated their readiness to withdraw from the general pattern of protection espoused by all democratic peoples those cases which in their opinion threatened the very continuation of the regime. Their decision to maintain such exceptional methods until 1956 was the more remarkable because of the opportunities they have had to control the final outcome of any case. Through the appellate courts, they always have had the opportunity to bring an undesirable decision of a lower court before judges chosen for the appellate courts because of their extensive political training. There would seem to have been no danger in permitting a defendant to appeal through the usual procedure to the court next higher above the one in which his trial occurred. The appellate bench for the peoples' court is the provincial court, and appeals from the provincial court when it sits as a court of original jurisdiction go to the supreme court of the republic concerned. Perhaps in recognition of the protection provided by the appellate procedure, Stalin's heirs made their decision in 1956 to eliminate the political exceptions to ordinary procedural rights. In doing so, they have probably won praise from those who do not appreciate the controls remaining.

When a court hears an appeal, it has no lay judges on the bench. All three judges are selected from the panel of professional judges available at that level. Under such circumstances, the policy-makers' decision under Stalin to allow no appeals seems to have been a vote of no confidence in the political wisdom of the professional judges in the higher courts. This conclusion is fortified by the fact that, even if the appellate court should have taken a position contrary to the desires of the policy-makers at the highest level, the procedural code provided before 1956 and still provides another chance for the government to require a review. Under the code, either the Prosecutor-General of the U.S.S.R. or the President of the Supreme Court of the U.S.S.R. may ask for a review of the record by the appellate college of the Supreme Court of the U.S.S.R. Should the appellate college of the Supreme Court of the U.S.S.R. again decide against the interests of the state, as interpreted by the highest policy-makers of the Communist party, another review may be had by the Plenum of the Supreme Court of the U.S.S.R., on which sit all judges of the various colleges of the Supreme Court.

With so many possibilities to change the decision of the trial court on appeal to the next higher court and on subsequent review by courts right up to the level of the full bench of the Supreme Court of the U.S.S.R., the denial prior to 1956 of the right of appeal in political cases could have had only one object, to deter potential assassins and those seeking to bring about a new revolution by striking terror into their hearts. They were being advised that they could be assured of no escape from execution. In this is another example of the value the Communist party has found in terrorizing as an instrument of government to prevent the unseating of the regime. The good will of the people at home and abroad that was gained from the adoption of procedural due process for the routine cases was sacrificed when the vital cord of the regime was in danger.

The Status of the Presumption of Innocence

Another element of what the American court considers vital to the concept of due process of law is missing from Soviet codes. This is the presumption of innocence, which operates to require the state, through the prosecutor, to prove that the crime has actually been committed. Under the system in use in most Western countries, the prosecutor may not lay his charge before the judge and ask the defendant to disprove it. The prosecutor must prove his charge, even when the defendant refuses to take the stand and respond to questions. While this procedural protection of the defendant is often exasperating to a prosecutor who feels that he has a good case, so good in fact that he can presume the defendant guilty and especially if the defendant will not take the stand in his own defense, mankind throughout the centuries has reached the conclusion that the only fair trial is the one in which the defendant must be presumed innocent at the outset.

Soviet law contains no such written statement of presumption of innocence, but Soviet text writers have said that the presumption exists. They argue that it exists because the law guarantees the right of counsel and they say that such a guarantee is meaningless unless the attorney retained by the defendant can have an opportunity to present his client's defense. These authors seem to feel that if a citizen were presumed guilty, there would be no reason to give him any chance to defend himself, so that any right to defense naturally carries with it the presumption of innocence.

This view was restated in 1958 when new fundamental principles for criminal procedure were adopted. Although jurists on the drafting committee urged specific declaration of the existence in Soviet law of a presumption of innocence, non-jurists argued that common people would not understand what it meant, for they could not but suppose that when an accused was brought to trial, the prosecutor and the preliminary investigator must have had good reason to conclude him guilty. The presumption was not incorporated, although the President of the Supreme Court of the U.S.S.R. restated in his speech to the Supreme Soviet as a deputy, perhaps in an effort to make his point in the stenographic minutes, that the procedural guarantee of the new codes rested on the assumption of the existence of a presumption of innocence, even though it was not stated explicitly.

Westerners have been rather doubtful of the effectiveness of such an argument in times of stress. They would prefer having the presumption of innocence spelled out, and this is usually done in the West. It is particularly important in procedural systems structured upon the customary pattern of Continental European countries, as is the U.S.S.R., for in those countries there is always a lengthy preliminary investigation before trial, which is unknown to Anglo-American procedure. The Soviet preliminary investigation is a hearing before an investigator who is a civil servant subject to the administrative control of the prosecutor's office. Under the Soviet procedural code, he is supposed to conduct an impartial hearing like that of a judge, in spite of his administrative link to the prosecutor. He is required by law to hear not only those witnesses brought by the police and by the prosecutor but also all witnesses and evidence that the defendant wishes to introduce. On the basis of careful weighing of all of this evidence, the investigator prepares a conclusion supported by the record of his investigation, from which the prosecutor can prepare the indictment. The indictment and the record are then sent to the court for use in the trial, which means that at a Soviet trial the judges have before them a record, often in several volumes of typewritten and handwritten notes, of what every witness said on the occasion of the preliminary investigation. The judge has only to work through the material, calling the witnesses and seeing whether they adhere to their prior testimony.

It is a rare Soviet judge, on the admission of Soviet text writers themselves, who can resist the conclusion that the investigator's work must have proved guilt. While the judge is supposed to consider the accused innocent, he has a hard time approaching the case as if the accused were innocent. He is likely to try to prove the record before him rather than to verify it. Under Soviet rules of procedure, a judge may ask any question he wants and cross-examine witnesses himself. He is not limited to listening to the direct and cross-examination by prosecutor and defense attorney, as is the case in some American states. In consequence, the judge can, and often does, appear to be a second prosecutor acting on the basis of the record before him.

The great threat to the presumption of innocence presented by the preliminary investigation has caused even Soviet authors to argue that the accused should be permitted to have counsel at the preliminary investigation as well as at the trial. Their arguments were partially successful in obtaining reform in 1958, but only for juvenile delinquents. For them counsel is now to be permitted, but for adults the preliminary investigator may exclude counsel if he so desires from the preliminary investigation. Exclusion has been countenanced lest he obtain suggestions that would permit the concealing of evidence from the prosecution or learn secrets that might be harmful to the state.

The Soviet Lawyer

Such emphasis upon the importance of counsel must take into

consideration the character of the lawyer in Soviet circumstance. In all systems of the law, to be permitted to practice, the lawyer must be licensed by the court or by some administrative body such as a ministry of justice. Such licensing is thought to be necessary as a protection to clients against incompetency or criminality on the part of attorneys. In the U.S.S.R., lawyers are licensed by the ministry of justice of each republic under an instruction issued by the federal ministry. They must pass bar examinations administered by the ministry of the republic. The major differences between the Soviet and the American lawyers are not in licensing. They lie in other places.

On the organizational side, the Soviet lawyer practices in an office operated by the republic's college of advocates, to which he is admitted after passing the requirements of an educational and character nature. These offices are placed in areas believed to be convenient for clients, by the authorities in the ministry of justice of each republic. Although no law prohibits private practice, there are now no private practitioners. All lawyers work in the offices of a college of advocates. Within these offices, operations are conducted like those of a partnership. One member is selected as manager by vote of all of the members. When a client calls for assistance, he may choose his preferred lawyer, and, if he has none, the manager assigns one. When fees are paid, they are allocated first, in a given proportion, to meet the operating expense of the office, and the balance is paid to the lawyer who did the work. Fees are set by regulation in accordance with a scale based upon time spent and type of work done. Since the scale has to be flexible to meet the varying demands upon an attorney, there is still some room for negotiation of the fee with a client. Fees may even be waived, if the client is too poor to pay.

From the organization side, it is evident that there is more control over the activity of a lawyer than would be found in an American state in which lawyers conduct their practice on a private basis. In actuality, a Soviet attorney is rather free to choose the cases he will accept and reject and to decide upon the measures he will take to represent his client, but he is always mindful that the success of his career is subject to the pleasure of his colleagues in the office, and they in turn develop attitudes which they believe to be favored by the Communist party.

In this effort to please a monopoly political party lies the major difference between the Soviet attorney and his American counterpart. The difference will be seen to be deeper than any organizational framework of the bar. It lies at the base of the Soviet one-party system of government, as a result of which the lawyer will be wary of unpopular causes. There is no large and powerful opposition to which he can turn for protection in the event that his client's case is unpopular politically. In the routine case involving no politics, the Soviet lawyer seems to feel free to defend his client's interest as he will, but in the political case he has to limit his activities to what the Communist party policy-makers feel is permissible defense.

In the early days of the Soviet regime, the lawyer's lot was more difficult. There was a tendency on the part of the public and even of Communist party members to feel that a criminal defendant and a civil plaintiff were politically questionable characters. It was presumed that the police would not have arrested a person unless he were guilty and that a civil plaintiff in bringing suit was taking advantage of some poor workman who could not pay his debts. A lawyer taking such cases was associated in the public mind with the unpopular position of the client.

In the early days there was no appreciation of the attitude that Western societies have taken toward the role of lawyers, namely, that no one can be sure of what really happened until after the trial, for if one could be sure, why should there be a trial at all? Westerners believe that the trial will not produce the true facts unless all interested parties are given a chance to state their case. This requires a lawyer, for few individuals are sufficiently alert in the excitement of a courtroom, even if they have knowledge of legal procedures, to make the decisions necessary to present their case well. All this experience of the centuries with the conduct of a lawsuit was discarded by the Soviet citizens of the early years in their attitude toward trials and lawyers.

A Changed Attitude toward the Bar

During the last twenty years there has been creeping back in the U.S.S.R. an appreciation of the lesson of the centuries. Soviet authors now attempt to explain to their public that society is harmed if the innocent are punished or if a negligent driver is not made to pay for damage as the result of a civil suit to determine fault. If an innocent man is punished, the guilty one is left at large to commit the same crime again, to the injury of the state and of the society that it professes to protect. If a negligent driver does not have to pay damages as the result of a civil suit, he feels no restraint for the future. In consequence, effective defense is beneficial to the state and to society and should be encouraged. It makes certain that those who are really at fault are punished.

Even prosecutors have written to the editors of the journal of the Ministry of Justice of the U.S.S.R. urging that a defense attorney be permitted to appear at the preliminary investigation. The argument they give is that errors can creep into the most carefully prepared prosecution, and it would help the prosecutor to know that a lawyer representing the accused was watchful against such errors. In short, defense is desirable because it protects the state.

As in other areas of Soviet activity, the position has lost support up to the present time in highest quarters when a terrorist act was committed or when there was a conspiracy to overthrow the regime. It may have seemed to Soviet policy-makers that in such vital cases the prosecutor's staff could afford to assign to the matter a sufficient number of men to review all possibilities so as to make certain that the accused was guilty. One of the prosecutors could take the role of devil's advocate to make sure that no stone was left unturned. In the case of an assassination, the would-be assassin was usually caught in the act, so that there could be no question of guilt anyway. In consequence, a defense attorney may have seemed unnecessary to protect the state.

The world's interest in the presence of defense attorneys at a trial is so great, however, that in the purge trials of the late 1930's defense attorneys were assigned to some of the defendants by the college of advocates at the request of the court. Being in a situation where Stalin's own hand had formulated some of the charges and knowing that guilt was dictated by him before the trial began, the defense attorneys limited their defense. They acknowledged that their clients were guilty. They argued only that their clients had not been instigators of the alleged plot but had been led into it because of their weak wills after years of exemplary living. Clemency was asked and nothing more.

This being the political situation as it affects the activity of the Soviet lawyer, it can be seen that there are limitations on him that are not to be found in Western society. The Soviet state has, apparently, appreciated this danger. To compensate for it, there is placed upon the prosecution a duty to watch out for the interests of defendants and of parties to civil suits. It has already been indicated how the prosecutor may, and does, intervene in civil suits when he believes that the interests of the state are jeopardized by the impending defeat of one of the parties.

A Special Role for Prosecutors

The prosecutor of a republic may, and often does, intervene also in criminal cases, after a sentence has been pronounced and after a provincial or county prosecutor has obtained a verdict against the accused. The higher prosecutor is supposed to be more than a prosecutor. He is supposed to see to the correct application of the law. It may be that a lower prosecutor has made a mistake, and it is the superior's task to verify from time to time the work of the lower courts and to select for review by higher courts those cases that have not gone forward for review on appeal because the defendant did not press his case.

To assure that the prosecutor will not be influenced by the Communist party politicians at the local level, the structure of the prosecutor's office is completely centralized. Unlike the judges, who are named by the process of election at the local level and by the appropriate soviet at higher levels, the prosecutors from top to bottom are named by the Prosecutor-General of the U.S.S.R., although on the advice of the prosecutors of the republics. The Prosecutor-General in turn is named by the Supreme Soviet of the U.S.S.R. for a seven-year term. By this system, the prosecutors are always subject to influence by the highest Communist party circles, but they do not have to seek appointment by fawning upon local party bosses, nor need they fear for their jobs if they displease local party bosses who are tending to become local tyrants.

To the Western student of the Soviet system, it seems incredible that prosecutors, even under such structural protection, can think in two ways, as a prosecutor and as a defender. Yet the court reports are full of actions brought by prosecutors in the supreme courts of the republics and even before colleges of the Supreme Court of the U.S.S.R. to set aside a conviction of a trial court. The procedure does not appeal to those accustomed to a system that permits a series of appeals to the highest tribunals in the states of the United States, and sometimes to the Supreme Court of the United States, with the help of a fearless attorney who does not have to rely for his livelihood upon the political party in power. It is for this reason that the right to independent counsel in all cases and the right of appeal to the highest tribunal have been cherished so long in the West. These comprise some of the many marks distinguishing the Soviet system from those in the Western democracies.

CHAPTER 12

EMPLOYMENT BY THE STATE

State employment of labor has become a primary characteristic of the Soviet system of government, and it has affected vitally the lives of many Soviet citizens. To the Westerner, the result seems at times to be a new form of economic serfdom. To the Soviet propagandist, the system seems to provide the only way of achieving the maximum production that he believes essential to the working of a real democracy. An examination of the rules governing state employment and of the reaction of Soviet citizens to them will provide an opportunity to end this study of the Soviet system at a point close to the lives of individuals, where the impact of government is felt most strongly. In the final analysis, for a very large number of people in every country the ultimate acceptance or rejection of a system of government stems from the system's effect upon the job.

At the outset, it is necessary to recall that not everyone in the U.S.S.R. is employed by the state. The members of a collective farm are in theory co-owners of their agricultural enterprise, receiving not wages for their work but a share in the total net product of the farm. Although the activities of these farmers are prescribed by numerous laws and regulations, which are enforced in practice by the Communist party's discipline enforced on farm chairmen, the collective farmers are not state employees, as are their fellow farmers on the state farm.

There are still a considerable number of artisans at work in the U.S.S.R. Many of these perform their work as cobblers, tailors, repairmen, and wood-carvers at a popular crossing of two paths in a village or under the stairwell of an apartment house in a city. Most of these are now organized in artisan co-operative associations that have much the same organizational structure as the collective farms.

Membership meetings choose managers who conduct both the buying of raw materials available locally and the sale of the produce in the open markets or through consumers' co-operatives. Within these artisan co-operatives there is much more freedom than within the collective farms, because the government seems to feel that their items of manufacture are not as essential to the well-being of society as is the produce of the farms. Nevertheless, the government relies on these artisans for production of many small items such as coathangers, peasant furniture, table utensils, and individual farm implements, and their total produce is taken into consideration in making the annual state plan. The head of their national association reports on the operation of the system in the meetings of the Supreme Soviet, and the system clearly has an important place in satisfying some of the needs of consumers.

Considerable numbers of domestic servants are employed by private families so that wives and mothers can be freed of the duties of the home to pursue careers in the professions. Also, herdsmen are employed by collective farmers to watch those flocks that remain the private property of the households. While the number of these private employees is even today of some statistical importance, private employment is believed to be diminishing. This is because nurseries, laundries, and dining halls are lifting from the professional woman with a family some of the burdens that she has up to now been passing to a domestic servant or to the children's grandmother.

There are still some categories of professional persons who can be said to be self-employed. Lawyers perform their services in co-operative associations of lawyers organized under the auspices of the college of advocates, as has been indicated earlier. They receive no wage but a share of the fees commensurate with their work. Occasionally, up to very recent years, the most skilful of them have conducted private practice from their homes, but this time seems to have passed. Home practice is also a feature of the life of the medical doctors, but today this is always an after-hours practice, for the doctors are employed in clinics and hospitals by the Ministry of Public Health and spend the greater part of each day as state employees.

To support prospecting for precious metals and the trapping of furs, citizens are still encouraged to take to the trails of Siberia and of the Far North. It is these prospectors and trappers who, perhaps, alone retain the characteristics of what Americans have

called "rugged individualism." Yet, even these last of the individualists of the private enterprise era have no choice in the disposition
of their hauls. The gold and platinum must be sold to the State
Bank and the furs to the state enterprise dealing in this item. No
fur trapper can seek independent bids from firms interested in his
pelts.

Such private enterprise as there is suffers further discouragement
from the personal income tax statutes. While all Soviet citizens are
required to pay an income tax graduated in accordance with the
amount of their income, the private enterpriser is subjected to a
higher rate than those employed by the state. In consequence, the
doctor who is tempted to practice after hours in his home thinks
twice about the extent to which he may be able to retain the fees
he can collect. The social insurance rate for injury hampering employment is also lower by half for those domestic servants and
herdsmen of collective-farm households who choose private employment in the only areas still permitted instead of employment by
the state, and there is no social insurance for the self-employed
who loses his capacity to work.

Making a Career

For the ambitious young man or woman seeking a career in
Soviet society as it is today, the only thought will be of state employment. State employment opens the road to power, prestige, a
desirable apartment in the multiple dwellings maintained by state
agencies, and a steady income followed by a state pension. For the
most able of the young people, the road begins at graduation from
the compulsory eight-year state elementary schools. There are no
private schools of any kind. Because the Soviet school system entered upon a three- to five-year period of transition following the
school reform law of 1958, the route to a career is not as clear as
before the reform. Prior to 1958 the gifted student who completed
the combined elementary and high school program of ten years at
the age of seventeen or eighteen entered the university or a professional school without examination if he had demonstrated high
scholastic achievement. Those less brilliant took competitive examinations in mathematics, the Russian language and literature,
history of the peoples of the U.S.S.R., the Constitution of the
U.S.S.R., chemistry, physics, and one foreign language. Each institution had a quota for admission established with regard to open-
ings expected to be available on graduation. Community gossip
provided some idea to applicants of their opportunities.

The school reform of 1958 revolutionized the educational system with the stated purpose of preparing high school students not solely for university admission as in the past but for a life declared to require for the majority proficiency in manual skills. To provide this vocational approach the compulsory elementary school was set at eight years of general education combined with some vocational experience. Thereafter, the most gifted in the sciences, mathematics, music, and the graphic arts were to be permitted to proceed, as exceptions to the general rule, to one of a limited number of three-year schools preparing for university education in these fields. The others were to enter one of several types of schools offering different combinations of general and vocational education as well as practical work in industrial production and agriculture. After the three-year course those graduates wishing to proceed to professional education were to apply to the universities, demonstrating their scholastic proficiency and submitting letters of recommendation from Komsomol, Communist party, and trade-union officials as well as from directors of industrial plants or chairmen of collective farms. Priority in admission is to be given to those with records in production. For those who enter the university over this path there can be subsequent graduate programs leading to advanced degrees.

The age of fifteen or sixteen is, therefore, a momentous one for those hoping for a white-collar career. Very few individuals have been able subsequently to move into the coveted ranks of the "intellectuals" if they did not obtain entry at the point when professional education began. To be sure, there were much-heralded exceptions, as when a workman by some invention or rationalization of work proved his mental powers. In such cases he might be catapulted with great public acclaim into a professional school for further training, but these were the exceptions and not the rule. The separation of those who will eventually be favored as the technicians, the managers, and the intellectuals generally, from those who must remain throughout their lives at the level of the manual laborer, occurs at an early age.

Social Mobility

In the West, of recent years, the question has been discussed whether any real choice exists for the sons of workmen and peasants in the U.S.S.R. at the age of decision or whether they may be expected to continue their parents' activities at the work bench and at the plow. In an effort to determine whether the professed favoritism of Soviet leaders toward workmen and peasants in the new Russia had resulted in greater social mobility than is to be found in the West, the Harvard team of interviewers asked a series of questions of 2,725 refugees in Western Europe and in the United States during 1950 and 1951. The interviewers concluded that worker or peasant background had been a severe handicap to social mobility in the 1920's but that the situation had changed sharply in the 1930's.

The chances of a person who had been a worker or peasant before the Revolution to move into a white-collar or non-manual-worker group in the years between 1917 and 1929 were found to be only one-seventh as good as the chances for those who came from what the bolsheviks called the former "exploiter" classes. These had been the aristocracy, landowners, former Tsarist civil servants, intellectuals, army officers, merchants, and priests. While the interview sample may have been biased, in that probably fewer of those who had made the transition from one class to another had been sufficiently disgruntled with the Soviet system to flee, the statistics for the 1920's are not thought to be unduly unrepresentative since in all functionally specialized societies the rate of mobility possible within a single generation has been found to be low.

The rate of mobility in Soviet society during the 1920's, to be specific, was found by the interviewers to be 12.1 per cent. This meant that 102 persons out of the sample group of 840 members of the working class had been able to change their status. This contrasted with the success of 607 out of the sample group of 705 members of the former "exploiter" classes in retaining their white-collar status after the Revolution. The interviewers concluded that the high rate of retention of status by the former white-collar groups was due in part to the decision of the Communist party leaders to utilize specialists of the old regime in posts for which new specialists could not be trained quickly.

By the 1930's, the process of educating the masses had progressed markedly. The illiteracy rate, which had stood at 50 per cent as late as 1926, was pushed back to 20 per cent in 1939. The five-year plans were inaugurated to speed up industrialization, thus creating the need for large numbers of technicians and managers. The interview statistics indicate a reflection of these developments: the rate of mobility from the worker-peasant category to the non-manual category jumped from 12.1 per cent in the 1920's to 29.5 per cent in the 1930's.

The percentile increase is computed from the fact that 190 persons out of a group of 644 sons and daughters of working-class parents had been successful in moving into the white-collar or "intellectual" category. They did so, however, without pushing out the sons and daughters of persons who had been in the non-manual category before the Revolution, for the statistics show that 89.7 per cent of this group had been able to retain the favored position as compared with 73.9 per cent in the 1920's.

To determine how the Soviet rate of social mobility compared with a Western rate, the interviewers took a table prepared by Dewey and Anderson from a sample American community in 1933–34. This showed that 26.4 per cent of the persons who started their first permanent job as manual workers had been able to move into the non-manual category by the time of the investigation. Robert A. Feldmesser has concluded from his analysis of the Soviet statistics that social mobility in the U.S.S.R. has been the result of industrialization and that the figures are about what one would find in other industrialized societies. If this be so, the opportunity for choice of a profession at the age of decision in the U.S.S.R. is about what it is elsewhere. The children of parents who have the educational background associated with the non-manual categories of workers still have the greatest opportunity to gain admission to the professions. This is not because of any bias in their favor but simply because it is easier to maintain good records in school and to pass entrance examinations if parents are interested in such success and provide the environment in which academic pursuits find encouragement and stimulation.

Compulsory Assignment to Jobs

The Soviet youth who has been successful in placing his foot upon the ladder of the professions through completion of training at the university or at a professional school may have been chosen for his career through much the same process as is familiar to youths of the West, but at this point the structure of the Soviet system introduces a new feature. In the West, with the exception of students trained at state expense in military academies, a graduate is not required to pursue the profession for which he was trained, even if he has attended a state university. In the U.S.S.R. it is different.

Graduates of Soviet professional schools are required by law to serve for three years in the post to which they are assigned by the ministry for which they have been trained. It is argued by Soviet officials that it would be a social waste to do otherwise. Students have received stipends during their period of professional training, and they have been relieved of the duty to pay tuition. To a Soviet official mind, they owe service to the state in return for what they have received.

To avoid hardship, personal wishes are respected by the officials who make the assignments. Wives are not sent to cities apart from those in which their husbands are to work. Health factors are considered. Yet in most cases the jobs requiring recruits are in the remote provinces. It is the rare student who is assigned to Moscow, Leningrad, or Kiev, although the Soviet press has recently declared that some students have sought to use influence within the ministry to obtain the coveted posts in these cities. If a student refuses to go to the place of his assignment, or refuses to remain at the assigned post for the three years required, he is subject to prosecution.

From the foregoing, it is to be seen that the top ministerial administrators of the future, and the directors and technical directors of public corporations, are selected from the pool of experts created by the educational programs of the universities and of the professional schools. Those who have not been able to obtain admission to such schools are deprived of nearly all subsequent opportunity to cross the barrier between manual labor and the professional positions. These comprise the great pool from which employment directors meet their needs for unskilled labor.

A shortage of semiskilled personnel seems to have been felt just before World War II, for in 1940 a labor draft was instituted. Under the provisions of the labor-draft law, young men and women, on completion of their studies in the ten-year schools or at such time as they dropped out of school because of lack of ability or desire to continue beyond the required minimum of seven years, were subject to the labor draft. Local boards composed of the adult members of each rural and urban community decided which of the youths whom they knew were most suitable for a semiskilled education. Quotas were established for each community and filled from those young people who had not progressed to the university or to the professional school or who had not been drafted for military service under the conscription law.

The youths of both sexes who were drafted under the labor-reserve program had to serve four years. Their work began with a short course of technical training to fit them for an apprenticeship that led eventually to a position of foreman. They were uniformed and subjected to discipline only slightly less vigorous than that of the military. Eventually they were assigned to their place of work by the Ministry of Labor Reserves and its successor agency, to become the nucleus of a large industrial army of semiskilled workmen. In the first nine years of operation, the program trained four and a half million youths.

Since 1956 the labor-reserve officials have boasted that the system is filled by volunteers choosing this opportunity to rise above the level of common labor. If this is true—and it may be so, since manuals for officials show the draft to have been repealed in 1955—compulsion disappeared from recruitment to the labor-reserve system at the time that wartime legislation compelling adults to remain on the job was revoked, although the administrative manuals state that those who have received labor-reserve schooling must work at their place of assignment for four years. With the school reform of 1958 the labor-reserve schools are to be absorbed over a three- to five-year period in the regular school system, which will be oriented around vocational education except for the gifted few. There is no suggestion that a draft is contemplated to fill quotas.

Civil Service Regulation

For the unskilled workmen and clerks, there is no national recruitment program. The employment officers on the operating level of each ministry and of each public corporation are left completely free to choose whom they wish for the jobs they have to fill. No panel of available candidates is prepared by a civil service commission, as is the case generally in the West with state employment.

Regulations on such recruitment are few. The criminal code punishes any discrimination on the basis of race, religion, or sex. This latter basis for discrimination has been the subject of much trouble in the case of pregnant women who apply for jobs. Employment officers hesitate to employ a woman in this condition, for they know that soon she will take maternity leave, during which time she draws her regular pay, and at the end of her leave she must be returned to her job. Under the system of budgeted wages established for all state agencies, there will be costs from which there will be no return.

The policy-makers of the state have set up a budgeted wage system to assure maximum value from the wages expended; yet in the instance of the pregnant-woman worker they are faced with a competing value, the desire to increase the birth rate to provide a larger pool of labor supply and to man the armed services at the levels desired. Further, there is a public opinion problem, for there would be considerable hostility on the part of the women of the land if they found themselves excluded from jobs when about to bear children. In the face of these considerations, the policy-makers have found it necessary to include an article in the criminal code punishing managers of state enterprises who discriminate against pregnant women in their employment policies.

Close relationship by blood or marriage is the sole basis for legal discrimination in employment, and then only if one of the persons would be subject to the supervision of another. From this exclusionary rule are excepted technicians in a post office and in a telegraph agency, teachers, artists, musicians, medical doctors, agronomists, meteorologists, and laboratory workers. Presumably kinship makes no difference in the performance of duties by such professionals, or the demand for them may be so great that the risk of influence must be overlooked in the interest of getting things done.

No civil service examinations are given for positions in the state services and public corporations, it being assumed that the records in the schools are sufficiently uniform to provide a basis for judging the relative ability of every applicant. Further reason for the absence of a standard examination may be that with the present shortage of labor there is no pressure for admission to state employment, with the result that few if any allegations of favoritism in making appointments are made. Conditions are different from those in some other countries, in which employment is the subject of stiff competition and in which the civil service law requires that every candidate for a job be rated against his competitors on the basis of a uniform examination.

The functions to be performed in every job are described, as they are in the public services of other countries, in a civil service manual that provides uniformity throughout the entire country. Each job is given a rating to which is attached a specific wage scale. The scale varies with the qualifications of the incumbent, so that the wage will be higher if the incumbent has specified academic qualifications such as the Master's or Doctor's degree, if he accumulates years of service, or if he works in a remote location or in an especially dangerous place such as the psychiatric ward of a hospital. By this means, incentive encouragement is given those to whom the piecework system is inapplicable, such as medical doctors, teachers, directors of administrative bureaus, and the like.

Dismissals are a source of friction in any society. Even in private enterprise economies, the circumstances under which dismissals may occur are becoming the basis of contract regulation as the result of collective bargaining between management and labor unions. While there is no law in the United States forbidding a private employer to dismiss whom he will, there have come into being strict laws governing employment by state and federal governments in their respective civil services. For such employment, dismissals are regimented so that they may not occur without a hearing, meeting the tests of due process of law, in which the facts meriting dismissal are proved.

With its wide application of a system of public employment, the Soviet government found it necessary to define the circumstances under which dismissals might occur. This was done in the Code of Labor Laws, adopted in each Soviet republic in 1922 to meet the needs of the New Economic Policy when limited private enterprise was being reintroduced. While the rules were designed to restrain private employers, they were made equally applicable to the state managers, and they are presently of concern only to these, as private employment for productive purposes is now constitutionally forbidden. Their validity for conditions of monopoly state employment was restated in 1959 when they were incorporated with little change in the fundamentals for Soviet labor legislation published for discussion by the federal government prior to adoption in 1960.

The rules for dismissal are quite similar to those existing for the civil service of other lands. No one may be dismissed unless there is: compete or partial abolition of an office or reduction in its work load, termination of the position for which a person was employed, incompetency, recurrent failure without a satisfactory reason to perform duties assigned, commission of a criminal offense in connection with the work, failure to be present at work without excuse, failure to resume work for four consecutive months after restoration of capacity to work, or displacement by a reinstated person formerly performing the functions of the incumbent. During World War II absence for twenty minutes was made grounds for prosecution. While prosecution is no longer permitted, the twenty-minute rule probably represents the tolerance allowed before dismissal may occur.

Grievance Procedure

Established standards of conduct are always accompanied by disputes as to whether, in any given situation, the standards are met. A grievance procedure has been provided in private enterprise countries by management and labor, under which management and the labor union determine whether the provisions of a collective bargaining agreement relating to dismissal have been met. In the U.S.S.R. a grievance procedure is also provided, but it is established by law and not in collective bargaining agreement. Under the Soviet procedure, a system of grievance boards exists under the administrative supervision of each labor union's apparatus. These boards contain equal representation of the labor union to which the disgruntled workman belongs and of the management for which he works.

The very placing of the grievance boards under the supervision of one of the interested parties, namely, the labor union, rather than under an admittedly state agency such as a ministry of labor, which presumably would be impartial as between state manager and labor union, suggests the unusual position in which the labor union has been placed in the U.S.S.R. It has become in a sense a ministry of labor in the eyes of the policy-makers of the Communist party. Since 1930 it has been ordered not to take a position in defense of the interests of laboring men against those of the state managers, because the interests of both are supposed to be identical. To avoid development of any narrow syndicalist attitudes, the trade-union leadership has been related closely to the Communist party leadership, and, in consequence, the transfer of the grievance procedure to the trade-union organization is not the concession to labor that it appears to be. It is not the subordination of the state managers to the trade union, as would be charged in the United States if the Transport Workers Union in New York City were to be made responsible for the conduct of a grievance procedure to settle complaints brought by its members against the agency managing New York City's municipally owned subways. On the contrary, the Soviet labor unions have been so thoroughly absorbed into the state apparatus that the state managers need not ordinarily fear discrimination against them in the grievance boards. There would seem to exist an equal balance which permits decisions of a nature that both sides seem in the main to accept as fair, although some Soviet refugees have reported that management hesitates to tangle with the trade union before a grievance board.

The employee in a Soviet state agency is not bound under the 1959 general principles to bring his case before the grievance board in all situations. He may go directly to a court if he has been discharged from any but a supervisory position. In other cases, however, the law requires that he exhaust the remedy offered by the grievance boards, presumably on the assumption that the matter will usually be one of simple fact that can be determined quickly, informally, and accurately by men on the spot who know the conditions of employment. A disgruntled employee may appeal the grievance board's decision to the trade-union committee in the factory, shop, or locality concerned. Examination of the case is required by the trade-union committee if the grievance board is unable to agree on a solution.

If the trade-union committee fails to satisfy the employee or management, in cases unrelated to dismissal, the disgruntled party may take the case to court. Once he is there, he has available to him the usual route of an appeal to a higher court, and even intervention by a prosecutor or a president of a supreme court, to bring the matter before the supreme court of the republic or of the U.S.S.R.

Management is permitted to make some decisions without fear of review. Thus it may discharge employees who have the authority to hire or discharge other employees, and it may also discharge various officials having posts of such sensitivity as to preclude a public airing of their qualifications and their performance, such as, for example, agents of the Ministry of Internal Affairs.

Numerous judicial decisions having to do with labor disputes arising before the 1959 reform provide insight into Soviet society. In addition, there are reports of lawyers who have fled the Soviet Union after years of service as advisers on labor matters to Soviet managers. From these reports it is possible to conclude that, through the procedures provided to protect an employee in a job, the great majority of disgruntled Soviet employees have been able to obtain redress against a foreman who has been arbitrary in recommending a dismissal. The court will order reinstatement. Perhaps the most illuminating case involved the dismissal for incompetency of an elderly woman by the management of a village clinic. The case was pressed by the employee until it reached the Supreme Court of the U.S.S.R., which concluded that there had been insufficient study of the woman's qualifications by the lower tribunals through which the case had gone.

The Disadvantages of Monopoly Employment

The disadvantages of monopoly employment by state agencies would seem to be numerous, to one who is used to the private enterprise system. First and foremost is the disadvantage created by the Soviet government's attitude toward employees of the Soviet state. The government has tended over the years to treat employees as if they were resources, like cement or bricks or steel. The economic planners began their planning with control over the distribution of electrical power, on the theory that with limited control over a vital necessity of all industry they could influence industrial development as a whole. They moved into the planning of production and distribution of all key resources, leaving outside the allocation system only those locally produced and consumed. As Soviet planners have found themselves plagued by the tendency of employees to move from job to job in search of better conditions, they have tried to control labor turnover by prohibiting it, and, finally, under the strain of World War II, they moved to the allocation of labor to meet production needs.

In anticipation of war, all employees were frozen in their respective jobs in June, 1940, and became subject to prosecution if they left the job without permission of management. Management was required to give permission only if an employee was in ill-health or had been admitted to a school of higher learning to improve his or her skills. When entire factories were moved to new locations behind the Urals from areas of the Ukraine and western Russia threatened by the German advance, the employees were required to accompany the plant. Permanent cities were built for the employees, from which they were not permitted to depart after the war. From the state officials' point of view, production would have been lost if the individuals had been permitted to return to the Ukraine of their childhood. Since the welfare of all was thought to depend on maintenance of production, attention to personal desires was not permitted.

Mobility from one job to another was, therefore, reduced sharply in the U.S.S.R. after 1940. Reports coming from the U.S.S.R. as early as 1951 suggested that there was beginning even before Stalin's death a relaxation in the strict restraints formerly enforced against those who wanted to leave their jobs. In 1956 this suggestion was confirmed when the 1940 law was publicly repealed. There has been, however, a renewed propaganda drive to urge employees to remain on the job because of the wastefulness involved in labor turnover. Managers have been asked to discourage moving about, especially on the part of those employees whose training has involved time and expense.

Soviet reliance on the criminal code rather than on economic incentive is to be found in other situations. As in the case of preventing labor turnover by means of criminal law, penalties have been established to encourage faithful performance at the job. Thus, a manager of a state enterprise, as well as the chief engineer or the chief of technical inspection, is subject to prosecution if employees produce goods below standard quality. While the law was not enforced generally during the war, because of the difficulty in obtaining information from consumers in time to take the prescribed measures against the managers and seems under postwar conditions to remain a dead letter, it indicates Soviet attitudes. In a private enterprise system, the quality of goods finds quick reflection in the action of consumers, who will boycott poor quality or demand a reduced price. Managers who are unable to meet consumers' demands will find their enterprise losing money, and they will either lose their jobs, if they are employees themselves, or find themselves insolvent, if they are owners of the establishment. In the U.S.S.R., they are prosecuted if they are found to have been personally at fault.

The Soviet planners have tried to introduce some of the economic controls that result from the application of consumers' choice in a private enterprise system. They have placed identifying symbols in the form of trade marks on state-produced products of different plants, hoping that consumers will boycott the products which they have found by consumption in the past to be poor and choose the ones they have found to be good. The difficulty has been that the rate of production has been so much lower than necessary to meet consumers' desires that the economic method of weeding out poor managers has failed. There have not been enough commodities to give the consumer a choice. The criminal code has been made, therefore, to bear the burden of policing the efficiency of the managers. Rising production may change this situation.

Enforcement of planning directives has also influenced industrial freedom, for the authority of managers to operate the plant as they think best to achieve results has been limited. It happens, apparently, that errors in allocations, or faulty deliveries of goods, result in the accumulation of machine parts or of other supplies that cannot be used in the production process or in the operation of an office. Before 1940, if we may believe the statements of Soviet refugees, managers used to sell these surpluses to managers of other enterprises who had need of them in exchange for items for which they had need. This practice aroused the antagonism of the planning authorities, and an article was added to the criminal code prohibiting it on pain of prosecution.

The criminal penalty did not frighten the managers. They continued to do as they had done and to rely upon the results that they could show in terms of completing a job to justify their violation of the law. Reports of refugees, as analyzed by Joseph S. Berliner, indicate that flouting the details of the law in order to achieve production quotas became so common that scarcely a manager was free of guilt. Many were tried and sentenced, but it is indicative of the hostility that these prosecutions evoked that immediately after Stalin died in 1953 there was a general amnesty of certain categories of prisoners, prominent among whom were the managers who had been convicted of "economic crimes." Further, in 1955 the criminal penalty for disposal of surpluses was revoked, and a review of procedures for distribution of the unneeded products was ordered.

Psychological Reaction to Controls

In spite of the many restraints on job mobility and the criminal penalties for activities that are regulated in private enterprise countries by the operation of the free market system, the Soviet citizen seems to have found compensations that have satisfied him. It has been found almost universally true among the refugees from the Soviet system that they dislike searching for jobs under the free enterprise system. Many of them find themselves unable to become accustomed to an economy in which individuals find their own jobs and enjoy the mobility that such freedom of choice makes possible.

Within the U.S.S.R. itself, students graduating from professional schools have expressed amazement that the graduates of an American law school do not have waiting for them assigned employers to whom to report. It seems to the Soviet students that the security offered them in the assurance of a job, once they gain admission to an educational institution, is essential to their peace of mind. While they often object to the particular assignment that they receive, they seem to be willing to accept restraints on their freedom of choice of jobs because of the apparently no-risk society that they think it makes possible. Their objections, when they have them, are not against the elimination of the economic risks at the expense of job mobility but against the personal political risks in Stalin's system from which they hope now to depart. They want to be assured of just determination of guilt when there is a charge of mismanagement. They want to avoid being purged under circumstances over which they have no control, merely because the man at the top thinks he can achieve a political result by maintaining instability throughout the population.

Lack of job mobility has, however, created strains within the society. During the period that employees were unable to leave their jobs and seek other employment, they were less free from the evil intentions of supervisors than they were in a prosperous free enterprise economy. Dishonest managers in the U.S.S.R. have been said to force bookkeepers into their schemes for defrauding the government. They have made the bookkeeper show profits when there were none, so that bonuses might be paid. The bookkeepers are reported by Soviet refugees often to have been unable to escape the situation because they could not leave and seek employment elsewhere. If they remained without helping falsify the records, they found themselves subject to the managers' discriminatory treatment in the allocation of bonuses from the director's fund.

Court cases indicate that sex crimes also occur in situations where women employees are unable to escape from their jobs and are forced under various ruses to submit to attentions that they abhor. In one reported court case, it was found that actresses were thwarted in their careers in the theater unless they submitted to the desires of the theater manager. Only a plea to the prosecutor can bring relief from the ordeal, yet some have been fearful to make the plea lest it subject them or their friends to the manager's vindictive anger if the prosecutor pays no heed.

To meet the dangers of such circumstances, the Soviet policy-makers have relied upon their law-enforcement agencies more than has been necessary in the private enterprise systems, where there has been possible a measure of self-help in resigning a position to find one elsewhere. For this reason the prosecutors of the U.S.S.R. are probably better known by the populace generally and are certainly more frequently consulted than in Western countries. They are feared for their severity when they turn against an individual, but they may also be a man's or woman's best friend when that man or woman is trapped in a job.

To counter such desires as Soviet citizens may still have for the freedom offered by the private enterprise system, with its opportunities for job mobility, the Soviet propagandists do their best to deny that real mobility exists in private enterprise systems. They seize upon the sad stories of New England towns whose residents are left jobless because they are unable to follow a mill when it moves south to seek more favorable conditions. They ask where mobility is to be found in this situation. They seek out unemployment figures from the period of the great depression to prove that there can be no moving to another job when one is fearful even of losing the one that he has.

The Soviet propagandists make the unusual hardship situation seem like the general rule of Western economies, saying that the Western systems depend for their very existence upon a reserve pool of the unemployed. They ignore the remarkable steps taken in the West since the great depression of the 1930's to iron out extremes from the business cycle. They give no publicity to the success stories of various New England towns whose citizens have banded together to develop new industries for which their skills are fitted and for which there is a market. They give no publicity to the argument that the costs, for a few, of economic dislocation and unemployment are not so great socially as the human cost to all Soviet citizens of their system's numerous restraints on job mobility and freedom of choice and of the frustrating effects of administrative red tape within the confines of a planned economy.

CHAPTER 13

THE PERIL-POINTS

Democratic forms do not assure democratic government. History has proved that there are places at which counterweights can be placed to prevent democratic functioning of the forms. Modern dictators have shown that it is possible to combine democratic forms with counterweights. This has sometimes been done so cleverly at the early stages of a dictator's bid for power that the general public does not see the peril. It does not realize that it is losing the possibility of influencing policy and choosing leaders.

The blending of popular and dictatorial institutions in a fashion that fools the public may be said to be one of the characteristics of the modern totalitarian state. It is here that the totalitarians have been able to improve upon the system of the authoritarians, typified by the Tsars of Russia. The totalitarians have found a way to please the majority of the people, for a time at least, by giving them a parliament, an electoral procedure, trade unions, co-operative associations, local autonomy, a bill of rights, and codes of law. At the same time they have been able to preserve power by the use of controls over the forms that they have established or inherited. The totalitarians have shown that a people can no longer feel safe from the loss of freedom merely because its system of government incorporates democratic forms.

Soviet experience provides an example of the points at which a dictator has been able to prevent the democratic functioning of democratic forms, and this example has importance because it shows the extremes to which it is possible to go. It is obvious that in those countries that have long enjoyed democracy the public would not easily be misled into thinking that its system was democratic if the forms were counterweighted as they are in the U.S.S.R. Yet, even

191

well-informed leaders of established democratic states have realized that there are points at which democracy can be counterweighted and eventually destroyed. These points may be called the "peril-points," because they are the places at which restriction of democratic functions imperils the future of a democratic state.

Abraham Lincoln worried about such peril during the crisis of the war between the states, when he wrestled with the necessity of suspending the historic writ of habeas corpus. The Supreme Court of the United States worried about such peril when it had to pass upon the constitutionality of restraints on freedom of speech and of the press enacted by state legislatures during the First World War. During the Second World War and into the subsequent decade, the issue has been faced in many lands. In the United States, first in connection with the problem of protecting society against potentially dangerous individuals of German and Japanese stock living within the United States, and later in connection with the problem of removing Communists from positions in which they could cause harm, the Supreme Court has again been testing these restraints to determine whether they go beyond the point of necessity and permanently endanger constitutional freedoms.

It is appropriate at the end of this study to review the principal lessons of the Soviet dictatorship. It bears repeating that the major danger to be avoided is the adoption of the underlying philosophy of the Soviet leaders. The danger lies not in the acceptance of Marxist ideology, for few thinking people in the established democracies have been prepared to accept the limited Marxist explanation of historical phenomena. The danger lies in something deeper than the specifics of Marxism. It lies in the philosophy of its high priests, namely, that one man or one group of men can be infallible in their determination of political policy.

A Sense of Infallibility

In contrast to the leaders of the democratic states, Soviet leaders have professed since the days of their Revolution confidence in their understanding of the forces of history. They believe that Marx and Engels developed a method of analyzing history that is unquestionably correct. They believe that only a small number of thoroughly trained people can understand the method and apply it. They do not imagine that the general public can be taught to understand the method for many years. They conclude for this reason that the public will require leadership for the foreseeable future and that the leaders must be selected from the narrow circle of people who have been reared in the Marxist method and who have the skill to apply it to an ever changing economic and political situation.

In contrast to the attitude of Soviet leaders, the men and women of the democratic states of the West who work their way to a position of leadership have no such purpose. They do not believe that a theory of history can be deduced with certainty from the events of past centuries, although they enjoy speculating on the plausibility of one or another theory as it is developed by men such as Arnold Toynbee. Having risen from the ranks themselves, whether it be from a farm, a haberdashery shop, or the rough and tumble of a British trade union, they do not believe that any group of men has a monopoly on wisdom or on leadership qualities. They believe that wise ideas may come from many sources, often quite unexpected, and that these sources cannot under any circumstances be limited to a certain school of thought.

Although Western democratic leaders sometimes express the wish that they be let alone for long enough to apply their own schemes for national prosperity, they are prepared to bow, as did Winston Churchill during the Potsdam Conference at what seemed to be the very pinnacle of his career, to the will of the majority, and to step down for political opponents with quite different backgrounds, education, and aims. To men such as these, a major purpose of democratic government is to maintain a route through which new views may be aired and new men chosen to give them a trial.

Discipline for Party Members

The Soviet leaders, with their belief in the special wisdom granted to them by their mastery of the Marxist method, have constructed a matrix of government that assures their retention of power. Its core is an apparatus called a political party within which there is preserved a discipline like that within an army. Yet, to win and maintain the adherence of the eight million members of this apparatus, the leaders have had to devise a procedure that can be thought to give the membership an opportunity to shape policy and to choose party leaders. Counterweights have been developed at the peril-points, namely, the selection of delegates to the higher echelons within the party and the manner in which minorities may express their views and organize their supporters within party meetings.

The counterweights to democratic elections within the party have been the establishment of the one-candidate ballot and the indirect election of delegates to the higher levels of the party apparatus. The counterweight to complete freedom of expression guaranteed by Communist party rules is the prohibition against the formation of voting blocs or "factions."

Western democratic parties usually provide that party members may vote for delegates to the national party conventions directly, in primaries, rather than indirectly. Further, Western political parties place no restriction upon the organization of voting blocs within a party, with the result that the world is often startled by such notorious party splits as that between the Clement Attlee and Aneurin Bevan factions in the British Labor Party, that between the Dixiecrats and the Truman leadership within the Democratic party of the United States, and the schism over Pierre Mendès-France in the Radical Socialist party of France.

When one moves beyond the political party to the representative bodies of the state, the contrast between the Soviet system and that familiar in Western democracies is even more noticeable. The principal feature of the contrast is the Soviet denial of the right to form a political party other than the Communist party to function within the representative bodies. The right of association in political parties is specifically limited by the constitution itself. In Western democracies, the multiplicity of parties is fundamental. It is appreciated by students of politics that influence upon choice of leaders or determination of policy can be had only by association with like-minded persons, and this means, in political terminology, a political party. The right of association means, therefore, the right to form political parties without hindrance.

Yet, even in democratic countries there are occasions when a single political party in fact exists for a long period of time for some historical reason. While the right to form other parties continues, the right has little practical value because of the traditional situation. Thus, in India the Congress party gained such prestige in its battle with the British prior to liberation that for a considerable period of time it has remained the dominant factor in Indian politics, although smaller parties have won some important local victories. Yet, no one questions the fact of Indian democracy because the primary party is itself democratic in structure, giving to the people who are its members ample opportunity to express their views on policy and leadership. The same is true in those regions of other countries in which one or another political party has held power for many years if primaries open to all permit the members of the party to choose their own candidates. Sometimes persons whose sympathies are with the permanent minority party move into the ranks of the majority party at primary time to gain an opportunity to cast an effective vote. A one-party system can be democratic in practice, in the view of the Supreme Court of the United States, if the party that has an effective monopoly of power preserves a democratic structure within itself. The Soviet system provides no such safeguard.

Having eliminated any possibility of effective challenge to their authority from a second political party, or from a faction within the Communist party, the Soviet leaders have turned their attention to other possible sources of pressure upon their determination of policy. One gains the impression that Soviet leaders have sought to find the points at which they are unable, because of public opinion either at home or abroad or, sometimes, both at home and abroad, to eliminate a source of power and hence of pressure. They have then made arrangements that have neutralized the actual or potential pressure groups, and sometimes they have been successful in bringing a group within their own orbit to exert pressure upon segments of the population or upon workmen throughout the world for the benefit of the Communist party leadership.

Limitations on Potential Pressure Groups

Organized religions have presented a real challenge to the Soviet leadership's monopoly of power, both because of the tenacity with which many Soviet citizens hold to worship of their God and also because foreign pressures have been great. The Soviet leaders have sought to dissuade those nearest to them from religious attitudes by expelling them from party membership if they practice religion. They have sought to win others away from religion through a vigorous campaign against religious belief on the ground that the natural sciences disprove the existence of God. They have sought to restrict the influence of those who will not be frightened away from their beliefs or propagandized out of them by limiting religious education and denying legal status to church communities. Only during World War II, when the Russian Orthodox Church gave its support to Stalin, was a respite granted. It is likely that if the church should become again, as it was in the early days after the Revolution, a strong pressure group against the government, it would find its activities circumscribed as before. By intensifying atheistic propaganda since 1956, the Communist party is losing no opportunity to weaken the church.

The trade unions have also presented a grave problem to Communist party leaders. The trade unions could not be abolished as they were by Hitler, for their strengthening had been one of the slogans of the Revolution, and their vigor was looked upon by many workmen outside Russia as evidence of the healthy policies of the Soviet government. Yet, they could not be permitted to function as a force capable of challenging the policies set by the Communist party. When they appeared to be moving in that direction in 1928, their leaders were purged. They were provided with new leaders and directed to support governmental policies calling for increased production.

The co-operative associations have also been a potential political threat. For economic reasons, the Communist leaders have had to expand the co-operatives in the agricultural field and in the artisan field also to fill the gaps in state-organized production. Such expansion has created a source of pressure. Yet the co-operatives have been prevented from becoming a national pressure group. The agricultural co-operatives have been subordinated to the Ministry of Agriculture and have been controlled by dictation of the choice of officers whenever the members' choice was undesirable to the Communist party. They were further controlled until 1958 by a system of machine tractor stations to which was transferred maintenance of the mechanical agricultural implements used by these co-operatives. Since abolition of machine tractor station control the party has relied on intensification of party activity within farms amalgamated to create large agricultural enterprises. The artisan co-operatives have been controlled by limiting their sources of supply and by regulating access to markets on which they may sell their produce.

Any pressure that might have been exerted upon leaders by an industrial lobby, a chamber of commerce, or a real estate lobby has been eliminated by the expedient of abolishing private ownership of industrial establishments, of land, and also of merchandising enterprises. Those who manage the public corporations that operate state industry, sell its produce, and use that part of the land not allocated to the co-operative societies are permitted to form no independent associations such as the National Association of Manufacturers or the United States Chamber of Commerce.

No associations in other fields, even for ostensibly cultural purposes such as the propagation of literature or music, are permitted to organize without state authorization, nor can meetings of any group concerned with members in an area larger than a county be held without a license on each occasion.

Leaders of Western democracies have had a very different philosophy as to the value of pressure groups. They have believed that the functioning of the democratic process requires the existence of equally balanced pressure groups. When the balance has been unfavorable, efforts have been made to redress it; for example, the Wagner Act was adopted by the United States Congress to encourage the organization of trade unions, only to be superseded by the Taft-Hartley Act when the Congress thought it necessary to restore the balance between management and labor. When industry became so centralized as to threaten the development of monopolies, the Congress adopted antitrust laws to preserve competition and to fragment economic power. In the interests of fostering democratic practices, efforts were made by American experts in rebuilding Germany and Japan after World War II to limit the concentration of industry in a few hands and to prevent a return to the cartel system of prewar Europe.

Restrictions on Avenues of Expression

Having abolished the base for certain groups, such as those interested in the protection of productive property, and having limited severely the independence of other groups, such as the trade unions and co-operative associations, the Soviet leaders have taken great care to forestall the pressures that might be exerted by a free press. They have had to move carefully at this point, for one of the most obvious yardsticks of a democratic system of government is a free press. To satisfy their own people and win friends abroad, Soviet leaders have found it necessary to guarantee freedom of the press in the Soviet Constitution.

Having established the guarantee of a free press, Communist party leaders have provided counterweights to the guarantee. They have forbidden private citizens to operate even a mimeograph machine, much less a great modern newspaper press. They have created a state printing monopoly and a state censor for all potential publications. Further, they have provided that freedom of the press may be exercised only to the advantage of their system of government, and they have drafted a criminal code that permits prosecution of those who attempt to use press or speech to damage that system.

In sharp contrast to Soviet attitudes toward the press, citizens at all levels of Western democratic governments will fight to maintain a free press. No legal limitations are created in Western democracies on ownership by private persons or corporations of the essentials to publish newspapers, magazines, handbills, and books. No censorship prior to publication is permitted by law, although in certain cases of military security the editors are asked to agree as patriots and gentlemen not to publish what they may learn. Although censorship subsequent to publication has been permitted, by means of confiscation of the offending issue, and although in very unusual cases further publication of a newspaper that has been consistently endangering the security of the state has been prohibited, the administration of censorship is carefully controlled by the courts. It has usually been necessary for the executive to prove to a court that the danger to the democratic regime is obvious and that it is immediate.

The Soviet regime has not silenced its public completely. It has found it advantageous to permit citizens to write letters to the editors of the Soviet press in complaint against mismanagement of Soviet institutions. Such letters have value not only in suggesting to the people that its leaders permit free expression but also because they provide an important source of information for the leaders on the faults of subordinate administrators and on the temper of the people. Yet such letters to the editor do not meet the requirements of a free press, for they need not be published, and the pattern established in them over the years suggests that the writers have created for themselves a code of criticism that limits the subject matter that they will discuss and the personages whom they will subject to abuse.

No Independence for the Judiciary

The courts of the U.S.S.R. are avowedly an arm of Communist party policy. Soviet jurists accept no doctrine of separation of powers. While lower courts are insulated by law from interference by local party tyrants, the Supreme Court is always subject to control by the highest policy body in the state apparatus, the Supreme Soviet, in which nearly 80 per cent of the deputies are members of the Communist party and, therefore, subject to strict political discipline. The courts do much to protect the citizen from mistaken application of state policy, and in so doing win the respect of many citizens for the fairness of the regime in matters affecting the employment relationship, family quarrels, and housing disputes, but they cannot be a bulwark against tyranny if the leaders of the party decide that some tyrannical measure is necessary in the interest of security.

The courts of Western democracies are not always considered an independent branch of government beyond the reach of the executive, for there is not always separation of powers in the West. Yet in countries such as England, in which the Lord Chancellor as head of the judiciary is at the same time a member of the government and the presiding officer of the House of Lords, there is a tradition of non-interference with the affairs of the judiciary by the Parliament and its government of the day. The courts of the West have indicated their willingness to enforce human rights, whether guaranteed in a written constitution or by tradition alone, against encroachment by the executive in the name of security.

Legal procedures in the U.S.S.R. exhibit many of the measures accepted by Western lawyers as constituting procedural due process of law and as helping to assure the defendant an opportunity to present his case. Yet, when the charge is one of attempting to unseat the regime, these very measures of protection had been withdrawn until the reform of 1956 by exceptions written into the procedural codes. It is at this point that procedural protections are needed most if democracy is to be preserved, and the West has always held to this view.

Again, the position of the Western democracies is not an absolute. There have been times when some of the elements of procedural due process of law have been withdrawn, as when the writ of habeas corpus has been suspended during wartime. The very torture of mind through which Abraham Lincoln went in deciding whether to suspend it during the war between the states, and the hesitation of the English prime minister when the Battle of Britain was at its height, suggest that the difference between the West and the Soviet approach is a matter of degree. Yet, in that difference of degree there is an element of difference of quality. In the U.S.S.R., procedural due process has been waived even in peacetime. The decision seems to have been made with little reluctance in 1934, at the moment when one of Stalin's aides was assassinated. In the Western democracies the writ has been waived only in wartime, and after the passing of the emergency it has been quickly restored.

Few Limitations on the Security Police

Both the U.S.S.R. and the Western democracies have found it necessary to establish a security police. Both systems of government seem to have approached the institution with caution. The Soviet security police, established in 1918 as the *Cheka,* was limited at the start in its authority, and there were many Communist party members who disliked the idea of having such an agency at all. Yet, it was established. It soon expanded its authority to such an extent that it aroused the anger of the Soviet Ministry of Justice and the Congress of Soviets. It was abolished in 1922 and replaced by an institution with more limited powers and subjected to great control by the cabinet. The new security police then expanded its power, until the leadership found it advisable to abolish it in 1934 to create a still more limited instrument. Yet, this in turn expanded its authority. Since Stalin's death the security police has been under attack, and measures have been taken to control it through a strengthened Prosecutor-General of the U.S.S.R.

While recognizing that real danger, even to the regime itself, lurks in a security police over which there is no line of supervision through an official in close touch with the highest policy-makers, the security problem of the Soviet leadership has been seemingly so great that the security police has been permitted throughout its history to make arrests and to try those whom it has arrested in its own tribunals without reference to the courts. Only the Prosecutor-General of the U.S.S.R. has had the right to interfere, and even he, and his subordinates through whom he must operate in the daily situation, have been reluctant to intervene, because of the prestige developed by the security police in leadership circles. It remains to be seen whether the Prosecutor-General will be more successful now that Stalin is dead.

The Western democracies have been alert at all times to the danger that a security police may get out of hand. There have been efforts to provide checks upon assumption of authority greater than intended by the legislature by making the security police a subordinate part of a Ministry of Justice or responsible to an attorney-general rather than an independent ministry, as it has been in the U.S.S.R. There have been efforts in the West to limit the powers of the security police by permitting it to make arrests only in wartime, rather than in peace and war as is the case in the U.S.S.R. There have been other efforts to check its activities—by making it deliver all arrested persons to the judiciary for trial within a fixed period of time or by denying to it the right to pass sentence of any kind against any person. This has been in sharp contrast to the broad rights of the security police in the U.S.S.R.

Perhaps the surest protection against unlawful assumption of authority by the security police in the Western democracies is the multiparty system. If the security police exceeds its authority to the point that it enrages the citizens, there is the opportunity in a democracy to vote out of power the party whose responsibility it has been to curb the police. This ultimate method of dealing with the problem through the ballot box is not available to the citizens of the U.S.S.R., as it was not available to the citizens of Hitler's Germany and of Mussolini's Italy, in both of which the excesses of the security police became symbolic of the character of the regimes.

Finally, among the agencies on which the Soviet regime rests for security when all else fails, there is the army. For the Soviet leaders, the army has been a necessary evil. Its existence is required to protect the regime at home and from foreign powers. It must be strong, yet in its strength lies latent danger to the political leadership, for it could unseat the regime if it were not controlled. The whole history of the relationship between the Communist party and the army has been dotted with experiments in control by the former over the latter so as to assure loyalty without reducing military efficiency. In contrast with the citizens' armies of Western democracies, the Soviet army seems to be under more formal and rigid political controls, although from Stalin's death in 1953 to Marshal Zhukov's ouster in 1957 its leaders appeared to be gaining more influence in policy-making circles.

The army was one of the two major forces that seemed after Stalin's death to be pressing for recognition in the formulation of policy and the selection of leaders. The other force, as has been indicated throughout this book, was the managerial and technical class. It was necessary for the Communist party leadership to expand this class, as it was necessary to expand the army. The managers and technicians were essential to the productive functioning of a modern industrial and agricultural plant. To encourage maximum effort, more was found necessary than exhortation on the basis of traditional political goals. It was necessary to give to the managers and technicians preferred status, not only in terms of greater monetary rewards but also in terms of medals, personal praise, and prestige.

Pressures for Change

Following Stalin's death it became evident that there was pressure for a lessening of the severity with which he had ruled and that this pressure was strong even within the Communist party. Statistics showed that this party had become under his regime a party predominantly of specialists, meriting classification as intellectuals. Most notable within this group were the senior officers in the Armed Forces, the managers of industrial enterprises, the agronomist-chairmen of collective and state farms, and the professional party functionaries.

As Marxist-trained individuals these intellectuals probably respected the doctrine that only the enlightened few were yet qualified to rule. It is unlikely that their dreams of the future contained thought of mass participation in the policy-making function. All evidence suggests that the new intellectuals held firmly to the necessity of maintaining the system of state ownership of production and monopoly political direction and rejected any thought of private enterprise or the multiparty system.

The new intellectuals exerted influence upon some of the senior members of the Communist party, if the outsider can judge by results. Khrushchev appears to have been frightened, for in 1957 he began to take a series of steps designed to reduce their power and reshape their thinking and the thinking of their children. The Armed Forces were returned to their completely subordinate position with the dismissal of Marshal Zhukov and the strengthening of political education. The industrial managers were subjected to audit by production conferences established by the trade unions and by supervisory commissions created within the factories by the Communist party.

A campaign was conducted within the Communist party to proletarianize its membership. Two-thirds of those admitted between 1956 and 1959 were bench workmen and dirt farmers. Within the Presidium of the Central Committee of the party Khrushchev re-established at least the semblance of Stalin's authority to forestall the active resistance of dissenters tending to think in terms of factions.

Reshaping of the thinking of the intellectuals took the form of extensive revision of the education law with the professed aim of bringing the next generation into close familiarity with the shop and the field. All but the students needing uninterrupted study to master complex disciplines will be required to undergo a period of schooling, including bench labor and dirt farming, before entering upon specialized study in the universities and technical institutes.

While moving to close the gates on potential dissension, Khrushchev continued to denounce Stalin's dictatorial rule as the "cult of the individual," although in less comprehensive form than his denunciation before the party in 1956. He and his colleagues within the Presidium have found it desirable, if not necessary, to assure the intellectuals on whom they rely that personal safety can be expected. This assurance has taken the form of redefining criminal law in the interest of precision and expanding the procedural code to facilitate in some measure defense of the innocent.

The changes introduced between 1957 and 1959 have obvious importance. They have required a re-evaluation of the potential power of the men who defend the frontiers and manage the economy and the lower levels within the Communist party, but they do not suggest an impending change in the Soviet system of government. The system remains, as it has been since 1936, the embodiment of some of the most publicized forms of democracy, but these are counterweighted to prevent their use to unseat the inner circle of the Communist party.

If one looks to the future, it can be predicted that the ranks of the educated will swell within the U.S.S.R. as elsewhere. Even given the Marxist formulation of Soviet instruction, this expansion of education cannot but have an effect upon the system. It is hard to imagine that the new intellectuals will be content for very long with a position as executives outside the circle that makes policy. Still, it is unlikely that the present system will be threatened in its essentials. At most there will be an expansion of the circle of the ruling elite.

There is as yet no hint that those who are moving to positions of responsibility as executives are coming to believe that the public generally can be trusted to choose leaders wisely or to formulate policy. There is no reason to think that Stalin's heirs intend to institute a democratic system of government.

STRUCTURE OF THE COMMUNIST PARTY OF THE SOVIET UNION

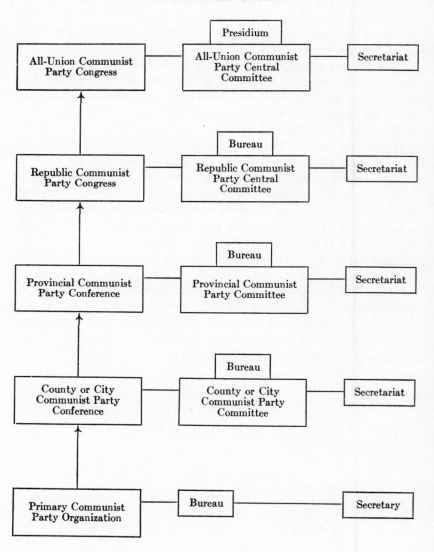

STRUCTURE OF THE SOVIET GOVERNMENTAL APPARATUS

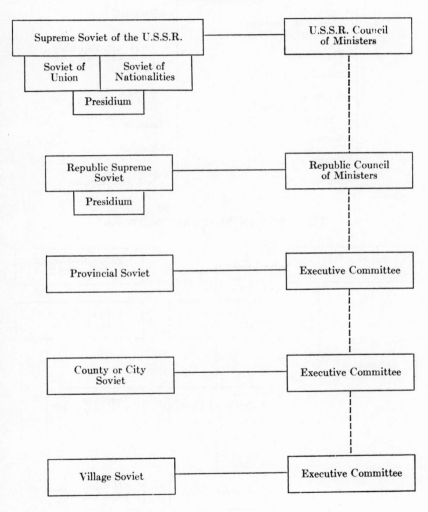

THE FEDERAL PATTERN

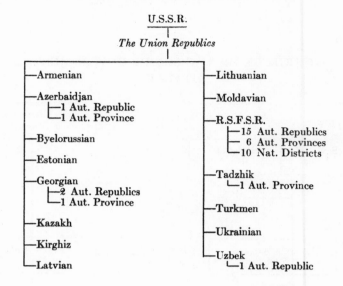

<u>U.S.S.R.</u>

The Union Republics

—Armenian

—Azerbaidjan
   ├—1 Aut. Republic
   └—1 Aut. Province

—Byelorussian

—Estonian

—Georgian
   ├—2 Aut. Republics
   └—1 Aut. Province

—Kazakh

—Kirghiz

—Latvian

—Lithuanian

—Moldavian

—R.S.F.S.R.
   ├—15 Aut. Republics
   ├— 6 Aut. Provinces
   └—10 Nat. Districts

—Tadzhik
   └—1 Aut. Province

—Turkmen

—Ukrainian

—Uzbek
   └—1 Aut. Republic

THE COURTS AND PROSECUTORS

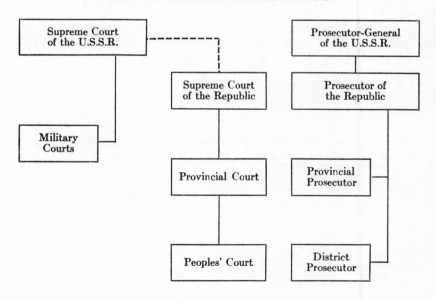

Supreme Court of the U.S.S.R.

Prosecutor-General of the U.S.S.R.

Supreme Court of the Republic

Prosecutor of the Republic

Military Courts

Provincial Court

Provincial Prosecutor

Peoples' Court

District Prosecutor

APPENDIX

CONSTITUTION
(FUNDAMENTAL LAW)

OF THE

UNION OF SOVIET

SOCIALISTIC REPUBLICS

As Amended to October 30, 1959

Chapter I
THE SOCIAL STRUCTURE

Article 1

The Union of Soviet Socialist Republics is a socialist state of workers and peasants.

Article 2

The political foundation of the U.S.S.R is the Soviets of Working People's Deputies, which grew and became strong as a result of the overthrow of the power of the landlords and capitalists and the conquest of the dictatorship of the proletariat.

Article 3

All power in the U.S.S.R. belongs to the working people of town and country as represented by the Soviets of Working People's Deputies.

Article 4

The economic foundation of the U.S.S.R. is the socialist system of economy and the socialist ownership of the instruments and means of production, firmly established as a result of the liquidation of the capitalist system of economy, the abolition of private ownership of the instruments and means of production, and the elimination of the exploitation of man by man.

Article 5

Socialist property in the U.S.S.R. exists either in the form of state property (belonging to the whole people) or in the form of co-operative and collective-farm property (property of collective farms, property of co-operative societies).

Article 6

The land, its mineral wealth, waters, forests, mills, factories, mines, rail, water and air transport, banks, communications, large state-organized agricultural enterprises (state farms, machine and tractor stations and the like), as well as municipal enterprises and the bulk of the dwelling-houses in the cities and industrial localities, are state property, that is, belong to the whole people.

Article 7

The common enterprises of collective farms and co-operative organizations, with their live-stock and implements, the products of the collective farms and co-operative organizations, as well as their common buildings, constitute the common, socialist property of the collective farms and co-operative organizations.

Every household in a collective farm, in addition to its basic income from the common, collective-farm enterprise, has for its personal use a small plot of household land and, as its personal property, a subsidiary husbandry on the plot, a dwelling-house, live-stock, poultry and minor agricultural implements—in accordance with the rules of the agricultural artel.

Article 8

The land occupied by collective farms is secured to them for their use free of charge and for an unlimited time, that is, in perpetuity.

Article 9

Alongside the socialist system of economy, which is the predominant form of economy in the U.S.S.R., the law permits the small private economy of individual peasants and handicraftsmen based on their own labour and precluding the exploitation of the labour of others.

Article 10

The personal property right of citizens in their incomes and savings from work, in their dwelling-houses and subsidiary home enterprises, in articles of domestic economy and use and articles of personal use and convenience, as well as the right of citizens to inherit personal property, is protected by law.

Article 11

The economic life of the U.S.S.R. is determined and directed by the state national-economic plan, with the aim of increasing the public wealth, of steadily raising the material and cultural standards of the working people, of consolidating the independence of the U.S.S.R. and strengthening its defensive capacity.

Article 12

Work in the U.S.S.R. is a duty and a matter of honour for every able-bodied citizen, in accordance with the principle: "He who does not work, neither shall he eat."

The principle applied in the U.S.S.R. is that of socialism: "From each according to his ability, to each according to his work."

Chapter II
THE STATE STRUCTURE

Article 13

The Union of Soviet Socialist Republics is a federal state, formed on the basis of a voluntary union of equal Soviet Socialist Republics, namely:

The Russian Soviet Federative Socialist Republic
The Ukrainian Soviet Socialist Republic
The Byelorussian Soviet Socialist Republic
The Uzbek Soviet Socialist Republic
The Kazakh Soviet Socialist Republic
The Georgian Soviet Socialist Republic
The Azerbaijan Soviet Socialist Republic
The Lithuanian Soviet Socialist Republic
The Moldavian Soviet Socialist Republic
The Latvian Soviet Socialist Republic
The Kirghiz Soviet Socialist Republic
The Tajik Soviet Socialist Republic
The Armenian Soviet Socialist Republic
The Turkmen Soviet Socialist Republic
The Estonian Soviet Socialist Republic

Article 14

The jurisdiction of the Union of Soviet Socialist Republics, as represented by its higher organs of state power and organs of state administration, embraces:

a) Representation of the U.S.S.R. in international relations, conclusion, ratification and denunciation of treaties of the U.S.S.R. with other states, establishment of general procedure governing the relations of Union Republics with foreign states;

b) Questions of war and peace;

c) Admission of new republics into the U.S.S.R.;

d) Control over the observance of the Constitution of the U.S.S.R., and ensuring conformity of the Constitutions of the Union Republics with the Constitution of the U.S.S.R.

e) Confirmation of alterations of boundaries between Union Republics;

f) Confirmation of the formation of new Autonomous Republics and Autonomous Regions within Union Republics;

g) Organization of the defence of the U.S.S.R., direction of all the

Armed Forces of the U.S.S.R., determination of directing principles governing the organization of the military formations of the Union Republics;

h) Foreign trade on the basis of state monopoly;

i) Safeguarding the security of the state;

j) Determination of the national-economic plans of the U.S.S.R.;

k) Approval of the consolidated state budget of the U.S.S.R. and of the report on its fulfilment; determination of the taxes and revenues which go to the Union, the Republican and the local budgets;

l) Administration of the banks, industrial and agricultural institutions and enterprises and also trading enterprises of all-Union subordination; general guidance of industry and construction of Union-Republic importance;

m) Administration of transport and communications of all-Union importance;

n) Direction of the monetary and credit system;

o) Organization of state insurance;

p) Contracting and granting of loans;

q) Determination of the basic principles of land tenure and of the use of mineral wealth, forests and waters;

r) Determination of the basic principles in the spheres of education and public health;

s) Organization of a uniform system of national-economic statistics;

t) Determination of the principles of labour legislation;

u) Legislation concerning the judicial system and judicial procedure; criminal and civil codes;

v) Legislation concerning Union citizenship; legislation concerning rights of foreigners;

w) Determination of the principles of legislation concerning marriage and the family;

x) Issuing of all-Union acts of amnesty.

Article 15

The sovereignty of the Union Republics is limited only in the spheres defined in Article 14 of the Constitution of the U.S.S.R. Outside of these spheres each Union Republic exercises state authority independently. The U.S.S.R. protects the sovereign rights of the Union Republics.

Article 16

Each Union Republic has its own Constitution, which takes account of the specific features of the Republic and is drawn up in full conformity with the Constitution of the U.S.S.R.

Article 17

The right freely to secede from the U.S.S.R. is reserved to every Union Republic.

Article 18

The territory of a Union Republic may not be altered without its consent.

Article 18-a

Each Union Republic has the right to enter into direct relations with foreign states and to conclude agreements and exchange diplomatic and consular representatives with them.

Article 18-b

Each Union Republic has its own Republican military formations.

Article 19

The laws of the U.S.S.R. have the same force within the territory of every Union Republic.

Article 20

In the event of divergence between a law of a Union Republic and a law of the Union, the Union law prevails.

Article 21

Uniform Union citizenship is established for citizens of the U.S.S.R. Every citizen of a Union Republic is a citizen of the U.S.S.R.

Article 22

The Russian Soviet Federative Socialist Republic includes the Bashkir, Buryat, Daghestan, Kabardinian-Balkar, Kalmyk, Karelian, Komi, Mari, Mordovian, North Ossetian, Tatar, Udmurt, Chechen-Ingush, Chuvash and Yakut Autonomous Soviet Socialist Republics; and the Adygei, Gorno-Altai, Jewish, Karachayevo-Cherkess, Tuva, and Khakass Autonomous Provinces.

Article 23

[Deleted, February 11, 1957]

Article 24

The Azerbaijan Soviet Socialist Republic includes the Nakhichevan Autonomous Soviet Socialist Republic and the Nagorno-Karabakh Autonomous Province.

Article 25

The Georgian Soviet Socialist Republic includes the Abkhazian Autonomous Soviet Socialist Republic, the Adjar Autonomous Soviet Socialist Republic and the South Ossetian Autonomous Province.

Article 26

The Uzbek Soviet Socialist Republic includes the Kara-Kalpak Autonomous Soviet Socialist Republic.

Article 27

The Tajik Soviet Socialist Republic includes the Gorno-Badakhshan Autonomous Province.

Article 28

Decision of questions relating to the provincial and territorial administrative structure of Union Republics is within the competence of Union Republics.

Article 29

[Deleted February 11, 1957]

Article 29-a

[Deleted February 11, 1957]

Article 29-b

[Deleted February 11, 1957]

Chapter III
THE HIGHER ORGANS
OF STATE POWER
IN THE UNION OF SOVIET
SOCIALIST REPUBLICS

Article 30

The highest organ of state power in the U.S.S.R. is the Supreme Soviet of the U.S.S.R.

Article 31

The Supreme Soviet of the U.S.S.R. exercises all rights vested in the Union of Soviet Socialist Republics in accordance with Article 14 of the Constitution, in so far as they do not, by virtue of the Constitution, come within the jurisdiction of organs of the U.S.S.R. that are accountable to the Supreme Soviet of the U.S.S.R., that is, the Presidium of the Supreme Soviet of the U.S.S.R., the Council of Ministers of the U.S.S.R., and the Ministries of the U.S.S.R.

Article 32

The legislative power of the U.S.S.R. is exercised exclusively by the Supreme Soviet of the U.S.S.R.

Article 33

The Supreme Soviet of the U.S.S.R. consists of two Chambers: the Soviet of the Union and the Soviet of Nationalities.

Article 34

The Soviet of the Union is elected by the citizens of the U.S.S.R. voting by election districts on the basis of one deputy for every 300,000 of the population.

Article 35

The Soviet of Nationalities is elected by the citizens of the U.S.S.R. voting by Union Republics, Autonomous Republics, Autonomous Provinces and National Districts on the basis of 25 deputies from each Union Republic, 11 deputies from each Autonomous Republic, 5 deputies from each Autonomous Province and one deputy from each National District.

Article 36

The Supreme Soviet of the U.S.S.R. is elected for a term of four years.

Article 37

The two Chambers of the Supreme Soviet of the U.S.S.R., the Soviet of the Union and the Soviet of the Nationalities, have equal rights.

Article 38

The Soviet of the Union and the Soviet of Nationalities have equal powers to initiate legislation.

Article 39

A law is considered adopted if passed by both Chambers of the Supreme Soviet of the U.S.S.R. by a simple majority vote in each.

Article 40

Laws passed by the Supreme Soviet of the U.S.S.R. are published in the languages of the Union Republics over the signatures of the President and Secretary of the Presidium of the Supreme Soviet of the U.S.S.R.

Article 41

Sessions of the Soviet of the Union and of the Soviet of Nationalities begin and terminate simultaneously.

Article 42

The Soviet of the Union elects a Chairman of the Soviet of the Union and four Vice-Chairmen.

Article 43

The Soviet of Nationalities elects a Chairman of the Soviet of Nationalities and four Vice-Chairmen.

Article 44

The Chairmen of the Soviet of the Union and the Soviet of Nationalities preside at the sittings of the respective Chambers and have charge of the conduct of their business and proceedings.

Article 45

Joint sittings of the two Chambers of the Supreme Soviet of the

U.S.S.R. are presided over alternately by the Chairman of the Soviet of the Union and the Chairman of the Soviet of Nationalities.

Article 46

Sessions of the Supreme Soviet of the U.S.S.R. are convened by the Presidium of the Supreme Soviet of the U.S.S.R. twice a year.

Extraordinary sessions are convened by the Presidium of the Supreme Soviet of the U.S.S.R. at its discretion or on the demand of one of the Union Republics.

Article 47

In the event of disagreement between the Soviet of the Union and the Soviet of Nationalities, the question is referred for settlement to a conciliation commission formed by the Chambers on a parity basis. If the conciliation commission fails to arrive at an agreement, or if its decision fails to satisfy one of the Chambers, the question is considered for a second time by the Chambers. Failing agreement between the two Chambers, the Presidium of the Supreme Soviet of the U.S.S.R. dissolves the Supreme Soviet of the U.S.S.R. and orders new elections.

Article 48

The Supreme Soviet of the U.S.S.R. at a joint sitting of the two Chambers elects the Presidium of the Supreme Soviet of the U.S.S.R., consisting of a President of the Presidium of the Supreme Soviet of the U.S.S.R., fifteen Vice-Presidents—one for each of the Union Republics—a Secretary of the Presidium and sixteen members of the Presidium of the Supreme Soviet of the U.S.S.R.

The Presidium of the Supreme Soviet of the U.S.S.R. is accountable to the Supreme Soviet of the U.S.S.R. for all its activities.

Article 49

The Presidium of the Supreme Soviet of the U.S.S.R.:

a) Convenes the sessions of the Supreme Soviet of the U.S.S.R.;

b) Issues decrees;

c) Gives interpretations of the laws of the U.S.S.R. in operation;

d) Dissolves the Supreme Soviet of the U.S.S.R. in conformity with Article 47 of the Constitution of the U.S.S.R. and orders new elections;

e) Conducts nation-wide polls (referendums) on its own initiative or on the demand of one of the Union Republics;

f) Annuls decisions and orders of the Council of Ministers of the U.S.S.R. and of the Councils of Ministers of the Union Republics if they do not conform to law;

g) In the intervals between sessions of the Supreme Soviet of the U.S.S.R., releases and appoints Ministers of the U.S.S.R. on the recommendation of the Chairman of the Council of Ministers of the U.S.S.R., subject to subsequent confirmation by the Supreme Soviet of the U.S.S.R.;

h) Institutes decorations (Orders and Medals) and titles of honour of the U.S.S.R.;

i) Awards Orders and Medals and confers titles of honour of the U.S.S.R.;

j) Exercises the right of pardon;

k) Institutes military titles, diplomatic ranks and other special titles;

l) Appoints and removes the high command of the Armed Forces of the U.S.S.R.;

m) In the intervals between sessions of the Supreme Soviet of the U.S.S.R., proclaims a state of war in the event of military attack on the U.S.S.R., or when necessary to fulfil international treaty obligations concerning mutual defence against aggression;

n) Orders general or partial mobilization;

o) Ratifies and denounces international treaties of the U.S.S.R.;

p) Appoints and recalls plenipotentiary representatives of the U.S.S.R. to foreign states;

q) Receives the letters of credence and recall of diplomatic representatives accredited to it by foreign states;

r) Proclaims martial law in separate localities or throughout the U.S.S.R. in the interests of the defence of the U.S.S.R. or of the maintenance of public order and the security of the state.

Article 50

The Soviet of the Union and the Soviet of Nationalities elect Credentials Committees to verify the credentials of the members of the respective Chambers.

On the report of the Credentials Committees, the Chambers decide whether to recognize the credentials of deputies or to annul their election.

Article 51

The Supreme Soviet of the U.S.S.R., when it deems necessary, appoints commissions of investigation and audit on any matter.

It is the duty of all institutions and officials to comply with the demands of such commissions and to submit to them all necessary materials and documents.

Article 52

A member of the Supreme Soviet of the U.S.S.R. may not be prosecuted or arrested without the consent of the Supreme Soviet of the U.S.S.R., or, when the Supreme Soviet of the U.S.S.R. is not in session, without the consent of the Presidium of the Supreme Soviet of the U.S.S.R.

Article 53

On the expiration of the term of office of the Supreme Soviet of the U.S.S.R., or on its dissolution prior to the expiration of its term of office, the Presidium of the Supreme Soviet of the U.S.S.R. retains its powers until the newly-elected Supreme Soviet of the U.S.S.R. shall have formed a new Presidium of the Supreme Soviet of the U.S.S.R.

Article 54

On the expiration of the term of office of the Supreme Soviet of the U.S.S.R., or in the event of its dissolution prior to the expiration of its term of office, the Presidium of the Supreme Soviet of the U.S.S.R. orders new elections to be held within a period not exceeding two months from the date of expiration of the term of office or dissolution of the Supreme Soviet of the U.S.S.R.

Article 55

The newly-elected Supreme Soviet of the U.S.S.R. is convened by the outgoing Presidium of the Supreme Soviet of the U.S.S.R. not later than three months after the elections.

Article 56

The Supreme Soviet of the U.S.S.R., at a joint sitting of the two Chambers, appoints the Government of the U.S.S.R., namely, the Council of Ministers of the U.S.S.R.

Chapter IV
THE HIGHER ORGANS
OF STATE POWER
IN THE UNION REPUBLICS

Article 57

The highest organ of state power in a Union Republic is the Supreme Soviet of the Union Republic.

Article 58

The Supreme Soviet of a Union Republic is elected by the citizens of the Republic for a term of four years.

The basis of representation is established by the Constitution of the Union Republic.

Article 59

The Supreme Soviet of a Union Republic is the sole legislative organ of the Republic.

Article 60

The Supreme Soviet of a Union Republic:

a) Adopts the Constitution of the Republic and amends it in conformity with Article 16 of the Constitution of the U.S.S.R.;

b) Confirms the Constitutions of the Autonomous Republics forming part of it and defines the boundaries of their territories;

c) Approves the national-economic plan and the budget of the Republic, forms economic administrative regions;

d) Exercises the right of amnesty and pardon of citizens sentenced by the judicial organs of the Union Republic;

e) Decides questions of representation of the Union Republic in its international relations;

f) Determines the manner of organizing the Republic's military formations.

Article 61

The Supreme Soviet of a Union Republic elects the Presidium of the Supreme Soviet of the Union Republic, consisting of a President of the Presidium of the Supreme Soviet of the Union Republic, Vice-Presidents, a Secretary of the Presidium and members of the Presidium of the Supreme Soviet of the Union Republic.

The powers of the Presidium of the Supreme Soviet of a Union Republic are defined by the Constitution of the Union Republic.

Article 62

The Supreme Soviet of a Union Republic elects a Chairman and Vice-Chairmen to conduct its sittings.

Article 63

The Supreme Soviet of a Union Republic appoints the Government of the Union Republic, namely, the Council of Ministers of the Union Republic.

Chapter V
THE ORGANS
OF STATE ADMINISTRATION
OF THE UNION OF SOVIET
SOCIALIST REPUBLICS

Article 64

The highest executive and administrative organ of the state power of the Union of Soviet Socialist Republics is the Council of Ministers of the U.S.S.R.

Article 65

The Council of Ministers of the U.S.S.R. is responsible and accountable to the Supreme Soviet of the U.S.S.R., or, in the intervals between sessions of the Supreme Soviet, to the Presidium of the Supreme Soviet of the U.S.S.R.

Article 66

The Council of Ministers of the U.S.S.R. issues decisions and orders on the basis and in pursuance of the laws in operation, and verifies their execution.

Article 67

Decisions and orders of the Council of Ministers of the U.S.S.R. are binding throughout the territory of the U.S.S.R.

Article 68

The Council of Ministers of the U.S.S.R.:

a) Co-ordinates and directs the work of the all-Union and Union-Republican Ministries of the U.S.S.R. and of other institutions under its jurisdiction, brings about guidance of the Councils of National Economy of the economic administrative regions through the Councils of Ministers of the Union Republics;

b) Adopts measures to carry out the national-economic plan and the state budget, and to strengthen the credit and monetary system;

c) Adopts measures for the maintenance of public order, for the protection of the interests of the state, and for the safeguarding of the rights of citizens;

d) Exercises general guidance in the sphere of relations with foreign states;

e) Fixes the annual contingent of citizens to be called up for military service and directs the general organization of the Armed Forces of the country;

f) Sets up, whenever necessary, special Committees and Central Administrations under the Council of Ministers of the U.S.S.R. for economic and cultural affairs and defence.

Article 69

The Council of Ministers of the U.S.S.R. has the right, in respect of those branches of administration and economy which come within the jurisdiction of the U.S.S.R., to suspend decisions and orders of the Councils of Ministers of the Union Republics and of the Councils of National Economy of the economic administrative regions and to annul orders and instructions of Ministers of the U.S.S.R.

Article 70

The Council of Ministers of the U.S.S.R. is appointed by the Supreme Soviet of the U.S.S.R. and consists of:

The Chairman of the Council of Ministers of the U.S.S.R.;

The First Vice-Chairmen of the Council of Ministers of the U.S.S.R.;

The Vice-Chairmen of the Council of Ministers of the U.S.S.R.;

The Ministers of the U.S.S.R.;

The Chairman of the U.S.S.R. Council of Ministers' State Planning Committee;

The Chairman of the U.S.S.R. Council of Ministers' Soviet Control Commission;

The Chairman of the U.S.S.R. Council of Ministers' State Committee on Labor and Wages;

The Chairman of the U.S.S.R. Council of Ministers' State Committee on Professional-Technical Education;

The Chairman of the U.S.S.R. Council of Ministers' State Committee on Automation and Machine Building;

The Chairman of the U.S.S.R. Council of Ministers' State Scientific and Technical Committee;

The Chairman of the U.S.S.R. Council of Ministers' State Committee on Aviation Technology;

The Chairman of the U.S.S.R. Council of Ministers' State Committee on Defense Technology;

The Chairman of the U.S.S.R. Council of Ministers' State Committee on Radio Electronics;

The Chairman of the U.S.S.R. Council of Ministers' State Committee on Shipbuilding;

The Chairman of the U.S.S.R. Council of Ministers' State Committee on Chemistry;

The Chairman of the U.S.S.R. Council of Ministers' State Committee on Construction;

The Chairman of the U.S.S.R. Council of Ministers' State Committee on Grain Products;

The Chairman of the U.S.S.R. Council of Ministers' State Committee on Foreign Economic Relations;

The Chairman of the U.S.S.R. Council of Ministers' State Committee on State Security;

The Chairman of the Board of the U.S.S.R. State Bank;

The Director of the U.S.S.R. Council of Ministers' Central Statistical Administration;

The Chairman of the U.S.S.R. Council of Ministers' State Scientific-Economic Council.

The Chairmen of the Union Republic Councils of Ministers are members ex officio of the Council of Ministers of the U.S.S.R.

Article 71

The Government of the U.S.S.R. or a Minister of the U.S.S.R. to whom a question of a member of the Supreme Soviet of the U.S.S.R. is addressed must give a verbal or written reply in the respective Chamber within a period not exceeding three days.

Article 72

The Ministers of the U.S.S.R. direct the branches of state administration which come within the jurisdiction of the U.S.S.R.

Article 73

The Ministers of the U.S.S.R., within the limits of the jurisdiction of their respective Ministries, issue orders and instructions on the basis and in pursuance of the laws in operation, and also of decisions and orders of the Council of Ministers of the U.S.S.R., and verify their execution.

Article 74

The Ministries of the U.S.S.R. are either all-Union or Union-Republican Ministries.

Article 75

Each all-Union Ministry directs the branch of state administration entrusted to it throughout the territory of the U.S.S.R. either directly or through bodies appointed by it.

Article 76

The Union-Republican Ministries, as a rule, direct the branches of state administration entrusted to them through corresponding Ministries of the Union Republics; they administer directly only a definite and limited number of enterprises according to a list confirmed by the Presidium of the Supreme Soviet of the U.S.S.R.

Article 77

The following Ministries are all-Union Ministries:

Foreign Trade
Merchant Marine
Transportation
Medium Machine Building
Power Plant Construction
Transport Construction

Article 78

The following Ministries are Union-Republic Ministries:

Internal Affairs
Higher and Specialized Secondary Education
Geology and Conservation of Mineral Resources
Public Health
Foreign Affairs
Culture
Defence
Communications
Agriculture
Finance

Chapter VI

THE ORGANS
OF STATE ADMINISTRATION
OF THE UNION REPUBLICS

Article 79

The highest executive and administrative organ of the state power of a Union Republic is the Council of Ministers of the Union Republic.

Article 80

The Council of Ministers of a Union Republic is responsible and accountable to the Supreme Soviet of the Union Republic, or, in the intervals between sessions of the Supreme Soviet of the Union Republic, to the Presidium of the Supreme Soviet of the Union Republic.

Article 81

The Council of Ministers of a Union Republic issues decisions and orders on the basis and in pursuance of the laws in operation of the U.S.S.R. and of the Union Republic, and of the decisions and orders of the Council of Ministers of the U.S.S.R., and verifies their execution.

Article 82

The Council of Ministers of a Union Republic has the right to suspend decisions and orders of the Councils of Ministers of its Autonomous Republics, and to annul decisions and orders of the Executive Committees of the Soviets of Working People's Deputies of its Territories, Provinces and Autonomous Provinces, and also decisions and orders of the Councils of National Economy of the economic administrative regions.

Article 83

The Council of Ministers of a Union Republic is appointed by the Supreme Soviet of the Union Republic and consists of:
The Chairman of the Council of Ministers of the Union Republic;

The First Vice-Chairmen of the Council of Ministers;
The Vice-Chairman of the State Planning Commission;
The Ministers;
The Chairmen of the State Committees, Commissions, and Directors of the other departments of the Council of Ministers, organized by the Supreme Soviet of the Union Republic in accordance with the Constitution of the Union Republic.

Article 84

The Ministers of a Union Republic direct the branches of state administration which come within the jurisdiction of the Union Republic.

Article 85

The Ministers of a Union Republic, within the limits of the jurisdiction of their respective Ministries, issue orders and instructions on the basis and in pursuance of the laws of the U.S.S.R. and of the Union Republic, of the decisions and orders of the Council of Ministers of the U.S.S.R. and the Council of Ministers of the Union Republic, and of the orders and instructions of the Union-Republican Ministries of the U.S.S.R.

Article 86

The Ministries of a Union Republic are either Union-Republican or Republican Ministries.

Article 87

Each Union-Republican Ministry directs the branch of state administration entrusted to it, and is subordinate both to the Council of Ministers of the Union Republic and to the corresponding Union-Republican Ministry of the U.S.S.R.

Article 88

Each Republican Ministry directs the branch of state administration entrusted to it and is directly subordinate to the Council of Ministers of the Union Republic.

Article 88a

The Councils of National Economy of the economic administrative regions direct the branches of economic activity entrusted to them, and they are subordinate directly to the Council of Ministers of the Union Republic.

The Councils of National Economy of the economic administrative regions within the limits of their jurisdiction issue decisions and orders on the basis of and in execution of the laws of the U.S.S.R. and of the Union Republic, and of the decisions and orders of the Council of Ministers of the U.S.S.R. and of the Council of Ministers of the Union Republic.

Chapter VII

THE HIGHER ORGANS
OF STATE POWER
IN THE AUTONOMOUS SOVIET
SOCIALIST REPUBLICS

Article 89

The highest organ of state power in an Autonomous Soviet Socialist Republic is the Supreme Soviet of the Autonomous Republic.

Article 90

The Supreme Soviet of an Autonomous Republic is elected by the citizens of the Republic for a term of four years on a basis of representation established by the Constitution of the Autonomous Republic.

Article 91

The Supreme Soviet of an Autonomous Republic is the sole legislative organ of the Autonomous Republic.

Article 92

Each Autonomous Republic has its own Constitution, which takes account of the specific features of the Autonomus Republic and is drawn up in full conformity with the Constitution of the Union Republic.

Article 93

The Supreme Soviet of an Autonomous Republic elects the Presidium of the Supreme Soviet of the Autonomous Republic and appoints the Council of Ministers of the Autonomous Republic, in accordance with its Constitution.

Chapter VIII
THE LOCAL ORGANS
OF STATE POWER

Article 94

The organs of state power in Territories, Provinces, Autonomous Provinces, Areas, Counties, Cities and rural localities (Stanitsas, Villages, Hamlets, Kishlaks, Auls) are the Soviets of Working People's Deputies.

Article 95

The Soviets of Working People's Deputies of Territories, Provinces, Autonomous Provinces, Areas, Counties, Cities and rural localities (Stanitsas, Villages, Hamlets, Kishlaks, Auls) are elected by the working people of the respective Territories, Provinces, Autonomous Provinces, Areas, Counties, Cities or rural localities for a term of two years.

Article 96

The basis of representation for Soviets of Working People's Deputies is determined by the Constitutions of the Union Republics.

Article 97

The Soviets of Working People's Deputies direct the work of the organs of administration subordinate to them, ensure the maintenance of public order, the observance of the laws and the protection of the rights of citizens, direct local economic and cultural affairs and draw up the local budgets.

Article 98

The Soviets of Working People's Deputies adopt decisions and issue orders within the limits of the powers vested in them by the laws of the U.S.S.R. and of the Union Republic.

Article 99

The executive and administrative organ of the Soviet of Working People's Deputies of a Territory, Province, Autonomous Province, Area, County, City or rural locality is the Executive Committee elected by it, consisting of a Chairman, Vice-Chairman, a Secretary and members.

Article 100

The executive and administrative organ of the Soviet of Working People's Deputies in a small locality, in accordance with the Constitution of the Union Republic, is the Chairman, the Vice-Chairman and the Secretary elected by the Soviet of Working People's Deputies.

Article 101

The executive organs of the Soviets of Working People's Deputies are directly accountable both to the Soviets of Working People's Deputies which elected them and to the executive organ of the superior Soviet of Working People's Deputies.

Chapter IX
THE COURTS AND
THE PROSECUTOR'S OFFICE

Article 102

In the U.S.S.R. justice is administered by the Supreme Court of the U.S.S.R., the Supreme Courts of the Union Republics, the Courts of the Territories, Provinces, Autonomous Republics, Autonomous Provinces and Areas, the Special Courts of the U.S.S.R. established by decision of the Supreme Soviet of the U.S.S.R., and the People's Courts.

Article 103

In all Courts cases are tried with the participation of lay judges, except in cases specially provided for by law.

Article 104

The Supreme Court of the U.S.S.R. is the highest judicial organ. The Supreme Court of the U.S.S.R. is charged with the supervision of the judicial activities of all the judicial organs of the U.S.S.R. as well as of the judicial organs of the Union Republics within the limitations established by law.

Article 105

The Supreme Court of the U.S.S.R. is elected by the Supreme Soviet of the U.S.S.R. for a term of five years.

The presidents of the Supreme Courts of the Union Republics are members ex officio of the Supreme Court of the U.S.S.R.

Article 106

The Supreme Courts of the Union Republics are elected by the Supreme Soviets of the Union Republics for a term of five years.

Article 107

The Supreme Courts of the Autonomous Republics are elected by the Supreme Soviets of the Autonomous Republics for a term of five years.

Article 108

The Courts of Territories, Provinces, Autonomous Provinces and Areas are elected by the Soviets of Working People's Deputies of the respective Territories, Provinces, Autonomous Provinces or Areas for a term of five years.

Article 109

People's judges of county (city) People's Courts are elected by citizens of the county (city) on the basis of universal, equal, and direct suffrage by secret ballot for a term of five years.

People's lay judges of county (city) People's Courts are elected at general meetings of workers, clerks, and peasants at their place of work or residence and of soldiers at their military unit for a term of two years.

Article 110

Judicial proceedings are conducted in the language of the Union Republic, Autonomous Republic or Autonomous Province, persons not knowing this language being guaranteed the opportunity of fully acquainting themselves with the material of the case through an interpreter and likewise the right to use their own language in court.

Article 111

In all Courts of the U.S.S.R. cases are heard in public, unless otherwise provided for by law, and the accused is guaranteed the right to defence.

Article 112

Judges are independent and subject only to the law.

Article 113

Supreme supervisory power to ensure the strict observance of the law by all Ministries and institutions subordinated to them, as well as by officials and citizens of the U.S.S.R. generally, is vested in the Prosecutor-General of the U.S.S.R.

Article 114

The Prosecutor-General of the U.S.S.R. is appointed by the Supreme Soviet of the U.S.S.R. for a term of seven years.

Article 115

Prosecutors of Republics, Territories, Provinces, Autonomous Republics and Autonomous Provinces are appointed by the Prosecutor-General of the U.S.S.R. for a term of five years.

Article 116

Area, County and city prosecutors are appointed by the Prosecutors of the Union Republics, subject to the approval of the Prosecutor-General of the U.S.S.R., for a term of five years.

Article 117

The organs of the Prosecutor's Office perform their functions independently of any local organs whatsoever, being subordinate solely to the Prosecutor-General of the U.S.S.R.

Chapter X
FUNDAMENTAL RIGHTS
AND DUTIES OF CITIZENS

Article 118

Citizens of the U.S.S.R. have the right to work, that is, the right to guaranteed employment and payment for their work in accordance with its quantity and quality.

The right to work is ensured by the socialist organization of the national economy, the steady growth of the productive forces of Soviet society, the elimination of the possibility of economic crises, and the abolition of unemployment.

Article 119

Citizens of the U.S.S.R. have the right to rest and leisure.

The right to rest and leisure is ensured by the establishment of an eight-hour day for industrial, office, and professional workers, the reduction of the working day to seven or six hours for arduous trades and to four hours in shops where conditions of work are particularly arduous, by the institution of annual vacations with full pay for industrial, office, and professional workers, and by the provision of a wide network of sanatoria, rest homes and clubs for the accommodation of the working people.

Article 120

Citizens of the U.S.S.R. have the right to maintenance in old age and also in case of sickness or disability.

This right is ensured by the extensive development of social insurance of industrial, office, and professional workers at state expense, free medical service for the working people, and the provision of a wide network of health resorts for the use of the working people.

Article 121

Citizens of the U.S.S.R. have the right to education.

This right is guaranteed by universal compulsory eight-year education, by extensively developed general secondary polytechnical education, professional technical education, secondary special and higher education on the basis of maintaining a link between education and life and production, by extensively developed evening and correspondence schools, by a system of state living allowances, by education in schools in a native language, by organization in factories, in state farms, and in collective farms of production, technological, and agronomic study for toilers without charge.

Article 122

Women in the U.S.S.R. are accorded equal rights with men in all spheres of economic, government, cultural, political and other public activity.

The possibility of exercising these rights is ensured by women being accorded an equal right with men to work, payment for work, rest and leisure, social insurance and education, and by state protection of the interests of mother and child, state aid to mothers of large families and unmarried mothers, maternity leave with full pay, and the provision of a wide network of maternity homes, nurseries and kindergartens.

Article 123

Equality of rights of citizens of the U.S.S.R., irrespective of their nationality or race, in all spheres of economic, government, cultural, political and other public activity, is an indefeasible law.

Any direct or indirect restriction of the rights of, or, conversely, the establishment of any direct or indirect privileges for, citizens on account of their race or nationality, as well as any advocacy of racial or national exclusiveness or hatred and contempt, is punishable by law.

Article 124

In order to ensure to citizens freedom of conscience, the church in the U.S.S.R. is separated from the state, and the school from the church. Freedom of religious worship and freedom of anti-religious propaganda is recognized for all citizens.

Article 125

In conformity with the interests of the working people, and in order to strengthen the socialist system, the citizens of the U.S.S.R. are guaranteed by law:

a) freedom of speech;
b) freedom of the press;
c) freedom of assembly, including the holding of mass meetings;
d) freedom of street processions and demonstrations.

These civil rights are ensured by placing at the disposal of the working people and their organizations printing presses, stocks of paper, public buildings, the streets, communications facilities and other material requisites for the exercise of these rights.

Article 126

In conformity with the interests of the working people, and in order to develop the organizational initiative and political activity of the masses of the people, citizens of the U.S.S.R. are guaranteed the right to unite in public organizations: trade unions, co-operative societies, youth organizations, sport and defence organizations, cultural, technical and scientific societies; and the most active and politically-conscious citizens in the ranks of the working class, working peasants and working intelligentsia voluntarily unite in the Communist Party of the Soviet Union, which is the vanguard of the working people in their struggle to build communist society and is the leading core of all organizations of the working people, both public and state.

Article 127

Citizens of the U.S.S.R. are guaranteed inviolability of the person. No person may be placed under arrest except by decision of a court or with the sanction of a prosecutor.

Article 128

The inviolability of the homes of citizens and privacy of correspondence are protected by law.

Article 129

The U.S.S.R. affords the right of asylum to foreign citizens persecuted for defending the interests of the working people, or for scientific activities, or for struggling for national liberation.

Article 130

It is the duty of every citizen of the U.S.S.R. to abide by the Constitution of the Union of Soviet Socialist Republics, to observe the laws, to maintain labour discipline, honestly to perform public duties, and to respect the rules of socialist intercourse.

Article 131

It is the duty of every citizen of the U.S.S.R. to safeguard and fortify public, socialist property as the sacred and inviolable foundation of the Soviet system, as the source of the wealth and might of the country, as the source of the prosperity and culture of all the working people.

Persons committing offences against public, socialist property are enemies of the people.

Article 132

Universal military service is law.

Military service in the Armed Forces of the U.S.S.R. is an honourable duty of the citizens of the U.S.S.R.

Article 133

To defend the country is the sacred duty of every citizen of the U.S.S.R. Treason to the Motherland—violation of the oath of allegiance, desertion to the enemy, impairing the military power of the state, espionage—is punishable with all the severity of the law as the most heinous of crimes.

Chapter XI
THE ELECTORAL SYSTEM

Article 134

Members of all Soviets of Working People's Deputies—of the Supreme Soviet of the U.S.S.R., the Supreme Soviets of the Union Republics, the

Soviets of Working People's Deputies of the Territories and Provinces, the Supreme Soviets of the Autonomous Republics, the Soviets of Working People's Deputies of the Autonomous Provinces, and the Area, County, City and rural (Stanitsa, Village, Hamlet, Kishlak, Aul) Soviets of Working People's Deputies—are chosen by the electors on the basis of universal, equal and direct suffrage by secret ballot.

Article 135

Elections of deputies are universal: all citizens of the U.S.S.R. who have reached the age of eighteen, irrespective of race or nationality, sex, religion, education, domicile, social origin, property status or past activities, have the right to vote in the election of deputies, with the exception of persons recognized as insane in accordance with the procedure established by law.

Every citizen of the U.S.S.R. who has reached the age of twenty-three is eligible for election to the Supreme Soviet of the U.S.S.R., irrespective of race or nationality, sex, religion, education, domicile, social origin, property status or past activities.

Article 136

Elections of deputies are equal: each citizen has one vote; all citizens participate in elections on an equal footing.

Article 137

Women have the right to elect and be elected on equal terms with men.

Article 138

Citizens serving in the Armed Forces of the U.S.S.R. have the right to elect and be elected on equal terms with all other citizens.

Article 139

Elections of deputies are direct: all Soviets of Working People's Deputies, from rural and city Soviets of Working People's Deputies to the Supreme Soviet of the U.S.S.R., are elected by the citizens by direct vote.

Article 140

Voting at elections of deputies is secret.

Article 141

Candidates are nominated by election districts.

The right to nominate candidates is secured to public organizations and societies of the working people: Communist Party organizations, trade unions, co-operatives, youth organizations and cultural societies.

Article 142

It is the duty of every deputy to report to his electors on his work and on the work of his Soviet of Working People's Deputies, and he may be recalled at any time upon decision of a majority of the electors in the manner established by law.

Chapter XII
ARMS, FLAG, CAPITAL

Article 143

The arms of the Union of Soviet Socialist Republics are a sickle and hammer against a globe depicted in the rays of the sun and surrounded by ears of grain, with the inscription "Workers of All Countries, Unite!" in the languages of the Union Republics. At the top of the arms is a five-pointed star.

Article 144

The state flag of the Union of Soviet Socialist Republics is of red cloth with the sickle and hammer depicted in gold in the upper corner near the staff and above them a five-pointed red star bordered in gold. The ratio of the width to the length is 1:2.

Article 145

The Capital of the Union of Soviet Socialist Republics is the City of Moscow.

Chapter XIII
PROCEDURE FOR AMENDING THE CONSTITUTION

Article 146

The Constitution of the U.S.S.R. may be amended only by decision of the Supreme Soviet of the U.S.S.R. adopted by a majority of not less than two-thirds of the votes in each of its chambers.

RULES OF THE COMMUNIST PARTY
OF THE SOVIET UNION

Adopted by the Nineteenth Party Congress
and as amended by the Twentieth
Party Congress

I

THE PARTY. PARTY MEMBERS, THEIR DUTIES AND RIGHTS

1. The Communist Party of the Soviet Union is a voluntary militant union of like-minded people, Communists, consisting of members of the working class, working peasants and working intellectuals.

The Communist Party of the Soviet Union, having organized an alliance of the working class and the labouring peasantry, achieved, as a result of the Great October Socialist Revolution of 1917, the overthrow of the power of the capitalists and landlords, the establishment of the dictatorship of the proletariat, the elimination of capitalism and the abolition of the exploitation of man by man, and ensured the building of a socialist society.

The principal objects of the Communist Party of the Soviet Union today are to build a communist society through gradual transition from socialism to communism, continuously to raise the living and cultural standards of society, to educate the members of society in the spirit of internationalism and fraternal ties with the working people of all countries, and to strengthen to the utmost the active defence of the Soviet Motherland against aggressive actions on the part of its enemies.

2. Membership of the Communist Party of the Soviet Union is open to any working citizen of the Soviet Union who does not exploit the labour of others, accepts the Party's Program and Rules, actively helps to carry them into effect, works in one of the organizations of the Party and fulfils all Party decisions.

Party members shall pay the established membership dues.

3. It is the duty of a Party member:

a) To protect the unity of the Party might and main, as the chief requisite for its power and strength;

b) To be an active fighter for the implementation of Party decisions. It is not enough for a Party member merely to agree with Party decisions; it is incumbent upon him to strive actively to have them put into effect. A passive and formal attitude on the part of Communists towards Party decisions undermines the Party's efficiency and is therefore incompatible with continuance in its ranks;

c) To set an example in work, to master the technique of his job, constantly to improve his trade or professional skill, and assiduously to protect and fortify socialist social property as the sacred and inviolable foundation of the Soviet system;

d) Constantly to strengthen the ties with the masses, promptly to respond to the needs and requirements of the working people, and to explain to the non-party masses the policy and decisions of the Party, always remembering that the strength and invincibility of our Party lies in its vital and unbreakable bond with the people;

e) To raise his level of political understanding and to broaden his knowledge of the principles of Marxism-Leninism;

f) To observe Party and state discipline, which is equally binding on all Party members. There cannot be two disciplines in the Party—one for leaders, the other for rank-and-file members. The Party has one discipline, one law for all Communists, irrespective of their past services or the positions they occupy. Violation of Party or state discipline is a serious evil, which is detrimental to the Party and therefore incompatible with continuance in its ranks;

g) To develop self-criticism and criticism from below, to bring to light shortcomings in work and to strive to eliminate them, to combat every tendency to make a pretence of all being well and to indulge in raptures over achievements in work. Suppression of criticism is a grave evil. He who stifles criticism, who substitutes ostentatious parade and adulation for it, can have no place in the ranks of the Party;

h) To inform leading Party bodies, up to and including the Central Committee, of shortcomings in work, irrespective of person. A Party member has no right to conceal an abnormal state of affairs, to close his eyes to reprehensible actions which injure the interests of the Party or the state. He who hinders a Party member in the performance of this duty should be sternly punished as a violator of the will of the Party;

i) To be truthful and honest with the Party and not conceal or distort the truth. Untruthfulness or deception practised by a Communist towards the Party is a grave evil and is incompatible with continuance in the Party's ranks;

j) To guard Party and state secrets and to display political vigilance, always remembering that vigilance on the part of Communists is essential on all sectors and in all circumstances. Divulgence of Party or state secrets is a crime against the Party and incompatible with continuance in its ranks;

k) In any post entrusted to him by the Party, undeviatingly to observe the Party's injunction regarding the proper selection of personnel on the basis of their political and professional qualifications. Infringement of this injunction, selection of personnel from considerations of friendship, personal loyalty, home town ties or kinship, is incompatible with continuance in the ranks of the Party.

4. A Party member has the right:

a) To take part in the free and businesslike discussion at Party meetings or in the Party press of questions of Party policy;

b) To criticize any Party worker at Party meetings;

c) To elect and be elected to Party bodies;

d) To demand to be present in person whenever decisions are taken regarding his activities or conduct;

e) To address any question or statement to any Party body, up to and including the Central Committee of the Communist Party of the Soviet Union.

5. Members are admitted to the Party only individually. New members are admitted from among the candidate members who have been through the specified probationary period. Membership of the Party is open to politically conscious and active workers, peasants and intellectuals who are devoted to the cause of communism.

Persons may join the Party on attaining the age of eighteen.

The procedure of admission of candidate members to full Party membership is as follows:

a) Applicants for Party membership must submit recommendations from three Party members who have a Party standing of not less than three years and who know the applicants from having worked with them for not less than one year.

Note 1. In the case of members of the Leninist Young Communist League applying for membership of the Party, the recommendation of a county committee of the Y.C.L. is equivalent to the recommendation of one Party member.

Note 2. Members and alternate members of the Central Committee of the Communist Party of the Soviet Union shall refrain from giving recommendations.

b) Applications for Party membership are discussed and decided by the general meeting of the primary Party organization, whose decision takes effect after endorsement by the county (borough) Party committee, or by the city Party committee in cities with no borough divisions.

The presence of the recommenders at the discussion of applications for Party membership is not essential.

c) Persons up to the age of twenty inclusive may join the Party only through the Young Communist League.

d) Former members of other parties require for admission to the Party the recommendations of five Party members: three of ten years' Party standing and two of prerevolutionary Party standing. They may be admitted only through a primary Party organization, and the endorsement of the Central Committee of the Communist Party of the Soviet Union is essential.

6. Persons recommending applicants for admission to the Party are responsible for the soundness of their recommendations.

7. The Party standing of a candidate member admitted to full membership dates from the day of the decision of the general meeting of the primary Party organization to adopt him as full member.

8. A member of one Party organization who removes to the locality of another Party organization shall be entered on the membership rolls of the latter.

Note. The transfer of Party members from one organization to another is effected in accordance with regulations laid down by the Central Committee of the Communist Party of the Soviet Union.

9. A Party member or candidate member who fails to pay membership dues for three months in succession without sufficient reason is regarded as having automatically ceased to be a member of the Party; the primary Party organization shall pass a decision to this effect, which shall be subject to endorsement by the county or city Party committee.

10. The question of the expulsion of a Communist from the Party is decided by the general meeting of the primary Party organization to which he belongs and must be endorsed by the county or city Party committee. The decision of a county or city committee to expel a mem-

ber takes effect only when endorsed by the provincial or territorial[1] Party committee, or by the Central Committee of the Communist Party of a Union Republic.

Until such time as the decision to expel him is endorsed by the provincial or territorial Party committee or the Central Committee of the Communist Party of a Union Republic, the Party member retains his membership card and is entitled to attend closed Party meetings.

11. A primary Party organization cannot pass a decision on the expulsion of a Communist from the Party, or on his demotion to the status of candidate member, if he is a member of the Central Committee of the Communist Party of the Soviet Union, or of the Central Committee of the Communist Party of a Union Republic, or of a territorial, provincial, area,[2] city or county Party committee.

The expulsion of a member of the Central Committee of the Communist Party of a Union Republic, or of a territorial, regional, area, city or county Party commitee from the given committee or from the Party, or his demotion from full membership to candidate membership, is decided at a plenary meeting of the committee concerned, and only if the necessity for it is recognized by two thirds of the votes.

12. The expulsion of a member of the Central Committee of the Communist Party of the Soviet Union from the Central Committee or from the Party, or his demotion to candidate membership, is decided by the Party Congress, or, in intervals between congresses, by the Plenum of the Central Committee of the Communist Party of the Soviet Union, the assent of a two-thirds majority of the members of the C.C. Plenum being required. The expelled member of the Central Committee is automatically replaced by an alternate member of the C.C., in the order established by the Congress when electing the C.C. alternate members.

13. Should a Party member commit an offence punishable by court of law, he shall be expelled from the Party and the administrative or judicial authorities informed of the offence.

14. When the question of expelling a member from the Party is discussed, the maximum caution and comradely consideration must be exercised, and the grounds for the charges preferred against him must be thoroughly investigated.

In the case of minor offences, measures of Party education and influence should be applied (admonition, reprimand, etc.), and not expulsion from the Party, which is the supreme Party penalty.

Should the necessity arise, Party organizations may, as a Party penalty, demote members to the status of candidate member for a period of not more than one year. The decision of the primary Party organization demoting a Party member to candidate membership requires the endorsement of the county or city Party committee. On the expiration of his

[1] To simplify understanding of party structure, the territories have been grouped with provinces in the text, since their position in the party hierarchy is identical.—J. N. H.

[2] Areas have not been mentioned in the text. They are analogous sometimes to provinces and sometimes to counties in the party hierarchy.—J. N. H.

period of demotion to candidate membership he shall be admitted to full membership of the Party in accordance with the regular procedure, but he shall retain his former Party standing.

15. Appeals against expulsion from the Party, and also decisions of Party organizations to expel members from the Party, must be examined by the appropriate Party bodies within not more than twenty days from date of their receipt.

II
CANDIDATE MEMBERS

16. All persons desirous of joining the Party must pass through a probationary period as candidate members, the object of which is to give them an opportunity to familiarize themselves with the Program, Rules and tactics of the Party and to enable the Party organizations to test the personal qualities of the candidates.

17. The procedure of admission of candidate members (individual admission, submission of recommendations and their verification, decision of the primary organization as to admission and its endorsement) is identical with the procedure of admission of Party members.

18. The period of probationary membership shall be one year.

It is the duty of Party organizations to assist candidates to prepare for admission to the Party. On the expiration of a candidate member's probationary period, the Party organization shall discuss his fitness for admission at a general meeting. If a candidate was unable to prove his fitness for reasons which the primary Party organization considers sufficient, it may prolong his probationary period for a term of not more than one year. Should it be found in the course of his probationary period that a candidate member does not possess the personal qualities warranting his admission to the Party, the Party organization shall pass a decision to remove him from the list of candidate members. A decision of a primary Party organization to prolong the probationary period of a candidate member, or to remove him from the list of candidate members, takes effect after it has been endorsd by the county or city Party committee.

19. Candidate members attend the meetings of the organization to which they are attached, and have a voice but no vote.

20. Candidate members pay the usual membership dues to the local Party committee.

III
STRUCTURE OF THE PARTY.
INNER-PARTY DEMOCRACY

21. The guiding principle of the organizational structure of the Party is democratic centralism, which signifies:

a) Election of all leading Party bodies, from the highest to the lowest;

b) Periodical reports of the Party bodies to their Party organizations;

c) Strict Party discipline and subordination of the minority to the majority;

d) Absolutely binding character of the decisions of higher bodies upon lower bodies.

22. The Party is built on the territorial-industrial principle: a Party organization serving a given area is regarded as higher than any Party organization serving part of that area; and a Party organization serving a whole branch of work is regarded as higher than any Party organization serving part of that branch of work.

23. All Party organizations are autonomous in the decision of local questions, provided that their decisions do not conflict with decisions of the Party.

24. The highest governing body in each party organization is the general membership meeting (in the case of primary organizations), conference (e.g., in the case of county or provincial organizations), or congress (in the case of Communist Parties of Union Republics and the Communist Party of the Soviet Union).

25. The general meeting, conference or congress elects a bureau or committee which acts as its executive body and directs all the current work of the given organization.

26. Voting by lists of candidates in the election of Party bodies is forbidden. Each candidate shall be voted upon separately, every Party member being ensured the unlimited right to challenge the candidates and to criticize them. Voting of candidates shall be by secret ballot.

27. In cities and county centres, meetings of active members of the city and county Party organizations shall be convened for the discussion of the more important decisions of the Party and the government. They shall be convened not for parade and the formal and ceremonial approval of the decisions, but for their genuine discussion.

28. The free and businesslike discussion of questions of Party policy in individual organizations or in the Party as a whole is the inalienable right of every Party member and logically follows from inner-party democracy. Only on the basis of inner-party democracy is it possible to develop self-criticism and to strengthen Party discipline, which must be conscious and not mechanical.

But wide discussion, especially discussion on a national scale, of questions of Party policy must be so organized as to prevent it leading to attempts by an insignificant minority to impose their will upon the majority of the Party, or to attempts to form factional groupings, which break the unity of the Party, attempts to cause splits, which may shake the strength and stability of the socialist system.

Wide discussion on a national scale can be regarded as necessary only:

a) If this necessity is recognized by at least several local Party organizations of regional or republican scale;

b) If there is not a sufficiently solid majority in the Central Committee of the Communist Party of the Soviet Union on important questions of Party policy;

c) If, in spite of the existence of a solid majority in the Central Committee holding a definite opinion, the Central Committee deems it necessary to test the correctness of its policy by means of a discussion in the Party.

Only compliance with these conditions can safeguard the Party against abuse of inner-party democracy by anti-party elements, only these conditions can give the assurance that inner-party democracy will be beneficial and not be used to the detriment of the Party and the working class.

IV

HIGHER PARTY ORGANS

29. The highest organ of the Communist Party of the Soviet Union is the Party Congress. Ordinary congresses are convened at least once in four years. Extraordinary congresses are convened by the Central Committee of the Party on its own initiative or at the demand of not less than one third of the total membership represented at the preceding Party Congress. The convocation of a Party Congress and its agenda shall be announced at least six weeks before the Congress. Extraordinary congresses shall be convened within two months.

A congress is regarded as properly constituted if not less than one half of the total Party membership represented at the last ordinary congress are represented at it.

The basis of representation at a Party Congress is determined by the Central Committee.

30. Should the Central Committee of the Party fail to convene an extraordinary congress within the period specified in Article 29, the organizations which demanded it have the right to form an Organization Committee which shall enjoy the powers of the Central Committee of the Party as regards the convocation of the extraordinary congress.

31. The Congress:

a) Hears and acts on the reports of the Central Committee of the Party, of the Central Auditing Commission, and of the other central organizations;

b) Revises and amends the Program and Rules of the Party;

c) Determines the tactical line of the Party on major questions of current policy;

d) Elects the Central Committee of the Communist Party of the Soviet Union and the Central Auditing Commission.

32. The number of members to be elected to the Central Committee of the Party and to the Central Auditing Commission is determined by the Congress. In the event of members falling out of the Central Committee their places are filled from among the alternate members elected by the Congress.

33. The Central Committee of the Communist Party of the Soviet Union holds not less than one plenary meeting every six months. Alternate members of the Central Committee attend its plenary meetings with voice but no vote.

34. The Central Committee of the Communist Party of the Soviet Union sets up a Presidium to direct the work of the Central Committee between plenary meetings, and a Secretariat to direct the current work, chiefly the organization of verification of fulfilment of Party decisions, and selection of personnel.

35. The Central Committee of the Communist Party of the Soviet Union sets up a Party Control Committee of the C.C.

The Party Control Committee of the C.C.:

a) Verifies how Party members and candidate members observe Party discipline, and takes action against Communists who violate the Program and Rules of the Party, or Party and state discipline, and against violators of Party ethics (against those who deceive the Party or are dishonest and insincere with it, against slanderers or bureaucrats, against persons guilty of moral delinquency in private life, etc.);

b) Reviews appeals against decisions of Central Committees of Communist Parties of Union Republics, or of territorial and regional Party committees expelling members from the Party or imposing Party penalties upon them;

36. The Central Committee of the Communist Party of the Soviet Union directs the entire work of the Party in the interval between Congresses, represents the Party in its relations with other parties, organizations and institutions, sets up various Party institutions and directs their activities, appoints the editors of central press organs under its control and confirms the appointment of the editors of the Party organs of big local organizations, organizes and manages enterprises of a public character, distributes the forces and resources of the Party, and manages the central funds.

The Central Committee guides the work of the central Soviet and public organizations through the Party groups within them.

37. In order to strengthen leadership and political work, the Central Committee of the Party has the right to create Political Departments and to assign Party Organizers of the Central Committee to individual sectors of socialist construction which have acquired special importance for the national economy and the country in general; and, in the measure that the Political Departments complete their tasks, to abolish them or to convert them into ordinary Party bodies on the industrial-territorial principle.

The work of the Political Departments is governed by special instructions endorsed by the Central Committee.

38. The Central Committee of the Communist Party of the Soviet Union keeps the Party organizations regularly informed of its work.

39. The Central Auditing Commission *a*) investigates whether affairs are handled expeditiously and properly by the central bodies of the Party and whether the apparatus of the Secretariat of the Central Committee is working smoothly, and *b*) audits the accounts of the treasury and the enterprises of the Central Committee of the Party.

V

PROVINCIAL, TERRITORIAL AND REPUBLICAN PARTY ORGANIZATIONS

40. The highest organ of a provincial, territorial or republican Party organization is the provincial or territorial Party Conference or the Congress of the Communist Party of the Union Republic, and, in the

interval between them, the provincial committee, territorial committee or Central Committee of the Communist Party of the Union Republic. They guide themselves in their activities by the decisions of the Communist Party of the Soviet Union and its leading bodies.

41. Ordinary provincial and territorial conferences and congresses of the Communist Parties of Union Republics are convened once every two years by the particular provincial or territorial committee or Central Committee of the Communist Party of the Union Republic. Extraordinary conferences or congresses are convened by decision of the particular provincial committee, territorial committee or Central Committee of the Communist Party of the Union Republic, or at the demand of one third of the total membership of the organizations belonging to the provincial, territorial or republican Party Organization. Congresses of the Communist Parties of Union Republics, containing provincial subdivisions (the Ukraine, Byelorussia, Kazakhstan, Uzbekistan), may be conducted once in four years.

The basis of representation at provincial and territorial conferences and congresses of Communist Parties of the Union Republics is determined by the particular provincial committee, territorial committee or Central Committee of the Communist Party of the Union Republic.

Provincial and territorial conferences and congresses of Communist Parties of Union Republics hear and act on the reports of the respective provincial or territorial committee or Central Committee of the Communist Party of the Union Republic, of the auditing commission and of other provincial, territorial or republican organizations, discuss questions of Party, Soviet, economic and trade union work in the particular province, territory or republic, and elect a provincial committee, territorial committee or Central Committee of the Communist Party of the Union Republic, as the case may be, an auditing commission and delegates to the Congresses of the Communist Party of the Soviet Union.

42. The provincial and territorial committees and Central Committees of the Communist Parties of Union Republics each elect an executive body, consisting of not more than eleven members, including three secretaries, the appointment of the latter being subject to the confirmation of the Central Committee of the Party. The secretaries must have a Party standing of not less than five years.

The provincial committees, territorial committees and Central Committees of Communist Parties of Union Republics each set up a secretariat for the examination of current questions and for verification of fulfilment. The secretariats report the decisions they adopt to the bureaus of their respective provincial or territorial Party committees or Central Committees of the Communist Parties of Union Republics.

43. The provincial committees, territorial committees and Central Committees of the Communist Parties of Union Republics organize various Party institutions within their particular province, territory or republic and direct their activities; ensure faithful observance of Party directives, development of criticism and self-criticism, and education of Communists in a spirit of intolerance of shortcomings; direct the study of Marxism-Leninism by Party members and candidate members; organ-

ize the communist education of the working people; appoint the editors of the provincial, territorial or republican Party press organ which works under their control; guide the activities of the provincial, territorial or republican Soviet and public organizations through the Party groups within them; organize and manage their own enterprises of general importance in the particular province, territory or republic; distribute within the limits of their organization the forces and resources of the Party; manage the Party funds of the region, territory or republic; send regular information to the Central Committee of the Party and at fixed intervals present reports to it on their activities.

44. Plenary meetings of provincial committees, territorial committees and Central Committees of the Communist Parties of Union Republics are convened at least once every four months.

45. Party organizations in autonomous republics and in national and other provinces forming part of a territory or Union Republic work under the direction of their particular territorial committee or Central Committee of the Communist Party of the Union Republic, and guide their internal life by the regulations set forth in Section V of the Party Rules relating to regional, territorial and republican organizations.

VI
AREA PARTY ORGANIZATIONS

46. Area Party organizations are formed in provinces, territories and republics which have areas.

The highest organ of an area Party organization is the area Party Conference, which is convened by the area Party committee at least once in two years; extraordinary conferences are convened by decision of the area Party committee or at the demand of one third of the total membership of the organizations belonging to the area organization.

The area conference hears and acts on the reports of the area committee, of the auditing commission and of other area Party organizations, and elects the area Party committee, the auditing commission, and delegates to provincial or territorial conferences and to congresses of the Communist Party of the Union Republic.

47. Each area committee elects a bureau, consisting of not more than nine persons, including secretaries of the area committee. The secretaries must have a Party standing of not less than three years. Secretaries of area committees must be confirmed by the provincial committee, territorial committee or Central Committee of the Communist Party of the Union Republic, as the case may be.

Plenary meetings of area committees are convened not less than once in three months.

48. An area committee organizes various Party institutions within its particular area and directs their activities; ensures faithful observance of Party directives, development of criticism and self-criticism, and education of Communists in a spirit of intolerance of shortcomings; directs the study of Marxism-Leninism by Party members and candidate members; organizes the communist education of the working people; appoints the

editors of the area Party press organ which works under its direction and control; guides the activities of the area Soviet and public organizations through the Party groups within them; organizes its own enterprises of general importance to the area; distributes the forces and resources of the Party within the limits of its area, and manages the area Party funds.

VII

CITY AND COUNTY (RURAL AND URBAN) PARTY ORGANIZATIONS

49. City and county Party conferences are convened by the city and county committees at least once a year; extraordinary conferences are convened by decision of the particular city or country committee, or at the demand of one third of the total membership of the organizations in the city or county. In cities containing borough subdivisions, city Party conferences are convened once in two years.

The city or county conference hears and acts on the reports of the city or county committee, of the auditing commission and of other city or county organizations, and elects the city or county committee, the auditing commission and the delegates to territorial or provincial conferences or congresses of the Communist Party of the Union Republic.

50. Each city or county committee elects a bureau consisting of from seven to nine persons, including secretaries of the city or county committee. Secretaries of city or county committees must have a Party standing of not less than three years. Their appointment is subject to the confirmation of the provincial committee, territorial committee or Central Committee of the Communist Party of the Union Republic.

51. A city or county committee organizes and confirms the primary Party organizations in industrial enterprises, state farms, machine and tractor stations, collective farms and offices, directs their activities and keeps a register of Communists; ensures the observance of Party directives, development of criticism and self-criticism, and education of Communists in a spirit of intolerance of shortcomings; organizes the study of Marxism-Leninism by Party members and candidate members; conducts the communist education of the working people; appoints the editors of the city or county Party press organ which works under its direction and control; guides the activities of the city or county Soviet and public organizations through the Party groups within them; distributes the forces and resources of the Party in the city or county, and manages the city or county Party funds. The city or county committee submits to the provincial committee, territorial committee or Central Committee of the Communist Party of the Union Republic reports on its activities at the times and in the form established by the Central Committee of the Party.

52. Plenary meetings of city or county committees are convened not less than once in three months.

53. In big cities, borough organizations subordinate to the city committees may be set up with the permission of the Central Committee of the Communist Party of the Soviet Union.

VIII

PRIMARY PARTY ORGANIZATIONS

54. The primary Party organizations are the basis of the Party.

Primary Party organizations are formed in mills, factories, state farms, machine and tractor stations and other economic enterprises, in collective farms, units of the Soviet Army and Navy, in villages, offices, educational establishments, etc., where there are not less than three Party members.

In enterprises, collective farms, offices, etc., where there are less than three Party members, candidate member groups or Party and Young Communist League groups are formed headed by a Party organizer appointed by the district or city Party committee or by the Political Department.

Primary Party organizations are confirmed by the county or city committees or by the competent Political Departments.

The highest organ of a primary Party organization is the general meeting of its members, which is convened not less than once a month.

55. In factories, offices, collective farms, etc., where there are over one hundred Party members and candidate members, shop, sectional, departmental, etc., Party organizations may be formed within the general primary Party organization covering the whole factory, office, etc., subject to the approval in each particular case of the county or city committee or of the competent Political Department.

Within shop, sectional, etc., organizations, and also within primary Party organizations having less than one hundred members and candidate members, Party groups may be formed in the brigades or units of the establishment.

56. In large factories and offices where there are over three hundred Party members and candidate members, Party committees may be formed with the sanction in each particular case of the provincial or territorial committee or of the Central Committee of the Party of the Union Republic, the shop Party organizations in such establishments being granted the rights of primary Party organizations.

57. A primary Party organization connects the mass of the workers, peasants and intellectuals with the leading organs of the Party. Its task is:

a) To conduct agitational and organizational work among the masses for the carrying out of Party calls and decisions, and to ensure direction of the primary press (printed bulletins, wall newspapers, etc.);

b) To recruit new members for the Party and to take care of their political training;

c) To organize the political education of Party members and candidate members and to see that they acquire an essential minimum knowledge of Marxism-Leninism;

d) To assist the county committee, city committee or Political Department in all its practical work;

e) To mobilize the efforts of the masses in factory, state farm, collective farm, etc., for the fulfilment of the production plan, for the strengthening of labour discipline and for the development of socialist emulation;

f) To combat inefficiency and mismanagement in factory, state farm and collective farm, and to show a daily concern for the improvement of the living and cultural standards of factory and office workers and collective farmers;

g) To develop criticism and self-criticism and to educate Communists in a spirit of intolerance of shortcomings;

h) To take an active part in the economic and political life of the country.

58. In order to enhance the role of the primary Party organizations in production and trading establishments, including state farms, collective farms and machine and tractor stations, and their responsibility for the state of the work in their enterprises, these organizations have the right to exercise control over the activities of the management of their particular enterprise.

It is the duty of Party organizations of Ministries, which, owing to the specific nature of the work in government institutions, cannot exercise functions of control, to draw attention to defects in the work of their institutions, to be alive to shortcomings in the work of the Ministry and of any of its personnel and to commuicate their information and opinions to the Central Committee and to the heads of the Ministry.

Secretaries of primary Party organizations of Ministries are confirmed by the Central Committee of the Party.

All Communists working in the central apparatus of a Ministry belong to one general Party organization of that Ministry.

59. For the conduct of its current business each primary Party organization elects a bureau consisting of not more than eleven persons for a term of one year.

Bureaus of primary Party organizations are formed if the organization has not less than fifteen Party members.

In Party organizations having less than fifteen Party members, no bureaus are formed, but a secretary of the primary Party organization is elected.

With the object of rapidly training and educating Party members in collective leadership, a shop Party organization having not less than fifteen and not more than fifty Party members has the right to elect a bureau of the shop Party organization consisting of from three to five persons; a shop organization having over fifty Party members may elect a bureau of from five to seven persons.

In primary Party organizations having not more than one hundred Party members, the persons who conduct the Party work are as a rule not exempted from their regular work.

Secretaries of primary and shop Party organizations must have a Party standing of not less than one year.

IX

THE PARTY
AND THE YOUNG COMMUNIST LEAGUE

60. The Leninist Young Communist League conducts its activities under the guidance of the Communist Party of the Soviet Union. The

Central Committee of the Y.C.L., as its leading body, is subordinated to the Central Committee of the Communist Party of the Soviet Union. The activities of the local organizations of the Y.C.L. are directed and controlled by the appropriate republican, territorial, provincial, city and county organizations of the Party.

61. Members of the Y.C.L. shall retire from that body from the moment they become members or candidate members of the Party, provided they do not hold leading posts in Y.C.L. organizations.

62. The Y.C.L. is an active assistant of the Party in all state and economic affairs. The Y.C.L. organizations must be in effect active vehicles of the Party's directives in all spheres of socialist construction, especially where there are no primary Party organizations.

63. Y.C.L. organizations enjoy wide initiative in discussing and submitting to the appropriate Party organizations all questions designed to remove shortcomings in the work of the particular factory, collective farm, state farm or office, and in helping them to improve the work, in organizing socialist emulation, in conducting mass campaigns, etc.

X

PARTY ORGANIZATIONS
IN THE SOVIET ARMY AND NAVY
AND IN THE TRANSPORT SERVICES

64. The guidance of Party work in the Soviet Army and Navy is exercised by the Chief Political Administration of the Ministry of Defense, which functions as a department of the Central Committee of the Communist Party of the Soviet Union.

Party organizations in the Soviet Army and Navy work on the basis of special instructions confirmed by the Central Committee.

65. The chiefs of the political administrations of military areas, fleets and armies must be Party members of five years' standing, and the chiefs of political departments of divisions and brigades Party members of three years' standing.

66. The political organs must maintain close contact with the local Party committees through constant participation of the heads of the political organs in the local Party committees, as well as through regular reports made at meetings of the Party committees by the chiefs of the political organs on political work in the military units.

XI

PARTY GROUPS IN NON-PARTY ORGANIZATIONS

67. At all congresses and conferences and in all elective bodies of Soviet, trade union, cooperative and other mass organizations having not less than three Party members, Party groups are formed whose task is to strengthen the influence of the Party in every way and to carry out the Party policy among the non-party people, to strengthen Party and state discipline, to combat bureaucracy, and to verify fulfilment of Party and Soviet directives. Each such group elects a secretary to conduct its current work.

68. The Party groups are subordinated to the appropriate Party organizations (Central Committee of the Communist Party of the Soviet Union, Central Committee of the Communist Party of the Union Republic, territorial, provincial, area, city or county Party committee).

In all questions the groups must strictly and unswervingly govern themselves by the decisions of the leading Party bodies.

XII

PARTY FUNDS

69. The funds of the Party and its organizations consist of membership dues, income from Party enterprises and other revenues.

70. The membership dues payable monthly by Party members and candidate members are as follows (per cent of earnings):

Monthly Earnings	Dues
Up to 500 rubles	½ per cent
From 501 to 1,000 rubles	1 per cent
From 1,001 to 1,500 rubles	1½ per cent
From 1,501 to 2,000 rubles	2 per cent
Over 2,000 rubles	3 per cent

71. Candidate members upon admission pay an entrance fee amounting to 2 per cent of their monthly earnings.

ANNOTATED BIBLIOGRAPHY

Many books and articles on various aspects of the Soviet system of government have been published since World War II. From this number, there follows a selection of some of the books that can be read to advantage in supplementing the material included in this volume. None of the many available articles is included specifically, for the articles are usually highly technical, but many may be found in the specialized periodicals listed below. While the books selected often include material pertinent to several parts of this study, they are included only under the heading of the chapter for which they are believed to be most valuable. One book of documents is pertinent to the discussion in several chapters, and is therefore placed at the head of the list.

Documentation:

MEISEL, JAMES H., and KOZERA, EDWARD S. (eds.). *Materials for the Study of the Soviet System: State and Party Constitutions, Laws, Decrees, Decisions and Official Statements of the Leaders in Translation.* 2d ed.; Ann Arbor, Mich.: George Wahr Publishing Co., 1953. lxxxiv+ 613 pp.
Invaluable as a source book for Soviet documents.

Chapter 1:

EBENSTEIN, WILLIAM. *Today's Isms: Communism, Fascism, Capitalism, Socialism.* New York: Prentice-Hall, Inc., 1954. x+191 pp.
A description of principles and practices. Designed for college teaching and admirable for comparative study. Bibliography.

HAIMSON, LEOPOLD H. *The Russian Marxists and the Origins of Bolshevism.* Cambridge, Mass.: Harvard University Press, 1956. 246 pp.
A clarification of the various trends among revolutionary Russian intellectuals from 1880 to 1905. Profiles of the leaders. Helpful in identifying political influences on the Russian Revolution.

HARCAVE, SIDNEY. *Russia: A History.* Philadelphia: J. B. Lippincott, 1952. 668 pp.
A widely used one-volume history prepared for college teaching. Devoted primarily to the one hundred years since 1855. Largely factual and a minimum of interpretation. Maps, chronologies, illustrations, and bibliography.

246

MEYER, ALFRED G. *Leninism.* Cambridge, Mass.: Harvard University Press, 1957. 324 pp.

A philosophical discussion in highly readable form of Lenin's theories and their relation to classical Marxist doctrine.

Chapter 2:

FAINSOD, MERLE. *How Russia Is Ruled.* Cambridge, Mass.: Harvard University Press, 1953. xi+575 pp.

A thorough analysis of the Communist party as the core of the Soviet power structure, using official Soviet documents and interviews with Soviet refugees now in the West. Also contains material on the structure of the Soviet state apparatus.

FAINSOD, MERLE. *Smolensk under Soviet Rule.* Cambridge, Mass.: Harvard University Press, 1958. 484 pp.

A reconstruction on the basis of secret Soviet archives captured by the German army of political life in one province of the U.S.S.R. during the late 1920's and 1930's.

GRULIOW, LEO (ed.). *Current Soviet Policies: The Documentary Record of the Nineteenth Communist Party Congress and the Reorganization after Stalin's Death.* New York: Frederick A. Praeger, Inc., 1953. vi+268 pp.

The full record of Communist party developments just prior to, and immediately after, Stalin's death.

GRULIOW, LEO (ed.). *Current Soviet Policies.* II. New York: Frederick A. Praeger, Inc., 1957. 247 pp.

A full documentary record of the twentieth Communist party congress, as well as related events of 1956.

SCHAPIRO, LEONARD. *The Origin of the Communist Autocracy.* Cambridge, Mass.: Harvard University Press, 1956. 397 pp.

A history and analysis of the rise of the Communist party: prerevolutionary relations with the non-Communist revolutionary parties, and dissensions within the Communist party up to inauguration of the New Economic Policy.

SCOTT, DEREK T. R. *Russian Political Institutions.* New York: Rinehart, 1958. 265 pp.

A textbook analysis of the Soviet political process valuable for its minute detail on selected issues.

Chapter 3:

KULSKI, W. W. *The Soviet Regime: Communism in Practice.* Syracuse: Syracuse University Press, 1954. xiv+807 pp.

A vigorous indictment of the Soviet regime, utilizing Soviet documents and textual explanations to indicate through Soviet mouths that professedly democratic institutions are not democratic in practice.

STEINBERG, I. N. *In the Workshop of the Revolution*. New York. Rinehart & Co., Inc., 1953. xiv+306 pp.

The development of the Soviet state in the early months of its life, as witnessed by a left-wing Socialist Revolutionary who collaborated as Commissar of Justice but finally broke with Lenin and was arrested.

TOWSTER, JULIAN. *Political Power in the U.S.S.R. 1917–1947: The Theory and Structure of Government in the Soviet State*. New York: Oxford University Press, 1948. xvii+443 pp.

A painstaking analysis of the Soviet system, with full documentation. Especially valuable on the role played by the state apparatus.

VYSHINSKY, ANDREI Y. *The Law of the Soviet State*. Translated by HUGH W. BABB. New York: Macmillan Co., 1948. xvii+749 pp.

A translation of the official Soviet University textbook on the Soviet state. Permits Americans to glimpse Soviet methods of mass indoctrination as well as to obtain some otherwise unrevealed detail.

Chapter 4:

CARSON, GEORGE BARR. *Electoral Practice in the U.S.S.R.* New York: Frederick A. Praeger, Inc., 1955. v+160 pp.

A specialized study utilizing every scrap of available evidence to portray the actual functioning of the Soviet electoral system.

DEUTSCHER, ISAAC. *Soviet Trade Unions*. London and New York: Royal Institute of International Affairs, 1950. ix+156 pp.

The history of the Soviet trade unions, with emphasis on the conflict of views regarding their function in Soviet society and on their ultimate absorption into the system of government.

INKELES, ALEX. *Public Opinion in Soviet Russia: A Study in Mass Persuasion*. Cambridge, Mass.: Harvard University Press, 1950. xviii+379 pp.

An analysis of Soviet press controls and mass propaganda techniques, by a sociologist, utilizing material from interviews with Soviet refugees now in the West.

Chapter 5:

BECK, F., and GODIN, W. *Russian Purge and the Extraction of Confession*. Translated by ERIC MOSBACHER and DAVID PORTER. New York: Viking Press, 1951. x+277 pp.

An account by two prisoners of the Soviet, one of them a German, of the operation of the terror apparatus as they saw it, and the setting of the operation within the framework of Soviet ideology.

LENIN, V. I. *The State and Revolution*. Revised translation. New York: International Publishers, 1935. 104 pp.

The official Soviet justification for proletarian dictatorship from which rationalization of terror as an instrument of dictatorship has been developed. This little volume is something of a handbook for Soviet political theorists.

MAYO, H. B. *Democracy and Marxism*. New York: Oxford University Press, 1955. xi+364 pp.

A readable digest of Marxist argument in support of the proletarian dictatorship and a systematic criticism of the argument by comparing it with the theory of democracy prevailing in the West.

MOORE, BARRINGTON, JR. *Soviet Politics: The Dilemma of Power: The Role of Ideas in Social Change*. Cambridge, Mass.: Harvard University Press, 1950. xviii+503 pp.

A consideration of Soviet policies in the light of the official theory, concluding that theory has some real influence upon the development of policy because Soviet leaders accept some elements of it.

MOORE, BARRINGTON, JR. *Terror and Progress—U.S.S.R.: Some Sources of Change and Stability in the Soviet Dictatorship*. Cambridge, Mass.: Harvard University Press, 1954. xvii+261 pp.

An argument that Soviet leaders use terror as a political instrument to achieve economic progress.

WOLIN, SIMON, and SLUSSER, ROBERT M. (eds.). *The Soviet Secret Police*. New York: Frederick A. Praeger, Inc., 1957. ix+408 pp.

A documented chronology from 1917 to 1956 with commentary by former Soviet citizens in the form of essays on various aspects of the security police.

Chapter 6:

BARGHOORN, FREDERICK C. *Soviet Russian Nationalism*. New York: Oxford University Press, 1956. ix+330 pp.

Exhaustive examination of the printed record to determine the place of the Great Russians and their culture within the Soviet federation and Stalin's effort to create a new chauvinistic national pride for the U.S.S.R. as a whole.

CRESSEY, GEORGE B. *The Basis of Soviet Strength*. New York: McGraw-Hill Book Co., Inc., 1945. ix+287 pp.

A geographer's popularized account of the physical structure of the U.S.S.R. and of its various peoples and their republics.

PIPES, RICHARD. *The Formation of the Soviet Union: Communism and Nationalism, 1917–1922*. Cambridge, Mass.: Harvard University Press, 1955. xii+355 pp.

Soviet concepts of federalism and the steps taken to create the federation of the U.S.S.R.

SHABAD, THEODORE. *Geography of the U.S.S.R.* New York: Columbia University Press, 1951. xxxii+584 pp.

A technical and detailed description of Soviet geography and population, with many maps.

Chapter 7:

ARAKELIAN, A. *Industrial Management in the U.S.S.R.* Translated by ELLSWORTH L. RAYMOND. Washington, D.C.: Public Affairs Press, 1950. 168 pp.

An official Soviet description of the administrative mechanism developed to operate Soviet industry. Includes organization charts.

BERLINER, JOSEPH S. *Factory and Manager in the U.S.S.R.* Cambridge, Mass.: Harvard University Press, 1957. xv+386 pp.

An economist's evaluation of the role of the industrial manager, utilizing material from émigré interviews as well as conventional sources.

BIENSTOCK, GREGORY, SCHWARZ, SOLOMON M., and YUGOW, AARON. *Management in Russian Industry and Agriculture.* New York: Oxford University Press, 1944. xxxii+198 pp.

The managerial problems in a state-owned and planned economy and the Soviet attempts at solution and elimination of administrative delay.

GRANICK, DAVID. *Management of the Industrial Firm in the U.S.S.R.: A Study in Soviet Economic Planning.* New York: Columbia University Press, 1954. xiii+346 pp.

An account of the Soviet administrative apparatus as it must appear to a Soviet state industrial manager. The study is based upon minute analysis of the Soviet press.

HAZARD, JOHN N. *Soviet Housing Law.* New Haven: Yale University Press, 1939. iv+178 pp.

An examination of the administrative problems met in dealing with tenants in state-owned dwellings and the mechanism developed to resolve them.

HOLZMAN, FRANKLYN D. *Soviet Taxation: The Fiscal and Monetary Problems of Planned Economy.* Cambridge, Mass.: Harvard University Press, 1955. 376 pp.

A full explanation by an economist of the tax system and its history.

Chapter 8:

DINERSTEIN, HERBERT S., and GOURE, LEON. *Two Studies of Soviet Controls.* Glencoe, Ill.: Free Press, 1955. xviii+254 pp.

The first study, "Communism and the Russian Peasant," presents Soviet agriculture as seen from the farm itself.

HUBBARD, LEONARD E. *The Economics of Soviet Agriculture.* London: Macmillan Co., 1939. xii+316 pp.

A factual account of the operation of the collective-farm system, including the model charter. Includes a summary of the agricultural pattern existing before the Revolution.

ROBINSON, GEROID TANQUARY. *Rural Russia under the Old Regime: A History of the Landlord Peasant World and a Prologue to the*

Peasant Revolution of 1917. New York: Macmillan Co., reprint 1949. ix+342 pp.

A detailed but readable account of the historical background of the peasant problem in the U.S.S.R.

VUCINICH, ALEXANDER. *Soviet Economic Institutions: The Social Structure of Production Units.* Stanford, Calif.: Stanford University Press, 1952. vii+150 pp.

A monograph using sociological techniques to analyze the structure of the Soviet productive units and, in particular, the co-operatives and the methods by which the Communist party controls them.

Chapter 9:

BERMAN, HAROLD J. *Justice in Russia: An Interpretation of Soviet Law.* Cambridge, Mass.: Harvard University Press, 1950. x+322 pp.

An interpretation of Soviet law as "parental" in contrast to Western attitudes. Includes a short history of prerevolutionary legal development.

CURTISS, JOHN S. *The Russian Church and the Soviet State, 1917–1950.* Boston: Little, Brown & Co., 1953. x+387 pp.

A complete account of the measures taken by the Soviet government to discourage the church and the countermeasures taken by the church. Includes the wartime relaxation of policy.

GSOVSKI, VLADIMIR. *Soviet Civil Law: Private Rights and Their Background under the Soviet Regime: Comparative Survey and Translation.* 2 vols. Ann Arbor, Mich.: University of Michigan Law School, 1948–49. xxxvi+909, xx+907 pp.

An encyclopedic compendium of information on the extent to which the Soviet state intervenes in private affairs. One volume contains translation of codes and statutes.

SCHLESINGER, RUDOLPH. *Changing Attitudes in Soviet Russia: The Family.* London: Routledge & Kegan Paul, 1949. ix+408 pp.

A description, through the use of documents, of the progression of state policy from laxness in family relationships to the current policy of fostering a closely knit family unit.

Chapter 10:

BERMAN, HAROLD J., and KERNER, MIROSLAV. *Documents on Soviet Military Law and Administration.* Cambridge, Mass.: Harvard University Press, 1955. xi+164 pp.

Texts of documents, including judicial decisions, believed by the authors to support their conclusions in the principal volume.

BERMAN, HAROLD J., and KERNER, MIROSLAV. *Soviet Military Law and Administration.* Cambridge, Mass.: Harvard University Press, 1955. xiv+208 pp.

A detailed study not only of military law but of the means by which the Communist party and police penetrate the army. One author had personal experience in the army.

BRZEZINSKI, ZBIGNIEW. *Political Controls in the Soviet Army: A Study Based on Reports by Former Soviet Officers*. New York: Frederick A. Praeger, Inc., 1954. viii+93 pp.

A study based on the recollections of six Soviet refugees now in the West, containing material previously unavailable in published sources.

LEE, ASHER (ed.). *The Soviet Air and Rocket Forces*. London: Weidenfeld & Nicolson, 1959. 311 pp.

Chapters written by non-Soviet and former Soviet experts on Soviet air strategy and equipment. For political scientists the chapter on politics by a former Soviet officer provides the first account since Marshal Zhukov's dismissal of Communist party and police controls within the Armed Forces.

Chapter 11:

HAZARD, JOHN N. *Law and Social Change in the U.S.S.R.* London: Stevens & Sons, Ltd., and Toronto: Carswell Company, Ltd., 1953. xxiv+310 pp.

A review of various branches of Soviet law, designed to indicate the function of law and courts in changing the Soviet social structure. Contains abstracts of 150 judicial decisions.

KONSTANTINOVSKY, BORIS A. *Soviet Law in Action: The Recollected Cases of a Soviet Lawyer,* ed. HAROLD J. BERMAN. Cambridge, Mass.: Harvard University Press, 1953. viii+77 pp.

A brief account of the actual functioning of courts, especially in labor cases, by a former legal adviser to the Odessa Bread Trust. Copious notes by Professor Berman indicate the structure and procedure of Soviet courts.

SCHLESINGER, RUDOLPH. *Soviet Legal Theory: Its Social Background and Development*. New York: Oxford University Press, 1945. viii+299 pp.

A legal philosopher's closely written evaluation of the course of Soviet law, with explanation of the structure and procedure of courts.

Chapter 12:

BERGSON, ABRAM. *The Structure of Soviet Wages: A Study in Socialist Economics*. Cambridge, Mass.: Harvard University Press, 1946. xvi+253 pp.

An economist's consideration of inequalities in Soviet wages. Includes information on the method of wage administration.

DEWITT, NICHOLAS. *Soviet Professional Manpower—Its Education, Training, and Supply*. Washington, D.C.: National Science Foundation, 1955. 400 pp.

In addition to a description of professional education, the volume contains a survey with chart of primary and secondary education on the eve of the 1958 reform, comparing the system with that of the U.S.A. Much statistical information on enrolments and time allotted in the curriculum.

KOROL, ALEXANDER G. *Soviet Education for Science and Technology.* New York: John Wiley & Sons, 1957. 513 pp.

A careful study of Soviet education prior to the 1958 reform, containing much detail.

Periodicals:

American Slavic and East European Review. Quarterly. Columbia University Press, New York 27, N.Y.

A major source for interpretive articles on Soviet politics and the historical, economic, and cultural base on which they rest. Edited by scholars from ten American universities. Book reviews include criticism of all major publications in English on the Eastern European area.

Current Digest of the Soviet Press. Weekly. 405 West 117th Street, New York 27, N.Y.

A thorough coverage in translation of all major news items and articles in the Soviet daily and periodical press. Contains no comment or explanation by editors. Sponsored by the Joint Committee on Slavic Studies of the American Council of Learned Societies and the Social Science Research Council. Ideal as research source for current Soviet events and official Soviet documents. Fully indexed in quarterly supplements.

The Russian Review. Quarterly. 235 Baker Library, Hanover, N.H.

Edited by Professor Dmitri von Mohrenschildt and a small group of other scholars. Relatively brief but meaty articles on Russian history, literature, economics, and politics. Book reviews and bibliographies.

The Slavonic and East European Review. Quarterly. School of Slavonic Studies, University of London, Malet Street, London, W.C. 1, England.

The oldest review in English on Eastern Europe. Contains documents in translation. Critical articles usually relate to historical and literary themes, but book reviews concern all disciplines.

Soviet Studies. Quarterly. Basil Blackwell, Oxford, England.

Edited on behalf of the Department for the Study of the Social and Economic Institutions of the U.S.S.R. of the University of Glasgow, Scotland, by Professors J. Miller and R. A. J. Schlesinger. Contains articles primarily on political and economic themes and translations of Soviet articles. Book reviews include Soviet publications.

Bibliographies:

CAREW HUNT, R. N. *Books on Communism.* London: Ampersand, Ltd., 1959. x+333 pp.

A thoroughly competent compilation with annotations of books on communism published in all countries since 1945.

GRIERSON, PHILIP. *Books on Soviet Russia 1917–1942: A Bibliography and a Guide to Reading.* London: Methuen & Co., 1943. 354 pp.

ROBERTS, HENRY L. *Foreign Affairs Bibliography, 1942–1952.* New York: Council on Foreign Relations, 1955. 727 pp.
Includes volumes on Soviet domestic policies.

SWARTZ, HARRY. *The Soviet Economy: A Selected Bibliography of Materials in English.* Syracuse: Syracuse University Press, 1949. 93 pp.

WOOLBERT, ROBERT GALE. *Foreign Affairs Bibliography: A Selected and Annotated List of Books on International Relations, 1932–1942.* New York: Council on Foreign Relations, 1945. xxi+705 pp.
The section on Russia includes volumes on aspects of Soviet domestic as well as foreign policies.

INDEX